The Red Teamer's Handbook: Advanced Penetration Testing Techniques

Gabriel Visage

In the ever-evolving landscape of cybersecurity, adversaries are relentless in finding new ways to breach defenses, exploit vulnerabilities, and outsmart even the most advanced security systems. Organizations, in turn, must rise to the challenge by adopting not only defensive strategies but also offensive tactics that simulate real-world attacks. This is where red teaming comes into play—a discipline that goes beyond traditional penetration testing to embody the mindset, tactics, and creativity of the adversary.

This book, **The Red Teamer's Handbook: Advanced Penetration Testing Techniques**, is a practical guide for cybersecurity professionals, ethical hackers, and red teamers who aim to elevate their craft. It's designed to push you past the basics, arming you with advanced skills, strategic insights, and cutting-edge techniques to tackle today's most complex challenges. Whether you're new to red teaming or an experienced practitioner, this handbook will help you sharpen your edge, refine your approach, and deliver more impactful results.

Why Red Teaming Matters

The cybersecurity world is no longer about building walls high enough to keep the adversary out; it's about understanding the adversary's playbook and learning to think like them. Red teamers are at the forefront of this battle, working as ethical adversaries to uncover vulnerabilities, test assumptions, and reveal weaknesses that defenders might overlook. A successful red team engagement doesn't just expose technical flaws—it challenges processes, uncovers blind spots, and builds resilience against the most sophisticated threats.

What to Expect from This Book

This handbook is not a beginner's guide. It's a comprehensive resource for those ready to dive deeper into the art and science of red teaming. Across 13 chapters, you'll explore:

- **Advanced Tactics and Techniques**: From crafting complex phishing campaigns to exploiting zero-day vulnerabilities.
- **Realistic Simulations**: How to design and execute red team engagements that emulate advanced persistent threats (APTs).
- **Collaboration and Impact**: How to work effectively with blue teams and deliver insights that drive meaningful change.
- **Cutting-Edge Domains**: Expanding into emerging fields like cloud infrastructure attacks, physical intrusions, and social engineering.

Every chapter blends technical depth with strategic considerations, ensuring that you not only master the "how" but also understand the "why" behind each technique.

Who This Book is For

This book is written for cybersecurity professionals who are:

Red Team Practitioners: Looking to deepen their skills and expand their toolkit.

Blue Team Members: Interested in learning how attackers operate to better defend their environments.

Security Consultants: Seeking advanced methodologies to improve client engagements.

Ethical Hackers: Ready to elevate their penetration testing practices to full-fledged red teaming operations.

A Note on Ethics

With great power comes great responsibility. The techniques described in this book are intended solely for ethical purposes, under appropriate authorization and within the confines of the law. Red teamers must uphold the highest standards of integrity, ensuring their work strengthens security without causing harm.

Your Journey Starts Here

As you turn these pages, you'll embark on a journey that challenges you to think differently, adapt quickly, and act decisively. Red teaming is both an art and a science—a discipline that requires technical expertise, creativity, and a commitment to continuous learning. Let this handbook be your trusted guide as you navigate the thrilling, ever-changing world of offensive security.

Welcome to The Red Teamer's Handbook. Let's get to work.

About the Author

Gabriel Visage is a seasoned cybersecurity professional, ethical hacker, and red team strategist with over a decade of experience in offensive security. Known for his ability to think like an adversary while maintaining a deep commitment to ethical hacking, Gabriel has built a reputation as a trusted expert in helping organizations uncover their most elusive vulnerabilities.

Throughout his career, Gabriel has led red team engagements for Fortune 500 companies, critical infrastructure providers, and government agencies, simulating advanced cyberattacks to test and strengthen their defenses. His work spans a diverse range of domains, including network security, cloud infrastructure, social engineering, and physical penetration testing.

A Passion for Teaching and Sharing Knowledge

Gabriel's passion goes beyond breaking systems—he is dedicated to empowering others to defend them. Over the years, he has trained countless cybersecurity professionals through workshops, conference talks, and mentorship programs. His focus is not just on tools and techniques but on fostering a mindset of curiosity, creativity, and adaptability in the face of evolving threats.

A Voice in the Cybersecurity Community

As an active member of the cybersecurity community, Gabriel has contributed to industry standards, authored technical white papers, and collaborated on research initiatives exploring the latest in attack methodologies. He regularly speaks at leading conferences, including DEF CON, Black Hat, and BSides, where his presentations are lauded for their practical insights and real-world relevance.

Beyond Cybersecurity

When not immersed in the world of red teaming, Gabriel is an avid learner and a technology enthusiast. He enjoys exploring emerging technologies, experimenting with custom tool development, and delving into the psychology of social engineering. Outside of work, he is a strong advocate for cybersecurity awareness and regularly volunteers his time to educate students and aspiring professionals on the importance of digital security.

Why This Book?

Gabriel wrote The Red Teamer's Handbook to fill a gap he noticed in the industry—a lack of comprehensive, advanced resources tailored specifically for red teamers ready to push beyond the basics. This book represents years of hard-earned experience, countless hours spent refining tactics, and a desire to share practical knowledge that readers can apply directly in their engagomonto.

Through this handbook, Gabriel hopes to inspire a new generation of red teamers to elevate their craft, collaborate effectively, and ultimately, make the digital world a safer place.

1. Foundations of Red Teaming

Red teaming is more than just a technical exercise—it's a strategic approach to uncovering weaknesses by thinking like an adversary. This chapter lays the groundwork for understanding the philosophy and purpose behind red teaming, distinguishing it from penetration testing and other security assessments. We'll explore the historical evolution of red teaming, its role in modern cybersecurity, and the key methodologies that define successful engagements. By establishing a strong foundation, you'll be prepared to approach red teaming with the mindset, ethics, and precision needed to emulate real-world threats and drive meaningful improvements in security.

1.1 The History and Evolution of Red Teaming

The concept of "red teaming" in cybersecurity and military strategy can be traced back to its roots in military and intelligence operations, but its application in modern cybersecurity is a relatively recent development. The evolution of red teaming—from its origins as a tool for military preparedness to its current role in ethical hacking and security assessments—reflects the broader evolution of threat detection, strategy, and defense in both physical and digital environments.

Military Origins

Red teaming has its origins in military strategy, where it was used to simulate adversary tactics and challenge conventional thinking. The earliest recorded use of red teaming dates back to World War II, particularly in the United States military. During this time, military leaders began to recognize that traditional strategic planning often assumed that the enemy would follow predictable patterns. To overcome this limitation, the military established "Red Teams"—groups tasked with adopting the role of the enemy and devising strategies that could defeat their own defenses.

One of the most notable early examples of red teaming in a military context was the creation of the "Red Cell" within the U.S. Army. This group of adversarial thinkers was assigned to challenge military plans by adopting the perspective of enemy forces, helping to identify weaknesses in defensive positions, and stress-test strategies before implementation. By simulating adversary tactics, the Red Cells helped military leaders develop more robust plans and enhance their preparedness for unexpected threats.

Red Teaming in Intelligence and National Security

As red teaming evolved in the military, it found applications in national security and intelligence agencies. One of the most significant early uses was in war games and strategic simulations during the Cold War, where intelligence agencies in both the United States and the Soviet Union utilized red teams to simulate the actions of rival nations and test their responses to various threats. These simulations were used to explore potential scenarios in international conflicts, ranging from nuclear warfare to conventional military operations. The goal was to anticipate enemy strategies, better understand potential vulnerabilities, and refine defensive tactics.

In the 1970s, the U.S. government formally began using red teams within its intelligence agencies to simulate adversary behaviors and analyze vulnerabilities in national defense systems. One key example was the creation of "red cell" teams within the CIA and NSA, which were tasked with testing the U.S. government's security measures and identifying areas of weakness. This period marked the growing recognition that adversaries would always adapt, and security strategies needed to be dynamic and evolve as threats changed.

The Emergence of Red Teaming in Cybersecurity

The rise of the internet and digital technology in the late 20th and early 21st centuries led to the introduction of red teaming into the realm of cybersecurity. As organizations began to rely heavily on digital infrastructure, the importance of safeguarding critical systems and data became a priority. Traditional defense strategies focused primarily on preventing unauthorized access, but cybercriminals and state-sponsored actors were quickly evolving their tactics to exploit vulnerabilities in networks, applications, and systems.

In the early days of cybersecurity, penetration testing (often called "pen testing") became the standard method for evaluating security. Pen testers would attempt to exploit known vulnerabilities in systems to assess how easily they could gain unauthorized access. While valuable, pen testing was generally focused on technical weaknesses rather than simulating full-fledged, sophisticated attacks that mimic real-world adversaries. This is where red teaming came into play. Red teaming takes penetration testing a step further by focusing not just on identifying vulnerabilities but on emulating the tactics, techniques, and procedures (TTPs) of real attackers, such as cybercriminals, hacktivists, or nation-state adversaries.

The formal integration of red teaming into cybersecurity practices gained momentum in the late 1990s and early 2000s, as organizations started to recognize that conventional defenses were insufficient against the growing sophistication of cyber threats. Large corporations, government agencies, and military organizations began to establish red team operations to test their defenses against highly skilled, determined adversaries who would use complex, multi-stage attacks to infiltrate and exploit their systems.

Red Teaming in Modern Cybersecurity

As cyber threats have grown in sophistication, so too has the practice of red teaming. Today, red teaming is a critical component of proactive security programs and is increasingly used to simulate real-world attacks in order to identify weaknesses across an organization's entire security posture. Unlike traditional penetration testing, which tends to focus on a specific vulnerability or attack vector, red teaming takes a more holistic approach, simulating the actions of a determined adversary across all attack vectors.

Modern red teaming incorporates a wide array of techniques, from social engineering (such as phishing and pretexting) to advanced exploitation methods, lateral movement, and post-exploitation tactics. Red teams mimic the tactics of real-world adversaries, simulating attacks that range from cyber-espionage and data breaches to full-scale, sophisticated attacks that could disrupt critical infrastructure.

One of the key factors driving the evolution of red teaming is the growing recognition that cybersecurity is not just a matter of defending systems and networks—it's about developing an adversarial mindset and constantly testing and improving security measures in response to evolving threats. Red teams work closely with blue teams (defensive security teams) in what is known as "purple teaming," where offensive and defensive strategies are integrated to create a more robust security posture. In this collaborative environment, red teams not only simulate attacks but also help blue teams identify gaps in detection and response capabilities, ultimately strengthening an organization's overall defenses.

Tools and Techniques in Modern Red Teaming

With the advent of sophisticated tools and frameworks, modern red team operations are increasingly reliant on both custom and off-the-shelf solutions to conduct assessments. Popular tools like Metasploit, Cobalt Strike, and Empire allow red teamers to automate many of the tactics involved in exploitation and post-exploitation, enabling them to focus on more complex aspects of their engagement.

The development of techniques such as lateral movement, privilege escalation, and advanced evasion methods has made red teaming a critical activity for organizations seeking to defend against advanced persistent threats (APTs). These tools and techniques allow red teams to simulate the tactics of modern cybercriminals and nation-state actors, testing everything from network security and endpoint defenses to security awareness training and incident response protocols.

The Future of Red Teaming

As the cybersecurity landscape continues to evolve, the role of red teaming will become even more critical. The rise of cloud computing, artificial intelligence, and the increasing interconnectivity of devices (the Internet of Things, or IoT) present new challenges for red teams, requiring them to adapt their techniques to new attack surfaces and emerging technologies. Additionally, with the growing frequency of cyberattacks targeting both private organizations and government entities, red teaming will continue to play a central role in preparing defenses against sophisticated, multi-layered threats.

Furthermore, the practice of red teaming will increasingly integrate with other forms of cybersecurity assessments, such as threat hunting and active defense strategies. As attackers become more advanced and persistent, organizations will need to work collaboratively across all aspects of their cybersecurity programs, continually evolving to stay one step ahead.

The history and evolution of red teaming reflect the changing landscape of warfare, security, and technology. From its military roots to its current role in cybersecurity, red teaming has evolved into a vital tool for organizations seeking to protect themselves from sophisticated, evolving threats. By emulating adversaries' tactics, red teams help organizations identify weaknesses, challenge assumptions, and improve their defenses. As technology continues to evolve and cyber threats become more complex, the role of red teaming will remain a cornerstone of proactive, effective security programs.

1.2 Key Differences: Red Teaming vs. Penetration Testing vs. Purple Teaming

In the world of cybersecurity, various approaches are employed to assess an organization's defenses against potential threats. Among these, Red Teaming, Penetration Testing (Pen Testing), and Purple Teaming are three distinct methodologies that are often confused due to their similarities. While they all focus on identifying and mitigating security risks, each approach has its own unique objectives, scope, and techniques. Understanding the key differences between these practices is crucial for organizations to choose the most effective strategy for their cybersecurity needs.

Penetration Testing (Pen Testing)

Penetration Testing is a focused, time-bound, and tactical security assessment aimed at identifying vulnerabilities in specific systems or applications. It is a well-defined, scoped process, often executed with explicit permission from the organization, with the goal of discovering weaknesses that could be exploited by attackers.

Objective:

Penetration testing primarily aims to identify and exploit vulnerabilities in a defined system, application, or network. The focus is on specific assets, such as web applications, internal network configurations, or even a particular device like a server or firewall.

Scope:

Pen testing is typically narrow in scope. The tester is given a clear set of boundaries, such as a specific set of systems or applications to evaluate. It usually focuses on known vulnerabilities or weaknesses in a system's design and implementation.

Duration:

Penetration testing is generally time-limited and can range from a few days to a few weeks. Testers follow a structured engagement timeline, with clear phases such as reconnaissance, exploitation, and reporting.

Approach:

Penetration testing is more methodical and controlled compared to red teaming. It often relies on known attack vectors, vulnerability databases, and industry-standard tools to assess systems for weaknesses. It is often used to assess specific areas of concern, such as an organization's website or network perimeter.

Output:

The outcome of a penetration test is a detailed report that outlines discovered vulnerabilities, the exploitation process, and recommendations for remediation. The focus is primarily on technical details and specific security flaws.

Example:

A penetration tester might attempt to exploit a SQL injection vulnerability in an organization's e-commerce website or test a company's firewall configuration for weaknesses.

Red Teaming

Red Teaming, on the other hand, is a more holistic, adversarial simulation designed to test an organization's overall security posture by emulating the tactics, techniques, and procedures (TTPs) of real-world attackers, such as cybercriminals, hacktivists, or nation-state actors. Unlike penetration testing, which has a narrow focus, red teaming is a broader and more aggressive security exercise that simulates advanced, multi-stage attacks.

Objective:

The goal of red teaming is to simulate a real-world adversary attempting to breach an organization's defenses. Red teams don't just focus on technical vulnerabilities but take a comprehensive, adversary-focused approach that includes social engineering, physical penetration, and digital exploitation.

Scope:

Red team engagements typically have a wider scope compared to penetration tests. The team may have access to all aspects of the organization's security environment—both digital and physical systems, social engineering targets, and more. They are often tasked with attacking the organization through multiple vectors, such as email phishing, network penetration, and even physical security breaches.

Duration:

Red team engagements are usually longer and more complex than penetration tests. They can last anywhere from a few weeks to several months. The duration allows the red team to simulate a sustained attack campaign, testing detection, response, and resilience over time.

Approach:

Red teams operate with full autonomy to conduct their simulated attacks. They emulate the tactics of a real attacker, often using stealth, misdirection, and advanced techniques to evade detection. Red teams typically employ social engineering tactics, phishing, physical penetration, and sophisticated malware. Their objective is not just to identify vulnerabilities but to see how far they can go within the organization before being detected or stopped.

Output:

The final deliverable from a red team engagement is a comprehensive report that includes findings from multiple attack vectors. It includes a narrative of the red team's engagement, vulnerabilities found, how they were exploited, and recommendations for improving overall security. The focus is on building organizational resilience and improving detection and response capabilities, rather than just fixing specific vulnerabilities.

Example:

A red team might conduct a multi-phased operation, starting with a spear-phishing campaign, followed by exploiting a vulnerability in the company's internal network to escalate privileges, and eventually moving on to exfiltrating sensitive data while evading detection.

Purple Teaming

Purple Teaming is a collaborative approach that blends the strengths of both red and blue teams. The idea behind purple teaming is to foster collaboration between offensive (red team) and defensive (blue team) security experts to enhance the organization's overall security posture. While red and blue teams traditionally work separately, purple teams create an environment where they work together to improve detection, response, and prevention capabilities.

Objective:

The primary goal of purple teaming is to enhance the effectiveness of both red and blue teams through collaboration. Red teams simulate realistic attacks, while blue teams defend against them. The purple team approach emphasizes learning and improving in real time by analyzing attack scenarios, improving detection systems, and fine-tuning response strategies.

Scope:

Purple teaming can have a flexible scope. It can involve targeted scenarios, much like penetration testing, or broader, more extensive engagements, like red teaming. However, unlike red teaming, purple team engagements tend to have a shared focus on improving the organization's ability to detect and respond to adversary actions.

Duration:

Purple team engagements can range from shorter, focused exercises to longer, ongoing partnerships. They are often conducted in real-time, with red and blue teams collaborating to optimize defenses while a red team runs simulated attacks. In some cases, purple teams may be ongoing, as part of a continuous improvement cycle.

Approach:

The purple team methodology emphasizes communication and feedback. Red teams carry out attacks while blue teams monitor and defend, with both teams continuously exchanging information about tactics, tools, and vulnerabilities. This real-time interaction helps blue teams strengthen detection and response while providing red teams with valuable insights into the effectiveness of their attacks.

Output:

The output of a purple team engagement is not just a report of vulnerabilities and attacks, but a series of actionable insights that improve detection capabilities, defensive configurations, and overall incident response strategies. It's a more iterative approach than red teaming or penetration testing, focusing on improving the defensive side in real-time.

Example:

A purple team exercise might involve a red team launching a phishing campaign while the blue team attempts to detect it. After the attack, the two teams would meet to review the tactics, identify detection gaps, and improve the blue team's defensive measures for the future.

While pen testing, red teaming, and purple teaming are all critical methodologies in modern cybersecurity, they serve different purposes and offer distinct approaches to assessing and improving security. Penetration testing is ideal for finding specific vulnerabilities in a system, red teaming provides a comprehensive adversary simulation for testing an organization's resilience, and purple teaming fosters collaboration between attackers and defenders to optimize overall security posture. By understanding the key differences, organizations can choose the right approach based on their unique needs, helping them build stronger defenses and improve their ability to detect and respond to cyber threats.

1.3 Understanding Adversarial Mindsets

The concept of an adversarial mindset is crucial to red teaming, penetration testing, and cybersecurity defense. To effectively protect against and respond to cyber threats, security professionals must understand how adversaries—whether cybercriminals, hacktivists, insiders, or nation-state actors—think, plan, and execute their attacks. Developing an adversarial mindset helps security teams anticipate potential threats, improve defensive strategies, and ensure that they are not caught off-guard by sophisticated, evolving attacks.

This section explores the importance of adopting an adversarial mindset, the psychological and strategic elements that shape adversaries' decision-making processes, and how organizations can harness this understanding to strengthen their own security posture.

The Importance of Thinking Like an Adversary

An adversarial mindset is critical because cyberattacks rarely follow a linear or predictable path. Cybercriminals and other malicious actors constantly evolve their tactics, techniques, and procedures (TTPs) to circumvent defense mechanisms, making it vital for security professionals to think like the attackers they're defending against. This mindset shift requires security teams to step out of their defensive mindset and consider how attackers approach the same systems, networks, and data that they are tasked with protecting.

Understanding how adversaries think is not only useful for penetration testing or red teaming, but it also informs proactive defense strategies, incident response planning, and threat hunting. A security professional who adopts an adversarial mindset is better prepared to anticipate potential attack vectors, identify weaknesses, and create a more resilient cybersecurity architecture.

Key Elements of the Adversarial Mindset

1. Persistence and Patience

Adversaries, especially advanced persistent threats (APTs), tend to approach their attacks with patience and persistence. A well-funded, organized adversary, such as a nation-state actor, will often invest significant time and resources in developing sophisticated attack strategies. These attackers do not expect immediate success and are prepared to invest days, weeks, or even months to achieve their objectives. This requires a long-term view, with a focus on subtle, persistent tactics such as social engineering, stealthy malware deployment, and lateral movement within a network.

For example, an APT may conduct a phased attack: initially gaining access through phishing or exploiting a zero-day vulnerability, then establishing persistence via backdoors or other stealthy means. Once inside, the attacker will move laterally across the network, escalating privileges, and exfiltrating sensitive data without triggering detection.

Security professionals must recognize this persistence and design defenses that anticipate slow, incremental attacks that may evolve over time. This involves setting up systems that detect unusual activity across an extended period and analyzing network traffic and user behavior for signs of compromise, even if the attack is not immediately obvious.

2. Creativity and Resourcefulness

An adversarial mindset also involves creativity and resourcefulness. Attackers often find innovative ways to exploit system weaknesses that defenders may overlook. Cybercriminals and hacktivists, for instance, may craft highly targeted spear-phishing campaigns or exploit common misconfigurations within applications or networks. Rather than relying on common, well-known attack methods, sophisticated adversaries often take an unconventional approach, using tools and techniques that are harder to detect.

The creativity of an attacker can be seen in their use of social engineering techniques, where they manipulate human behavior to gain access to systems. For instance, attackers may impersonate a trusted individual within the organization, or exploit internal processes to trick employees into divulging sensitive information. In some cases, attackers may also develop custom malware or tools tailored to bypass specific security measures, avoiding signature-based detection mechanisms.

Security teams need to account for these creative methods in their defensive strategies, continuously adapting and evolving their security measures to prevent attackers from exploiting overlooked weaknesses. This includes training employees to recognize social engineering tactics, staying updated on emerging threats, and adopting flexible security frameworks that can adjust to new attack techniques.

3. Risk Tolerance

Another important aspect of an adversarial mindset is risk tolerance. Cyber attackers, particularly those with malicious intent, are often willing to take significant risks to achieve their goals. Unlike traditional business operations, where risk is typically minimized, adversaries frequently engage in risky behavior—such as attempting to breach systems in high-profile ways or triggering a system compromise that could alert defenders—to gain access to valuable assets or sensitive information.

This risk tolerance can manifest in several ways, such as the use of "living off the land" techniques, where attackers use tools already available within a compromised system to carry out their attacks, or in the deployment of highly destructive payloads that risk immediate detection.

For defenders, understanding an attacker's risk tolerance means adopting proactive detection methods that focus not just on preventing an attack but also on identifying risky or suspicious behavior patterns within the system. This could include implementing endpoint monitoring, identifying anomalies in user behavior, or setting up traps (honeypots) to deceive attackers into revealing themselves.

4. Adaptive and Opportunistic Behavior

Adversaries are adaptable and opportunistic by nature. When faced with obstacles—whether it's a patch in a software vulnerability or a security team detecting their actions—attackers will pivot quickly, altering their strategy or shifting tactics. For example, if an attacker discovers that their access method has been blocked, they may attempt another route, such as exploiting a different vulnerability, leveraging a social engineering attack, or finding new weaknesses to exploit.

Attackers are often highly opportunistic, looking for gaps in an organization's defenses that they can exploit. For instance, an adversary might take advantage of a neglected system that hasn't been patched or an employee who has weak password practices. In some cases, adversaries will target vulnerabilities in third-party vendors or supply chains, which may have weaker defenses than the primary target.

Organizations must stay ahead of attackers by implementing a robust, layered defense strategy that includes regular vulnerability assessments, threat hunting, and continuous monitoring for potential changes in attack tactics. The ability to quickly adapt to changing threat landscapes and identify new vulnerabilities is key to maintaining strong defenses.

Adversarial Mindset in Red Teaming and Pen Testing

For red teamers and penetration testers, adopting an adversarial mindset is essential to simulate realistic attack scenarios. In red teaming, the goal is not merely to exploit a vulnerability but to think like an adversary at every stage of the attack—from reconnaissance and initial access to lateral movement, persistence, and exfiltration. Red teamers are tasked with emulating real-world attackers by using the same tools, techniques, and procedures (TTPs) as cybercriminals, hacktivists, or state-sponsored actors. This requires adopting the mindset of an attacker to ensure that simulated threats are as realistic as possible.

In penetration testing, this mindset is also valuable, although the scope is typically narrower. A pen tester must still think like an attacker, finding the most effective attack vectors and considering how to exploit vulnerabilities in the system in creative and stealthy ways.

By simulating adversarial thinking in their operations, red teamers and penetration testers provide organizations with the insight they need to bolster defenses and close security gaps.

Training and Cultivating an Adversarial Mindset

Cultivating an adversarial mindset doesn't happen overnight. It requires security professionals to engage in continuous learning, exposure to real-world threat scenarios, and a proactive approach to understanding attacker behavior. Some key steps to develop an adversarial mindset include:

- **Studying Attacker Tactics and Techniques**: Reading reports from organizations like MITRE ATT&CK, which catalog adversary behavior, is essential for understanding how attackers operate and adapt their methods.
- **Hands-On Training**: Participating in red team exercises, Capture the Flag (CTF) challenges, or threat simulations can help hone the practical skills needed to think like an attacker.
- **Learning from Real-World Attacks**: Examining high-profile breaches or analyzing data from incident response cases allows security professionals to understand how real adversaries operate.

- **Collaborating with Offensive Security Teams**: Red teamers and penetration testers must continuously work with blue teams to enhance their knowledge and better understand the mindset of both attackers and defenders.

Understanding the adversarial mindset is fundamental to identifying vulnerabilities, anticipating attacks, and strengthening security defenses. By adopting the thinking patterns, strategies, and behaviors of real-world attackers, security professionals— whether in red teaming, penetration testing, or defensive roles—can develop better defenses, more accurate threat models, and more effective incident response strategies. The adversarial mindset requires persistence, creativity, risk tolerance, and adaptability— qualities that are critical not only to successfully attacking systems but also to defending them against ever-evolving threats. Through continuous learning and applying these principles, cybersecurity teams can stay one step ahead of adversaries and build stronger, more resilient systems.

1.4 The Importance of Rules of Engagement and Scope

In the world of cybersecurity, whether conducting a red team exercise, penetration testing, or any form of security assessment, establishing clear Rules of Engagement (RoE) and Scope is critical to the success and integrity of the operation. These elements are foundational to ensuring that the assessment is conducted ethically, legally, and with the full knowledge and consent of all relevant stakeholders. In this section, we'll explore what Rules of Engagement and Scope entail, their importance, and how they contribute to effective and responsible cybersecurity assessments.

What are Rules of Engagement (RoE)?

Rules of Engagement (RoE) define the boundaries and expectations for how a security assessment, such as a red team exercise or penetration test, will be conducted. They outline the specific actions that are allowed and prohibited, ensuring that both the offensive (red team or penetration testers) and defensive teams (blue teams or system owners) operate within a clearly defined framework. RoE are essentially the "ground rules" for the engagement and can vary significantly depending on the type of test being conducted, the maturity of the organization's security program, and the level of authorization provided.

RoE typically include:

- **Attack Techniques and Methods**: What techniques, tactics, and procedures (TTPs) the team can use (e.g., social engineering, phishing, exploiting specific vulnerabilities).
- **Allowed Tools and Tools Restrictions**: A list of approved tools or methods, and restrictions on using certain tools to avoid damaging production systems.
- **Duration of Engagement**: The timeframe in which the test can take place, whether it's a few hours, days, or weeks.
- **Areas of Focus**: Specific systems, applications, or assets to be tested, and any exclusions or areas that should not be tested.
- **Escalation Procedures**: Steps for reporting any critical findings or unexpected issues, such as system outages, during the engagement.
- **Ethical and Legal Boundaries**: Clear guidance on ethical behavior, including any legal considerations, such as respecting privacy and confidentiality, and staying within the bounds of local and international laws.

These rules protect the interests of the organization being tested and ensure that the engagement is conducted professionally and within ethical boundaries.

What is Scope?

The Scope of an engagement refers to the specific parameters and targets of the security assessment. It defines the assets, systems, or environments that are in-scope for the assessment, as well as those that are out-of-scope. Properly defining the scope ensures that the red team or penetration testers focus on the areas that are of most importance to the organization, without causing undue harm or unnecessary disruption to non-critical systems.

The scope should include:

- **Targeted Systems and Networks**: Which systems, applications, and networks are part of the assessment? For instance, does the test focus on internal systems, external facing services, or cloud-based infrastructure?
- **Exclusions**: What systems or areas should not be tested, such as certain critical production systems or sensitive data repositories? This could also include specific departments or environments that must remain undisturbed.
- **Attack Vectors**: Which attack vectors are included in the engagement? For example, social engineering, physical security testing, web application vulnerabilities, or wireless network penetration.

- **Stakeholder Access**: Does the engagement allow red teamers to interact with specific individuals or departments? Should they conduct physical penetration testing, or is it strictly a digital engagement?
- **Boundary Conditions**: This could include rules for not disrupting services, respecting user privacy, or operating within defined business hours.

Clear scoping helps ensure that the assessment remains focused on the most critical aspects of an organization's security posture, avoiding unnecessary risks to systems outside the intended test parameters.

Why are Rules of Engagement and Scope Important?

1. Protecting the Organization's Interests

Without clear RoE and scope, there's a risk that a security assessment could inadvertently disrupt critical business operations or compromise sensitive data. For instance, conducting a penetration test or red team exercise on a live production system without proper authorization or limitations could lead to downtime, data loss, or breach of confidentiality.

Having well-defined RoE and scope ensures that both the security team and the organization are on the same page regarding what is being tested, how it will be tested, and any risks associated with the process. This is particularly important for maintaining operational continuity and safeguarding the integrity of business-critical systems and services.

2. Legal and Ethical Considerations

RoE and scope are essential in ensuring that a security assessment is conducted ethically and within legal boundaries. Unauthorized testing, particularly involving sensitive data, can lead to legal repercussions, including privacy violations, non-compliance with regulatory frameworks, or even litigation. The scope and RoE provide a safeguard against potential breaches of privacy laws and ensure that data protection laws (such as GDPR or HIPAA) are respected.

For example, red teaming may involve accessing physical premises or engaging in social engineering attacks. These activities must be explicitly authorized to avoid accusations of fraud, trespassing, or invasion of privacy.

3. Clear Communication and Accountability

RoE and scope set expectations for both the red team and the organization's defenders (or blue team). By defining clear boundaries, everyone knows what is allowed and what is off-limits. This helps prevent misunderstandings, confusion, or the misapplication of attack techniques that could cause unintended damage or alert defenders prematurely.

The communication provided by RoE and scope also helps clarify roles and responsibilities during the engagement. If something unexpected happens—such as a critical vulnerability being exploited or an important service being impacted—the escalation procedures within the RoE provide a framework for responsible handling of the situation. This ensures that everyone involved is aligned on how to react to challenges, minimizing risks to the organization.

4. Ensuring Comprehensive Security Coverage

Properly defined RoE and scope ensure that the engagement covers all necessary areas without unnecessary overlap. In red team engagements, for example, the red team may be tasked with assessing multiple attack vectors, such as phishing, web application vulnerabilities, and physical security. Without a well-defined scope, there could be confusion over whether social engineering is included, or whether physical access to the premises is part of the engagement.

A comprehensive scope ensures that critical systems and areas are tested, while minimizing the chance that irrelevant or unnecessary systems are included. This improves the effectiveness of the security assessment by allowing the red team to focus on the most relevant threats, vulnerabilities, and attack vectors.

Key Aspects to Define in RoE and Scope

To ensure the success of any security engagement, consider the following key points when defining RoE and scope:

- **Authorization**: Clear consent and approval from senior management and relevant stakeholders must be documented before any engagement begins.
- **Impact Minimization**: Define protocols for ensuring that tests will not cause undue disruption or affect business operations. This includes specifying times when testing can occur and ensuring systems are fully backed up.
- **Test Boundaries**: Set strict boundaries for testing—what can and cannot be targeted, which tools can be used, and which tactics (e.g., denial-of-service attacks) are off-limits.

- **Timeframe**: Clearly define the start and end dates for the engagement to prevent any unauthorized testing from happening before or after the agreed-upon period.
- **Escalation Protocol**: Create a protocol for escalating issues if an attack unexpectedly impacts a critical system or if sensitive data is inadvertently accessed.

In cybersecurity assessments, especially those involving red teaming, penetration testing, or other forms of security testing, Rules of Engagement and Scope are not just formalities—they are essential tools for ensuring that the engagement is conducted ethically, legally, and effectively. By providing clear guidelines for what is allowed, what is excluded, and how the engagement will be conducted, these elements protect both the organization and the testing team. Establishing well-defined RoE and scope minimizes risks, ensures that resources are focused on the most relevant security challenges, and sets clear expectations for both offensive and defensive teams. Properly implemented, these frameworks provide the necessary structure for successful, safe, and productive security assessments.

2. Threat Modeling and Reconnaissance

Every successful red team operation begins with thorough planning and reconnaissance. In this chapter, we delve into the art of threat modeling—building a detailed understanding of your target's environment from the perspective of an adversary. You'll learn how to gather critical intelligence using OSINT techniques, identify attack vectors, and map potential paths to compromise. By combining technical tools with strategic insight, this chapter equips you to design realistic and impactful engagements that mimic the tactics of sophisticated threat actors.

2.1 Building Threat Models: Mapping the Adversary's Perspective

Threat modeling is a fundamental aspect of both red teaming and cybersecurity defense. It involves identifying, understanding, and prioritizing potential threats to an organization's systems, networks, and data. By building effective threat models, security professionals can proactively defend against cyberattacks, anticipate adversary tactics, and better secure critical assets. This section focuses on how to build threat models that map the adversary's perspective, helping organizations think like attackers to identify weaknesses and vulnerabilities from the "other side."

What is Threat Modeling?

Threat modeling is the process of identifying and evaluating potential threats to a system and its components. The goal of threat modeling is to predict where vulnerabilities might exist and how adversaries may exploit them. By understanding the system from the perspective of a potential attacker, organizations can prioritize their security efforts and make informed decisions about how to defend critical assets.

The process typically involves:

- **Identifying assets**: What information, systems, or services are most valuable and need to be protected?
- **Identifying threats**: What kind of threats (external or internal) are most likely to target these assets?
- **Identifying vulnerabilities**: What weaknesses or gaps could an attacker exploit?

- **Analyzing potential impact**: What would happen if an attacker successfully exploits a vulnerability or gains access to a sensitive asset?
- **Mitigation strategies**: What can be done to reduce the likelihood or impact of the identified threats?

By systematically approaching these questions, security professionals can better understand the threat landscape and implement appropriate defenses.

Why Map the Adversary's Perspective?

To build an effective threat model, it's crucial to adopt the adversary's perspective. This shift in mindset allows security teams to anticipate how an attacker might think, plan, and execute their strategies. By focusing on the attacker's perspective, security professionals can identify blind spots and weaknesses in their defenses that may otherwise be overlooked.

Several factors make this approach crucial:

Real-World Attack Scenarios: Cyberattacks rarely follow a simple, predictable path. Adversaries use varied methods, sometimes relying on social engineering, sometimes on technical exploits, and other times on insider threats. Mapping the adversary's perspective helps organizations anticipate and prepare for the most likely attack vectors, from phishing to advanced persistent threats (APTs).

Resource Allocation: Security resources are often limited, so it's important to prioritize defenses based on real-world threats. By understanding the tactics an adversary would use to target an organization, defenders can focus their efforts on the most critical areas.

Continuous Adaptation: Threat actors constantly evolve their tactics to bypass defenses. By staying focused on the adversary's perspective, security teams can keep pace with emerging threats and continuously refine their defense strategies.

Steps for Building a Threat Model from the Adversary's Perspective

1. Identify and Prioritize Critical Assets

The first step in threat modeling is to identify the assets that are most critical to the organization. These can include:

- Sensitive data (e.g., personally identifiable information, intellectual property, financial data)
- Critical infrastructure (e.g., network equipment, cloud servers, databases)
- Reputation and brand value (e.g., customer trust, public image)
- Intellectual property (e.g., proprietary software, trade secrets)

Once critical assets are identified, they should be prioritized based on their importance to the organization and the potential impact of their compromise. The adversary's goal is to either steal, destroy, or gain control of these assets, so understanding their value helps determine where to focus defensive efforts.

2. Identify Potential Adversaries

Next, the organization must define the types of adversaries that might target these critical assets. Adversaries vary widely in their motivations, techniques, and resources. Some common types include:

Cybercriminals: Often motivated by financial gain, these attackers typically target weaknesses in web applications, systems, or users to steal sensitive data or perform financial fraud.

Hacktivists: These attackers are motivated by political or social causes and typically target high-profile organizations to draw attention to their message.

Nation-State Actors: These attackers may have sophisticated tools and extensive resources, with objectives ranging from espionage to disruption of critical infrastructure.

Insiders: These threats originate from within the organization itself and may involve disgruntled employees or contractors with knowledge of the system.

By understanding the type of adversary, their goals, capabilities, and attack patterns, an organization can more accurately model how an attack might unfold and which areas of the system would be most vulnerable.

3. Map Attack Vectors

With the adversary and assets identified, the next step is to map out the possible attack vectors. An attack vector is any method an attacker can use to gain access to a system. Attack vectors can vary greatly depending on the adversary's capabilities, the target organization's defenses, and the overall security posture of the systems in place.

Common attack vectors to consider include:

External Attack Vectors: These may include remote access through the internet, exploiting vulnerabilities in public-facing web applications, email phishing campaigns, or DNS poisoning. Adversaries may target public services like email, web servers, and APIs to gain initial access to an organization's network.

Internal Attack Vectors: Once an attacker has gained a foothold in a network, they may attempt to escalate privileges, move laterally within the network, and exfiltrate data. These attack vectors may involve exploiting misconfigured internal systems, social engineering techniques targeting employees, or abusing legitimate credentials.

Physical Attack Vectors: Adversaries may attempt to access physical premises or systems, bypassing physical security measures to implant malware, steal devices, or gain unauthorized access to internal networks.

Mapping these attack vectors allows security teams to determine which areas are most exposed and need strengthening.

4. Identify Vulnerabilities and Weaknesses

Once attack vectors are identified, it's essential to assess where vulnerabilities and weaknesses may exist within the systems. Vulnerabilities can include:

- Unpatched software or operating systems with known security flaws.
- Weak authentication protocols, such as poor password policies or lack of multi-factor authentication (MFA).
- Misconfigurations in cloud environments, web applications, or internal servers.
- Human factors, including a lack of security awareness training or failure to recognize phishing attempts.

Understanding where these vulnerabilities exist helps in predicting how adversaries might exploit them and gain unauthorized access to systems or data. By addressing these weaknesses, an organization can reduce the attack surface and prevent adversaries from achieving their objectives.

5. Simulate the Adversary's Attack Path

After mapping out potential attack vectors and vulnerabilities, security teams should attempt to simulate the adversary's attack path. This involves imagining how the adversary might exploit identified weaknesses and progress through the system to achieve their goal. Attackers often follow a multi-phase process, which can include:

Initial Access: The attacker gains entry to the system, often through phishing, exploiting software vulnerabilities, or gaining physical access.

Persistence: Once inside, the attacker establishes ways to maintain access, such as by installing backdoors or modifying system configurations.

Lateral Movement: The attacker moves within the network, escalating privileges and gaining access to additional systems.

Exfiltration: Finally, the attacker may extract sensitive data or disrupt critical services, achieving their goal.

Simulating this attack path helps organizations understand how an attack could unfold and where defensive measures need to be improved to stop the attacker at each stage.

6. Develop Mitigation Strategies

Once the threat model is complete, the next step is to develop mitigation strategies. These should address the most critical vulnerabilities and attack vectors that could be exploited by adversaries. Common mitigation strategies include:

- Patching vulnerabilities and ensuring software is kept up to date.
- Implementing strong access controls, such as multi-factor authentication (MFA) and the principle of least privilege.
- Monitoring networks for unusual activity that might indicate a breach.
- User training to increase awareness of phishing attacks and social engineering tactics.

By addressing the highest-priority threats and weaknesses, organizations can significantly reduce the likelihood of successful attacks.

Building a threat model by mapping the adversary's perspective is a critical exercise for any organization looking to strengthen its cybersecurity defenses. By thinking like an attacker, security professionals can identify attack vectors, vulnerabilities, and weaknesses that might otherwise be missed. Through careful analysis of the adversary's potential strategies, organizations can develop more effective defenses, prioritize remediation efforts, and ensure a higher level of protection for their most critical assets. Threat modeling is a dynamic, iterative process that helps security teams stay ahead of evolving threats and adapt their strategies as new attack methods emerge.

2.2 OSINT Deep Dive: Extracting Critical Information from Public Sources

In the world of cybersecurity, one of the most potent tools for adversaries and defenders alike is Open-Source Intelligence (OSINT). OSINT involves gathering publicly available information from various sources, including websites, social media, public records, and other open platforms, to build a comprehensive understanding of a target's infrastructure, operations, or vulnerabilities. For red teams and penetration testers, mastering OSINT techniques is crucial to effectively mapping the attack surface and identifying entry points. In this section, we will delve deep into how to extract critical information from public sources and utilize it for red team engagements and security assessments.

What is OSINT?

Open-Source Intelligence (OSINT) is intelligence collected from publicly available sources. Unlike traditional intelligence-gathering methods, which may involve clandestine or unauthorized activities, OSINT focuses on leveraging data that is freely available on the internet or through other public channels. This information can provide invaluable insights into a target organization, its employees, technologies, and potential vulnerabilities.

OSINT can include:

- **Websites**: The target's corporate websites, blogs, and forums where details about their systems, services, and technologies may be shared.
- **Social Media**: Platforms like LinkedIn, Twitter, and Facebook can reveal personal information about employees, company activities, and even unintentional disclosures.
- **Public Records**: Documents such as business registrations, patents, court filings, and government reports.
- **Domain and Network Information**: DNS records, WHOIS data, and IP address ranges that can provide clues about a target's infrastructure.

- **Code Repositories**: Platforms like GitHub, GitLab, or Bitbucket, where an organization's developers may have exposed sensitive source code or credentials.

The advantage of OSINT is that it doesn't require breaking any laws or engaging in covert activities, making it a powerful tool for ethical hacking and security assessments.

The Importance of OSINT in Red Teaming

For red teams, OSINT serves as a critical starting point for understanding the target. The primary value of OSINT lies in its ability to help red teamers build an adversarial model of the organization, identify potential attack vectors, and uncover vulnerabilities before launching more invasive techniques. Here's why OSINT is so important for red teaming:

Reconnaissance Phase: OSINT plays a pivotal role in the initial reconnaissance phase, where red teamers gather information about the target. Knowing the target's public footprint helps in crafting realistic attack scenarios.

Social Engineering: Many successful attacks, especially in the early stages, are the result of social engineering. Red teamers can use OSINT to identify personal details about employees (such as email addresses, roles, and interests) to conduct phishing campaigns, impersonation attacks, or pretexting.

Mapping the Attack Surface: OSINT allows attackers to uncover exposed systems, services, and vulnerabilities in an organization's external-facing assets, like web applications or cloud environments. This information helps determine the most efficient path to gain unauthorized access.

Improving Attack Success Rate: Armed with knowledge gathered through OSINT, red teamers can tailor their attacks to be more effective and less likely to be detected early. Understanding the target's technology stack, network architecture, and employees' behaviors ensures that the attack is crafted to exploit the weakest points.

Techniques for Extracting Critical Information with OSINT

Building an effective OSINT strategy requires using a variety of techniques to extract meaningful data from multiple sources. Below are some of the most valuable methods for gathering and analyzing OSINT:

1. Domain and WHOIS Lookups

When targeting an organization, one of the first things a red team should do is identify the organization's domains and associated IP addresses. This provides a clear map of the organization's online presence and infrastructure.

WHOIS Data: WHOIS databases provide registration information about domain names, including registrants' names, contact information, and domain expiration dates. By querying WHOIS databases, red teamers can identify the owners of a domain and sometimes discover administrative contact information. Many organizations overlook the security of their WHOIS records, making them a valuable source of OSINT.

DNS Records: A Domain Name System (DNS) query can help uncover information about the organization's internal infrastructure, such as mail servers, name servers, and subdomains. For example, DNS queries can identify exposed services like FTP servers, mail servers, or even VPN infrastructure that might be vulnerable to attack.

2. Social Media Scraping

Employees often share a significant amount of information on social media platforms that can be leveraged for OSINT. Red teamers can scan platforms like LinkedIn, Twitter, Facebook, and even personal blogs for information about the target organization's personnel, software stacks, technologies, locations, and even ongoing projects.

Employee Information: LinkedIn profiles can reveal roles, job descriptions, work histories, and sometimes even connections to vendors or partners. In addition, LinkedIn can provide insights into the tools and technologies used by employees, which is crucial for identifying potential vulnerabilities in software or services.

Publicly Available Intelligence: Twitter and Facebook posts may include insights into upcoming initiatives, internal developments, or personal information that can be used for social engineering attacks like phishing or pretexting.

Photos and Locations: Geotagged photos on platforms like Instagram or Facebook may inadvertently reveal sensitive details about an organization's locations or even office layouts.

3. Search Engine Techniques and Google Dorks

Search engines like Google can be a goldmine for OSINT. By refining search queries and utilizing specific search operators, red teamers can unearth a wealth of information.

Google dorks, or advanced search queries, allow attackers to perform highly targeted searches to extract specific information from websites.

Example Queries: Some common Google dorks might include:

- **filetype**:pdf site:target.com to find PDF documents published by the target.
- **intitle**:"index of" "backup" to locate publicly accessible backup directories.
- **inurl**:"/wp-admin/" to find WordPress admin login pages exposed to the internet.

These targeted search queries help red teamers locate sensitive files, exposed login pages, or even potential misconfigurations that could lead to a security breach.

4. Social Engineering and Phishing

One of the most powerful forms of OSINT in a red team engagement is the ability to use gathered data for social engineering. By knowing the target organization's staff members, their roles, and their communications, red teamers can craft convincing emails or phone calls that trick employees into divulging sensitive information or clicking on malicious links.

Crafting Phishing Campaigns: Using social media and internal company websites, red teamers can extract the names, job titles, and even interests of employees to create highly personalized phishing emails. For instance, an email from "HR" with an employee's name in the subject line and references to an internal initiative could easily deceive a staff member into clicking on a link or opening an attachment.

Pretexting and Impersonation: Using publicly available information to impersonate someone the target trusts is a classic social engineering technique. OSINT can help red teamers build a believable pretext and manipulate employees into providing access to secure systems or physical locations.

5. Code Repositories and Open Source Platforms

Public code repositories such as GitHub, GitLab, and Bitbucket can contain vast amounts of sensitive information, including API keys, credentials, or insecure coding practices. Developers may unintentionally upload source code that includes hardcoded secrets, access keys, or even configuration files that could provide attackers with access to systems and applications.

Reviewing Repositories: By searching for specific keywords such as password, API key, or client_secret, red teamers can uncover sensitive data exposed in open repositories.

Even code snippets that describe internal systems or technologies used by the organization can provide useful clues for attack planning.

Challenges and Ethical Considerations in OSINT

While OSINT is an invaluable tool for red teamers, it's not without its challenges and ethical considerations:

Volume of Data: The sheer volume of publicly available information can be overwhelming. Effective OSINT requires skillful filtering and analysis to identify truly relevant data without getting bogged down in noise.

Data Privacy: Although OSINT involves public data, there are still ethical boundaries. Gathering information from social media platforms or private forums must be done carefully to avoid breaching privacy expectations or violating terms of service.

Legality: OSINT techniques should be used ethically and within the boundaries of the law. For example, scraping personal data or engaging in unauthorized data extraction from websites can violate privacy regulations or terms of use agreements.

Open-Source Intelligence (OSINT) is a critical component of red teaming and penetration testing. By extracting critical information from publicly available sources, red teamers can gain deep insights into an organization's vulnerabilities, systems, and employees. Techniques like domain lookups, social media scraping, and code repository analysis provide valuable intelligence that helps attackers craft precise and effective attack strategies. However, while OSINT is a powerful tool, it must be used ethically, legally, and responsibly. When done correctly, OSINT enables red teams to simulate realistic adversary behavior, identify weaknesses, and ultimately help organizations bolster their defenses against real-world threats.

2.3 Advanced Reconnaissance Techniques and Tools

Reconnaissance is a critical phase in red teaming and penetration testing, where the goal is to gather as much information as possible about the target organization. It sets the foundation for crafting an attack strategy and understanding the vulnerabilities in the target's network, systems, and personnel. In advanced reconnaissance, the techniques and tools used go beyond basic methods to provide deeper insights into the target's infrastructure, defenses, and weaknesses.

This section will explore advanced reconnaissance techniques and the tools commonly used to carry out these activities in red teaming engagements. From sophisticated network scanning to social engineering tactics, mastering these techniques will help red teamers better simulate real-world attackers and uncover hidden vulnerabilities in their targets.

What is Advanced Reconnaissance?

Advanced reconnaissance takes the process of information gathering to the next level by using more targeted and complex techniques to extract deep insights into a target organization. While basic reconnaissance (e.g., domain searches, WHOIS lookups, social media profiling) provides useful initial information, advanced reconnaissance aims to uncover additional layers of detail, often through covert or less obvious channels. This level of reconnaissance is particularly important for simulating advanced persistent threats (APTs), state-sponsored actors, or highly skilled cybercriminals who leverage specialized tools and methodologies to conduct thorough attacks.

Key Goals of Advanced Reconnaissance

- **Identify Hidden Infrastructure**: Beyond basic network mapping, advanced reconnaissance helps uncover hidden or obscure systems, servers, and services that may be exposed unintentionally or poorly secured.
- **Map Attack Vectors**: Advanced reconnaissance seeks to map out multiple paths an attacker could take to gain access to the network or escalate privileges within the environment.
- **Avoid Detection**: Unlike initial, noisy scans, advanced techniques often focus on avoiding detection by intrusion detection systems (IDS), firewalls, or honeypots.
- **Gather Detailed Information on Employees**: Deep insights into the target organization's personnel, their roles, and their online behavior can provide opportunities for social engineering attacks.

In the following sections, we will discuss some of the most advanced reconnaissance techniques, including DNS enumeration, passive network scanning, deep social media analysis, and the use of specialized tools.

Techniques for Advanced Reconnaissance

1. DNS and Subdomain Enumeration

DNS (Domain Name System) enumeration is an advanced reconnaissance technique used to gather information about a target's network, subdomains, and related infrastructure.

Why It's Important: Subdomain enumeration reveals hidden web applications, staging servers, backup sites, and internal network domains that may not be visible through regular searches. Attackers can exploit misconfigured subdomains to find vulnerable services that aren't normally visible to the public.

Techniques:

- **Brute Forcing**: Using wordlists to guess subdomains and identify hidden entries (e.g., staging.target.com, dev.target.com).
- **DNS Zone Transfer**: A poorly configured DNS server may allow unauthorized users to initiate a zone transfer. This can provide a full list of subdomains, IP addresses, and associated services within a domain.

Reverse DNS Lookup: Conducting reverse lookups on IP address ranges may reveal hidden subdomains or internal services that are not directly linked to the main website. Tools:

- **dnsdumpster.com**: An online DNS reconnaissance tool that helps map out a target's DNS records and associated infrastructure.
- **Sublist3r**: A popular Python-based tool for subdomain enumeration that uses search engines, DNS services, and brute-forcing techniques to gather subdomains.
- **Fierce**: A DNS reconnaissance tool designed to locate DNS records and enumerate subdomains.

2. Passive and Active Network Scanning

Network scanning can be broken down into passive and active scanning. Both techniques are vital in advanced reconnaissance, with passive scanning being used to avoid detection and active scanning providing more in-depth insights into the network.

Passive Network Scanning: This method involves gathering information without directly interacting with the target network. Passive scanning avoids triggering alarms or revealing the attacker's presence to intrusion detection systems (IDS).

Data Sources: Publicly available sources, like network traffic analysis, DNS, WHOIS, and even social media, can provide indirect information about the target network's architecture without the need for direct probing.

Tool Example:

- **Shodan**: A search engine that scans the internet for devices, such as routers, servers, webcams, and IoT devices, that are exposed to the internet. It can be used to passively gather information about open ports, services, and device configurations.
- **Censys**: Another powerful tool that provides a comprehensive search of exposed services and devices on the internet. It allows red teamers to search by certificate, IP address, or specific service details.

Active Network Scanning: Active scanning involves sending requests to a target network and analyzing responses to identify systems, services, and vulnerabilities. This method can be detected, so care must be taken to avoid alerting the target.

Network Scanning Tools:

- Nmap: One of the most widely used network scanning tools, Nmap is capable of discovering hosts, identifying services, and even detecting vulnerabilities.
- Masscan: Similar to Nmap, but faster and designed for large-scale scanning. Masscan can scan millions of IP addresses in a short amount of time and is ideal for discovering open ports.
- Netcat: Often called the "Swiss Army knife" of networking, Netcat can be used for banner grabbing, port scanning, and even creating reverse shells.

3. Social Media Analysis and Employee Profiling

Social media provides a goldmine of publicly available information that can be leveraged for advanced reconnaissance. Red teamers can analyze social media platforms such as LinkedIn, Twitter, Facebook, Instagram, and even GitHub to gather insights into a target's organizational structure, technologies, and even internal operations.

Why It's Important: By analyzing employees' social media profiles, an attacker can discover valuable information such as their job roles, the technologies they use, work habits, and even sensitive data that can be used for social engineering or spear-phishing campaigns.

Techniques:

- **LinkedIn Scraping**: LinkedIn provides detailed information about an employee's job role, skill sets, and work history. By mapping out the employees, their departments, and their titles, a red teamer can identify high-value targets for attacks.
- **Twitter Analysis**: Twitter posts can provide real-time insights into company activities, upcoming events, and potential vulnerabilities (e.g., a developer posting about a bug they are working on).
- **Geolocation Tagging**: Analyzing photos or posts that include geolocation data can reveal locations of offices, employees, and even security weaknesses (e.g., employees posting about leaving work after hours).

Tools:

- **Social-Engineer Toolkit (SET):** SET is a powerful framework for social engineering attacks, capable of crafting phishing emails and pretexting scenarios based on information gathered through OSINT.
- **Hunter.io**: A tool to find email addresses associated with a domain. By searching for employees' email patterns, you can identify staff members and their roles.
- **Maltego**: A data mining tool that aggregates information from multiple sources, including social media, and visualizes relationships between people, companies, and other entities.

4. Advanced OSINT Tools for Deep Reconnaissance

In addition to the tools mentioned earlier, several advanced OSINT tools are essential for deep reconnaissance. These tools allow red teamers to gather intelligence from hard-to-reach or obscure sources, further enhancing their understanding of the target.

Tools:

- **Recon-ng**: A powerful OSINT framework that offers a modular approach to gathering information. It automates the process of collecting intelligence from various sources such as social media, DNS, and WHOIS.
- **theHarvester**: A tool designed for gathering email addresses, subdomains, and domain information. It aggregates data from a wide variety of search engines and public databases.

- **SpiderFoot**: An open-source OSINT automation tool that scans the web and various data sources to find relevant information about the target. It can be used to collect data on domains, IP addresses, and social media profiles.
- **FOCA**: A tool used for analyzing metadata in documents that are available online. It can extract useful information like usernames, software versions, and server configurations from PDF files, Word documents, and other formats.

Advanced reconnaissance is a cornerstone of any effective red team engagement, and mastering these techniques and tools is essential for uncovering the full extent of an organization's attack surface. By using methods such as DNS enumeration, passive and active network scanning, social media analysis, and specialized OSINT tools, red teamers can gather the deep insights needed to simulate sophisticated cyberattacks. These methods not only help to identify vulnerabilities but also assist in mapping out attack paths, social engineering targets, and areas of opportunity to exploit. When executed carefully and thoroughly, advanced reconnaissance increases the effectiveness of red team engagements and helps organizations strengthen their defenses against real-world threats.

2.4 Identifying Attack Paths Using Threat Intelligence

In the world of cybersecurity, understanding potential attack paths is crucial for both offensive and defensive strategies. Threat intelligence plays a pivotal role in identifying these attack paths by providing valuable insights into how adversaries operate, what tactics they use, and where they focus their efforts. Red teaming, in particular, relies heavily on threat intelligence to simulate real-world cyberattacks and craft realistic attack paths that align with the most current threat landscape.

This section explores how threat intelligence is used to identify attack paths, how it enhances the red teaming process, and the tools and methodologies red teams can use to map out attack vectors. By utilizing up-to-date intelligence, red teamers can model realistic adversary behavior, simulate targeted attacks, and understand how to exploit vulnerabilities in their targets' defenses.

What is Threat Intelligence?

Threat intelligence refers to the process of collecting, analyzing, and interpreting data regarding potential or actual threats to an organization's security. This information helps organizations understand the tactics, techniques, and procedures (TTPs) used by cybercriminals, state-sponsored actors, hacktivists, and other malicious entities. Threat intelligence is often classified into different types based on its source, specificity, and the depth of the data.

- **Strategic Threat Intelligence**: High-level data focused on long-term trends, emerging threats, geopolitical factors, and general adversary behaviors.
- **Tactical Threat Intelligence**: More detailed information that focuses on specific adversary tactics, techniques, and tools used in cyberattacks.
- **Operational Threat Intelligence**: Focused on specific threats and campaigns, often involving current or ongoing attacks.
- **Technical Threat Intelligence**: The most granular form, consisting of details like malware hashes, IP addresses, attack infrastructure, vulnerabilities, and indicators of compromise (IOCs).

For red teams, tactical and operational threat intelligence is of particular importance as it provides actionable insights that can be used to simulate specific attack paths and adversarial tactics.

How Threat Intelligence Helps Identify Attack Paths

The process of identifying attack paths using threat intelligence involves understanding the possible ways that adversaries could breach an organization's defenses. Attack paths, also known as attack vectors, are the routes or methods through which an adversary gains unauthorized access to an organization's systems, data, or network. Threat intelligence helps red teamers identify these paths by providing the necessary context and insights into known tactics, vulnerabilities, and attack techniques.

Here's how threat intelligence contributes to identifying attack paths:

1. Mapping Adversary Tactics, Techniques, and Procedures (TTPs)

The MITRE ATT&CK framework is an invaluable tool for red teams when mapping attack paths. This framework categorizes adversary behaviors and helps identify the steps a threat actor may take during an attack. By studying these TTPs, red teamers can identify where the vulnerabilities are most likely to be exploited in an organization's defenses.

Example: If a red team is simulating a phishing attack that leads to initial access, threat intelligence will help them understand how a specific adversary group, such as a ransomware actor, typically uses social engineering to gain access. The red team can then tailor their approach using the same tools and techniques to match what is known about the actor.

By leveraging intelligence on the TTPs of specific threat groups, red teamers can map out the most probable attack paths and understand how best to exploit weaknesses in the target organization.

2. Identifying Vulnerabilities and Exposures

Threat intelligence feeds often include information about newly discovered vulnerabilities, zero-day exploits, and other weaknesses in software or hardware. This intelligence can be used by red teamers to focus their efforts on systems or services that are vulnerable to known exploits.

Example: A zero-day vulnerability in a popular content management system (CMS) like WordPress could present a viable attack path if the target organization uses the vulnerable version. Red teamers can use this intelligence to create an exploit scenario, simulating an attack that leverages this vulnerability.

Threat intelligence feeds can also include information about known exploitable vulnerabilities (CVE identifiers), patch management issues, or specific misconfigurations in commonly used systems. Armed with this knowledge, red teams can simulate targeted attacks that make use of these weaknesses, thereby identifying the path an adversary would most likely follow.

3. Mapping Attack Surface with External Reconnaissance

Threat intelligence also assists red teams in identifying exposed services, domains, and other external-facing assets that can be attacked. Threat actors frequently look for exposed attack surfaces, such as:

- Misconfigured DNS records
- Unpatched web servers
- Open ports or protocols
- Weak or exposed authentication mechanisms
- Outdated technologies with known vulnerabilities

Threat intelligence feeds provide real-time data on the most commonly targeted services and systems, as well as known attack paths associated with certain technologies. Red teams can use this data to conduct thorough reconnaissance and identify entry points that external attackers might use.

Example: If threat intelligence reveals that attackers are actively exploiting an old version of Apache Struts, the red team may prioritize scanning the organization's servers to check if that particular vulnerability is present, potentially allowing them to create a path to execute remote code.

4. Simulating Real-World Attacks Using Historical Data

Another way threat intelligence aids in identifying attack paths is by providing historical data on previous attacks. By analyzing attack campaigns that have been reported in the wild, red teamers can create realistic attack scenarios based on actual tactics used by adversaries. This includes historical attacks that leverage specific malware strains, lateral movement tactics, or privilege escalation techniques.

Example: If threat intelligence highlights a recent increase in RAT (Remote Access Trojan) malware usage by a specific threat group, the red team can simulate this attack by deploying similar tools or techniques to create an attack path that mimics real-world actions.

Using this intelligence, red teamers can recreate the exact steps taken by an attacker in a previous campaign and understand how they infiltrated the network, moved laterally, and escalated privileges. By doing so, the red team can identify attack paths that have been effective in the past and use them to exploit the target's defenses.

Tools and Resources for Threat Intelligence in Red Teaming

Several tools and platforms help red teams to ingest, analyze, and apply threat intelligence in identifying attack paths. Below are some of the most valuable resources:

1. Threat Intelligence Platforms (TIPs)

MISP (Malware Information Sharing Platform): An open-source platform designed to share, store, and collaborate on structured threat information. MISP helps red teams integrate intelligence feeds, such as IOCs, CVEs, and TTPs, to enrich their attack simulations.

ThreatConnect: A commercial platform that enables teams to manage threat intelligence and apply it in their security operations, including red teaming. It supports integrating external feeds and allows teams to track adversary activities across various vectors.

2. OSINT and Threat Intelligence Feeds

AlienVault Open Threat Exchange (OTX): An open-source threat intelligence platform that aggregates data from around the world, providing valuable insights into emerging threats, vulnerabilities, and attack patterns.

Anomali: A threat intelligence platform that collects, analyzes, and operationalizes threat intelligence from various sources. It provides a comprehensive view of the threat landscape, which is critical for identifying attack paths during red team engagements.

3. MITRE ATT&CK Framework

The MITRE ATT&CK framework is a widely used and essential tool in red teaming, offering detailed information on adversary behaviors across the entire attack lifecycle. It categorizes the TTPs employed by attackers, allowing red teams to align their strategies with real-world threat groups.

ATT&CK Navigator: A tool that helps visualize and map out the TTPs that correspond to a red team's planned attack path, which can be further customized to the target's environment.

Challenges in Identifying Attack Paths Using Threat Intelligence

While threat intelligence is a valuable tool for identifying attack paths, there are some challenges that red teams need to navigate:

Data Overload: Threat intelligence feeds can generate vast amounts of data, making it difficult to sift through and identify actionable insights. Red teams must be skilled in filtering and prioritizing the most relevant information.

Integration: Integrating threat intelligence into the red team's workflow can be complex, especially when combining multiple tools, platforms, and data sources. Red teams need a structured process to leverage intelligence effectively.

Accuracy: Threat intelligence data can sometimes be incomplete or inaccurate. A red team must validate the information they receive to ensure it accurately reflects the current threat landscape and is applicable to their target environment.

Threat intelligence is an indispensable tool for red teams, enabling them to identify and simulate realistic attack paths during engagement. By integrating intelligence into their attack planning and reconnaissance, red teamers can leverage detailed adversary TTPs, vulnerabilities, and real-world attack data to craft sophisticated and targeted attacks. Understanding how to apply threat intelligence effectively ensures that red teams simulate realistic adversary behavior, uncover potential weaknesses, and ultimately help organizations strengthen their defenses. When paired with solid reconnaissance techniques, threat intelligence allows red teamers to uncover hidden vulnerabilities, map attack paths, and provide actionable recommendations that improve security posture and resilience.

3. Building a Red Team Toolkit

A red team is only as effective as the tools at its disposal, and building a versatile, reliable toolkit is essential for success. This chapter guides you through assembling and managing a comprehensive set of tools for reconnaissance, exploitation, persistence, and evasion. From selecting industry-standard platforms like Metasploit and Cobalt Strike to creating custom scripts and payloads, you'll learn how to tailor your toolkit to the unique demands of each engagement. Additionally, we'll cover the critical aspects of securing your attack infrastructure and maintaining operational security to ensure stealth and efficiency throughout your operations.

3.1 Essential Reconnaissance Tools and Utilities

Reconnaissance is the first and one of the most critical stages of a red team engagement. It involves gathering information about a target organization to identify potential attack surfaces and develop attack paths. For red teamers, having a solid set of reconnaissance tools is vital to the success of the engagement. These tools help automate the data collection process, ensure a comprehensive analysis of the target, and uncover hidden vulnerabilities that could be exploited in later phases.

This chapter will cover the essential reconnaissance tools and utilities that red teamers use to gather publicly available information, map out the target's attack surface, and establish the foundation for a full-scale simulated attack. These tools span a range of use cases, from OSINT (Open Source Intelligence) collection to network scanning and DNS enumeration, and are indispensable for conducting thorough and efficient reconnaissance.

Key Categories of Reconnaissance Tools

Reconnaissance tools can be divided into several categories based on their specific functionalities. Below are the main categories, with a focus on the most essential utilities within each:

- OSINT Tools
- Network Scanning Tools
- DNS Enumeration Tools
- Web Application Recon Tools
- Social Engineering Tools

- Wireless Network Recon Tools

1. OSINT Tools

OSINT tools focus on gathering publicly available information from the internet. This includes information about the target organization, employees, infrastructure, and exposed services. These tools are invaluable for mapping the attack surface without direct interaction with the target's systems.

Key OSINT Tools:

theHarvester:

A popular tool for gathering emails, subdomains, hosts, employee names, and more from publicly available sources like search engines (Google, Bing), social media, and other databases. theHarvester is typically used during the initial phase of reconnaissance to collect basic data about the target.

- **Usage**: theHarvester -d example.com -b google
- **Key Features**: Email enumeration, subdomain discovery, company employee profiles.

Maltego:

Maltego is a powerful OSINT tool for mapping relationships between various entities like domains, email addresses, phone numbers, and people. It uses a graphical interface to visualize how different pieces of information are interconnected, which can be critical for identifying attack paths.

- **Usage**: Use Maltego to visualize a company's infrastructure and the relationship between employees, technologies, and services.
- **Key Features**: Data mining, social network analysis, footprinting.

Recon-ng:

Recon-ng is an advanced web reconnaissance framework written in Python. It provides a robust environment for gathering and analyzing OSINT data from public sources, offering a range of modules that can perform everything from domain and email harvesting to passive DNS enumeration.

- **Usage**: recon-ng provides an interactive environment to run various reconnaissance modules.
- **Key Features**: Full web reconnaissance, built-in APIs, modular architecture.

2. Network Scanning Tools

Network scanning tools are used to identify the target's infrastructure, including open ports, active services, and the structure of the network. These tools help red teamers determine which systems are vulnerable to attacks and discover hidden assets that may not be immediately visible.

Key Network Scanning Tools:

Nmap:

Nmap (Network Mapper) is one of the most widely used network scanning tools for discovering hosts and services on a network. It supports a variety of scanning techniques, including TCP, UDP, and SYN scans, and can be used to identify operating systems, services, and open ports.

- **Usage**: nmap -sS -p 1-65535 example.com
- **Key Features**: Host discovery, service detection, operating system fingerprinting, and vulnerability scanning.

Masscan:

Masscan is known for its ability to scan large networks very quickly. It is similar to Nmap but is optimized for high-speed scanning of IP addresses and ports, making it suitable for large-scale reconnaissance efforts. While faster than Nmap, it is less detailed.

- **Usage**: masscan -p0-65535 192.168.0.0/24
- **Key Features**: Fast port scanning, suitable for large networks.

Netcat:

Netcat is often called the "Swiss Army knife" of networking tools. It can be used for banner grabbing, port scanning, and even for creating reverse shells. It is a lightweight and highly versatile tool for manual network reconnaissance.

- **Usage**: nc -v -z 192.168.0.1 80-443

- **Key Features**: Banner grabbing, port scanning, raw socket connections.

3. DNS Enumeration Tools

DNS enumeration is a technique used to gather information about a target's DNS records, subdomains, and associated IP addresses. Red teamers use these tools to uncover hidden or less obvious parts of the target's infrastructure.

Key DNS Enumeration Tools:

Sublist3r:

Sublist3r is a tool designed for subdomain enumeration. It uses multiple search engines and DNS services to find subdomains of a given domain. This can reveal internal systems, staging servers, or misconfigured services.

- **Usage**: sublist3r -d example.com
- **Key Features**: Fast subdomain enumeration, uses multiple data sources like Google, Bing, and Yahoo.

DNSdumpster:

DNSdumpster is an online tool for discovering DNS records, including subdomains and associated IP addresses. It can also reveal internal assets and infrastructure that may not be publicly visible through regular web searches.

- **Usage**: Access via dnsdumpster.com, input the target domain.
- **Key Features**: Free, web-based DNS enumeration, graphical representation of DNS data.

Fierce:

Fierce is a domain scanner that focuses on finding misconfigured DNS and subdomains. It can help red teamers discover DNS zone transfers, which could reveal a full list of internal systems.

- **Usage**: fierce --domain example.com
- **Key Features**: Zone transfer detection, reverse lookups, subdomain enumeration.

4. Web Application Recon Tools

Web applications are prime targets for red team engagements, and specialized reconnaissance tools are necessary to enumerate web services, gather information on APIs, and detect vulnerabilities.

Key Web Application Recon Tools:

Burp Suite:

Burp Suite is an integrated platform for web application security testing. It contains a powerful proxy, scanner, and numerous tools for enumerating web applications, discovering security flaws, and performing vulnerability analysis.

- **Usage**: Set up a proxy to intercept HTTP/S traffic and use it to enumerate pages and services.
- **Key Features**: Web vulnerability scanning, proxying, request/response manipulation.

Dirbuster:

Dirbuster is a tool for brute-forcing directories and files within a web application. It can be used to discover hidden pages and resources, such as admin panels, configuration files, or backup systems.

- **Usage**: Run with custom wordlists to identify hidden directories.
- **Key Features**: Directory and file brute-forcing, customizable wordlists.

Wfuzz:

Wfuzz is another web application fuzzer, similar to Dirbuster, but with more flexibility. It allows users to fuzz web applications for hidden files, directories, and even vulnerabilities like SQL injection or XSS.

- **Usage**: wfuzz -c -w /usr/share/wordlists/dirbuster/directory-list-2.3-medium.txt http://example.com/FUZZ
- **Key Features**: HTTP fuzzing, customizable wordlists, brute-forcing directories.

5. Social Engineering Tools

Social engineering is an attack vector that preys on human behavior, often bypassing traditional technical defenses. Reconnaissance for social engineering typically involves collecting data about employees and organizational structure.

Key Social Engineering Tools:

SET (Social-Engineer Toolkit):

SET is a tool designed to automate social engineering attacks, such as phishing campaigns, credential harvesting, and pretexting. It can be used to craft realistic phishing emails and simulate real-world attacks.

- **Usage**: Use the SET framework to create phishing templates and attack payloads.
- **Key Features**: Phishing templates, credential harvesting, web attack simulations.

Social-Engineer Toolkit (SET):

A versatile social engineering tool that automates phishing campaigns, fake websites, and malicious USB payloads. Red teamers can use SET to target human vulnerabilities in addition to technical ones.

6. Wireless Network Recon Tools

For physical penetration tests, reconnaissance on wireless networks can uncover weak access points or poorly secured wireless configurations.

Key Wireless Network Recon Tools:

Aircrack-ng:

Aircrack-ng is a suite of tools used to audit wireless networks. It supports network monitoring, packet injection, and key cracking for WEP and WPA networks.

- **Usage**: airmon-ng start wlan0 to start wireless monitoring mode.
- **Key Features**: Wireless network monitoring, WEP/WPA cracking, packet injection.

Kismet:

Kismet is a wireless network detector, sniffer, and intrusion detection system. It can passively detect wireless networks and capture data packets to be analyzed.

- **Usage:** Run kismet to detect and log nearby wireless networks.
- **Key Features**: Passive wireless detection, AP enumeration, protocol analysis.

Reconnaissance is the cornerstone of any successful red team operation. The tools outlined above are essential for efficiently gathering critical information about a target, identifying potential attack surfaces, and mapping out a successful penetration strategy. Mastering these reconnaissance tools, and using them in tandem, allows red teamers to gather the intelligence needed to design sophisticated, real-world attack simulations that challenge organizations' security posture.

3.2 Exploit Frameworks: Metasploit, Cobalt Strike, and Beyond

When conducting a red team engagement, exploiting vulnerabilities to gain access to a target's systems is a critical phase. While identifying weaknesses is important, the tools and frameworks used to exploit those vulnerabilities are equally essential. Exploit frameworks like Metasploit and Cobalt Strike are invaluable assets in a red teamer's toolkit. These frameworks provide powerful capabilities to automate the exploitation process, simulate real-world attack scenarios, and move laterally within the target's network.

This section will explore some of the most widely used exploit frameworks—Metasploit and Cobalt Strike—along with other tools that extend the capabilities of red teams during exploitation.

What are Exploit Frameworks?

Exploit frameworks are software tools that provide pre-built, ready-to-use exploits for various vulnerabilities, as well as the infrastructure needed to carry out attacks in a controlled, systematic manner. These frameworks are designed to simplify and accelerate the exploitation phase, allowing red teamers to focus on crafting realistic attack scenarios while automating the technical aspects of exploitation.

Exploit frameworks typically come with the following core features:

- **Pre-built Exploits**: Common vulnerabilities and exposures (CVEs) in software are cataloged with ready-to-launch exploits.

- **Payloads**: Frameworks include various payloads that can be deployed after successful exploitation, such as reverse shells or Meterpreter sessions.
- **Post-Exploitation Modules**: Many frameworks offer post-exploitation modules that allow for further escalation of privileges, lateral movement, and persistence.
- **Customizability**: Red teamers can modify existing exploits and payloads to meet specific engagement needs or to target more sophisticated systems.
- **Reporting and Logging**: Advanced logging and reporting capabilities help document the red team's activities for later analysis and debriefing.

Now, let's dive deeper into the two most popular exploit frameworks used in red teaming: Metasploit and Cobalt Strike, followed by some other noteworthy tools that extend the exploitation capabilities of red teams.

1. Metasploit Framework

Metasploit is one of the most well-known and widely used exploit frameworks in the cybersecurity industry. It has become a go-to tool for penetration testers, red teamers, and security researchers due to its versatility and vast repository of exploits, payloads, and post-exploitation modules.

Key Features of Metasploit:

Extensive Exploit Collection: Metasploit has an extensive library of publicly disclosed exploits, allowing red teamers to target a wide range of vulnerabilities in various operating systems, services, and applications.

Metasploit Console: The interactive console, known as msfconsole, allows red teamers to manage and launch attacks efficiently. It provides a command-line interface for selecting exploits, setting payloads, and customizing attacks.

Exploit Development and Customization: Red teamers can write their own exploits using Metasploit's scripting language, Ruby, or modify existing exploits to suit the needs of their engagement.

Post-Exploitation Modules: After gaining access to a target system, Metasploit includes numerous modules to escalate privileges, gather system information, and pivot to other systems on the network.

Meterpreter: A specialized payload in Metasploit that allows for advanced post-exploitation actions like file manipulation, command execution, keylogging, and more. It also supports reverse shells and pivoting through firewalls and NATs (Network Address Translators).

Common Uses in Red Teaming:

Exploitation: After identifying a vulnerability, a red teamer uses Metasploit to launch an exploit to gain access to the system.

Post-Exploitation: Once inside the network, red teamers can use Metasploit's post-exploitation tools to escalate privileges, maintain access, and gather critical data.

Lateral Movement: Metasploit's integration with other tools like SMB and WinRM enables lateral movement through the target's network.

Social Engineering: Metasploit also contains modules to carry out phishing attacks and deliver payloads through web applications or email.

2. Cobalt Strike

Cobalt Strike is a premium, commercial exploit framework that has gained popularity among red teamers for its advanced capabilities, versatility, and focus on emulating real-world adversaries. It was designed to simulate the tactics, techniques, and procedures (TTPs) of advanced persistent threat (APT) actors and is widely used in engagements that require stealth and persistence.

Key Features of Cobalt Strike:

Beacon Payload: Cobalt Strike's core payload, known as Beacon, allows red teamers to control compromised systems via reverse shells or HTTP-based communication. Beacon supports encrypted communications, making it harder for defenders to detect.

Advanced Post-Exploitation Capabilities: Once a target system is compromised, Cobalt Strike provides powerful post-exploitation tools for data exfiltration, system enumeration, and privilege escalation. It also supports features like keylogging, screen capturing, and command injection.

Malleable C2 Profiles: Cobalt Strike's Command and Control (C2) framework can be customized using malleable C2 profiles to mimic traffic patterns associated with specific threat actors, making it difficult for defenders to distinguish between legitimate and malicious traffic.

Lateral Movement and Pivoting: Cobalt Strike excels at lateral movement within networks, allowing red teams to pivot from one compromised host to others using various protocols like SMB, RDP, and WinRM.

Red Team Simulation: Cobalt Strike includes modules designed to simulate real-world attack scenarios, including credential dumping, web shell deployment, and ransomware deployment, helping red teamers mirror the TTPs of advanced attackers.

Common Uses in Red Teaming:

Initial Access and Persistence: Cobalt Strike is often used to establish initial access via phishing, RDP, or web application exploits. Once access is gained, it ensures persistence on the target system with advanced C2 capabilities.

Stealth and Evasion: With its malleable C2 profiles, Cobalt Strike helps red teamers blend their traffic with legitimate network activities, avoiding detection by IDS/IPS systems and firewalls.

Advanced Exploitation: Cobalt Strike includes built-in exploits for a wide range of vulnerabilities, especially those targeting enterprise-level systems. It also provides privilege escalation and lateral movement tools for more complex engagements.

Red Team Operations: Cobalt Strike's focus on simulating APT-level attacks allows red teams to execute more sophisticated tactics, such as long-term compromise, data exfiltration, and simulated data destruction.

3. Beyond Metasploit and Cobalt Strike: Other Noteworthy Exploit Frameworks

While Metasploit and Cobalt Strike dominate the exploit framework landscape, there are other tools available that can augment or extend the capabilities of red teamers. These frameworks may not have the same comprehensive features but still offer significant advantages in specific scenarios.

Key Alternative Exploit Frameworks:

Empire:

Empire is a PowerShell-based post-exploitation framework used primarily for Windows environments. It focuses on providing flexible and powerful payloads that can evade detection by antivirus software. Empire supports powershell and Python scripts for lateral movement, persistence, and data exfiltration.

Use Case: Ideal for post-exploitation tasks in Windows environments, especially for environments with strict monitoring or detection systems.

BeEF (Browser Exploitation Framework):

BeEF is designed to exploit web browsers. It allows red teamers to conduct attacks on web browsers, leveraging social engineering and browser vulnerabilities to gain control over the target's machine.

Use Case: Primarily used for client-side attacks, exploiting web applications, phishing, or man-in-the-browser (MITB) attacks.

Nessus:

While Nessus is primarily known as a vulnerability scanner, it also features exploitable vulnerabilities detection, which can be used to confirm whether a vulnerability is actively exploitable in a target environment.

Use Case: For red teamers who need to identify security weaknesses and validate their exploitation potential without fully engaging in complex attack tactics.

Impacket:

Impacket is a collection of Python scripts that allows red teamers to manipulate network protocols and perform various attacks on Windows networks. It is highly effective for SMB, Kerberos, and NTLM exploitation and lateral movement within the network.

Use Case: Useful for Windows network exploitation, credential dumping, and lateral movement during post-exploitation.

Exploit frameworks are indispensable tools for red teamers, providing the ability to exploit known vulnerabilities, simulate advanced attack scenarios, and maintain persistent access to a compromised network. Metasploit and Cobalt Strike are the two most widely used frameworks, each offering distinct features and capabilities. Metasploit is perfect for vulnerability exploitation and testing, while Cobalt Strike excels at simulating APT-style attacks with a focus on stealth, persistence, and lateral movement. In addition to these, frameworks like Empire, BeEF, and Impacket offer specialized capabilities for specific environments or attack types.

By mastering these exploit frameworks, red teamers can efficiently simulate real-world cyberattacks and assess the robustness of their target's defenses. However, successful exploitation relies not just on the tools but on a deep understanding of attack techniques and how they can be applied to bypass security mechanisms and achieve the objectives of the engagement.

3.3 Crafting Custom Payloads and Scripts for Specific Objectives

In red teaming, crafting custom payloads and scripts is a vital skill. While exploit frameworks like Metasploit and Cobalt Strike come with pre-built payloads, there are often situations where a custom payload is needed to bypass security controls, target specific systems, or achieve specific objectives in a red team engagement. Custom payloads and scripts give red teamers the flexibility to tailor their attacks to the unique characteristics of the target environment, ultimately enhancing the effectiveness of their efforts.

This chapter delves into the process of crafting custom payloads and scripts, focusing on understanding the underlying concepts, choosing the right payloads for the job, and tailoring them to fit specific objectives. It will explore the use of custom scripting languages, payload obfuscation techniques, and modifying existing exploits to create sophisticated attack vectors.

What is a Payload?

A payload is the part of an exploit that carries out the malicious action once a vulnerability has been successfully exploited. The payload could be anything from gaining remote access to a system (a reverse shell), executing a command, dumping credentials, installing malware, or escalating privileges.

Custom payloads are often necessary when standard ones don't work due to the target's specific defenses or configurations. Crafting these payloads requires understanding both the target system's architecture and the environment where the payload will execute.

When to Craft Custom Payloads

Here are some typical scenarios where crafting custom payloads is necessary:

Bypassing Security Controls:

Many modern systems have antivirus software, intrusion detection systems (IDS), firewalls, and endpoint protection mechanisms in place. These tools often have signatures or heuristics designed to detect known payloads. Crafting a custom payload can help you evade these security measures.

Target-Specific Payloads:

In some cases, pre-built payloads may not align with the specific environment or system architecture of the target. Custom payloads allow red teamers to fine-tune their approach based on the target's operating system, network configuration, or security posture.

Advanced Exploitation:

Some advanced attacks, such as privilege escalation, credential dumping, or lateral movement, may require payloads that are either completely new or modified versions of existing ones to meet the specific needs of the red team operation.

Tailoring to Engagement Goals:

Red team engagements often have specific objectives, such as achieving persistence, exfiltrating data, or pivoting to other networks. Custom payloads allow the red teamer to tailor attacks for these goals, ensuring they can achieve the mission while remaining undetected.

Types of Payloads and Customization Considerations

When crafting a custom payload, red teamers must consider various factors related to their specific goals. The most commonly used payload types are:

Reverse Shells:

A reverse shell is one of the most common payloads, where a compromised system connects back to the attacker's system, providing command-line access. Custom reverse shells might be used to ensure compatibility with firewalls, proxies, or NAT traversal.

Customization Considerations:

- Protocol choice (TCP, UDP, HTTP, DNS)
- Port selection (non-standard ports to evade detection)
- Encryption for traffic obfuscation
- Encoding or obfuscating the payload to avoid detection by antivirus/IDS systems

Meterpreter:

Meterpreter is a flexible payload included in the Metasploit Framework that provides extensive post-exploitation capabilities, including file manipulation, keystroke logging, privilege escalation, and network pivoting. Custom versions of Meterpreter can be crafted to interact with specific tools or security features on the target.

Customization Considerations:

- Interaction with specific post-exploitation modules
- Integration with additional C2 servers or tools
- Customizing how it handles data exfiltration or maintains persistence

Web Shells:

Web shells allow remote control of a web server by exploiting web application vulnerabilities. Custom web shells might be crafted to provide more robust functionality or bypass certain web application security mechanisms, such as web application firewalls (WAFs).

Customization Considerations:

- Web shell obfuscation techniques (to avoid detection by WAFs)
- Adding advanced capabilities such as file uploading, command execution, or credential dumping
- Using unique methods of communication, such as HTTP-based reverse shells or web sockets

Beaconing Payloads:

A beacon payload is designed to periodically communicate with a command-and-control (C2) server, allowing the attacker to maintain persistence on a system. Custom beacon payloads can be tailored for low-and-slow attacks, where the attacker avoids raising alarms by limiting network activity.

Customization Considerations:

- Custom intervals for beaconing (making it harder to detect)
- Custom C2 protocols to evade detection by network monitoring systems
- Adding encryption to communication for increased stealth

Crafting Custom Payloads: Step-by-Step Process

Crafting a custom payload generally follows a structured approach. Here's an overview of the process:

1. Define the Objective

Start by defining the specific goal for the engagement. Is the objective to exfiltrate data, maintain persistence, escalate privileges, or access a specific system or network? Once the goal is defined, the payload can be designed accordingly.

2. Select the Appropriate Payload Type

Based on the objective, choose the payload type. For example:

- For remote access, a reverse shell or Meterpreter payload might be ideal.
- For maintaining persistence, a beaconing payload or web shell might be better.
- For privilege escalation, a custom local exploit or kernel exploit might be necessary.

3. Analyze the Target Environment

Before crafting the payload, gather detailed information about the target's environment, including:

- **Operating System**: Is the target running Windows, Linux, or macOS? This will affect the choice of payload and the tools used.
- **Network Configurations**: Is the target behind a firewall or NAT? Consider using reverse HTTP/HTTPS shells or DNS tunneling to bypass restrictions.
- **Security Software**: Is there antivirus, endpoint detection and response (EDR), or a web application firewall (WAF) in place? Ensure that the payload can bypass these defenses.

4. Write and Test the Payload

Once the requirements are clear, write the custom payload. This could involve:

- Using a scripting language like Python or PowerShell to craft a reverse shell.
- Modifying Metasploit's Meterpreter script to suit your needs.
- Writing custom shellcode in C or assembly for more low-level control.

After writing the payload, test it in a controlled environment (e.g., virtual machines) to ensure it works as intended without triggering security defenses.

5. Obfuscate and Encrypt the Payload

Obfuscation is a key step in avoiding detection by antivirus or intrusion detection systems. Tools like Veil-Evasion, MSFVenom, or shellter can help obfuscate or encrypt the payload, making it harder for security defenses to flag it.

Techniques for Obfuscation:

- **Code packing**: Compressing the payload code into a self-extracting file.
- **Encoding**: Encoding the payload using base64 or other encoding schemes to obscure its true intent.
- **Polymorphism**: Using techniques to modify the payload slightly each time it's executed, making detection more difficult.

6. Deliver and Execute the Payload

Once the payload is crafted, it must be delivered to the target system. This can be done using a variety of methods, including:

- Phishing (e.g., sending a malicious attachment or link)
- Exploiting vulnerabilities (e.g., using Metasploit's exploit/windows/smb/ms17_010_eternalblue)
- Social engineering (e.g., USB drop attacks, malicious websites)

7. Post-Exploitation

After the payload successfully executes and the attacker gains control of the target system, further post-exploitation tasks may need to be customized. This could include:

- **Privilege escalation**: Crafting or modifying local exploits to gain elevated privileges.
- **Data exfiltration**: Using custom scripts to extract sensitive data.
- **Lateral movement**: Developing custom scripts to pivot to other systems on the network.

Best Practices for Crafting Custom Payloads

- **Test Extensively**: Always test the payloads in a controlled, isolated environment before deployment to ensure they function as expected.
- **Avoid Over-Complicating**: While customization is important, avoid making the payload too complex. The simpler it is, the less likely it is to fail or raise red flags.
- **Maintain Stealth**: Focus on evading detection, both by antivirus systems and network monitoring tools. Use techniques like encryption, polymorphism, and low-and-slow tactics.
- **Stay Within the Rules of Engagement**: Custom payloads must be used ethically and within the agreed-upon scope of the engagement. Always be mindful of the organization's policies and the legal implications of your actions.

Crafting custom payloads and scripts is a critical skill for red teamers, offering the flexibility and precision needed to execute sophisticated attacks that meet specific engagement goals. By understanding the target environment, crafting tailored payloads, and leveraging tools for obfuscation and encryption, red teamers can bypass security defenses and maximize their chances of success. Custom payloads not only ensure a more tailored attack but also provide red teams with the capability to simulate advanced, real-world cyberattacks that would otherwise be difficult to execute with off-the-shelf tools alone.

3.4 Managing Your Attack Infrastructure with Anonymity and Security

In red teaming, managing the infrastructure that supports your operations is as crucial as executing the attack itself. The attack infrastructure, which includes servers, command-and-control (C2) channels, and tools used to perform the engagement, must be secured, anonymous, and resilient to detection. The security of this infrastructure is paramount to ensure that the red team's activities remain covert, that they don't inadvertently expose their actions, and that they can continue to operate without interruption.

This chapter covers the key principles and best practices for managing attack infrastructure securely and anonymously during red team operations. It will focus on anonymity, security measures for attack tools, and resilience to ensure uninterrupted operations and mitigate detection by the target or external observers.

Why Anonymity and Security Matter in Red Teaming

Red team engagements are designed to simulate real-world adversaries, which means that the infrastructure used for these operations should reflect that of sophisticated threat actors. In a real-world attack, adversaries make efforts to hide their identity, obfuscate their tracks, and ensure that their infrastructure is not detected by network monitoring systems, firewalls, or intrusion detection systems (IDS).

Here are a few key reasons why managing the attack infrastructure securely and anonymously is vital:

- **Avoid Detection by the Target**: Attack infrastructure must remain hidden to prevent the target from identifying the red team and counteracting its efforts.
- **Preserve the Integrity of the Engagement**: If the target discovers the red team's activities prematurely, it may interfere with the operation, leading to failed objectives or even damage to the organization's environment.
- **Maintain Legal and Ethical Boundaries**: A red team must follow the rules of engagement and avoid inadvertently breaking the law, especially when operating on external infrastructure or using techniques that could be misconstrued as malicious activity.
- **Operational Resilience**: Anonymizing and securing attack infrastructure ensures that if any one part of the infrastructure is compromised or blocked, the red team can pivot and continue its operation without losing momentum.

1. Building and Securing Command-and-Control (C2) Infrastructure

The C2 infrastructure is the central hub that coordinates all red team activities. This infrastructure typically includes web servers, VPNs, reverse shells, and remote access tools that control compromised systems. Ensuring that the C2 infrastructure is properly secured and anonymized is critical to maintaining the integrity of the operation.

Key Practices for Secure C2 Infrastructure:

Use of Proxy Servers and VPNs:

Employing proxy servers or VPNs to route C2 traffic is one of the most effective ways to anonymize attack infrastructure. Using Tor or I2P can add layers of obfuscation to prevent the traffic from being traced back to the attacker's origin.

Tools: Tor, Shadowsocks, I2P, or commercial VPN services with no logging policies.

Decentralized C2 Servers:

Instead of relying on a single C2 server, set up multiple distributed C2 servers across different geographic regions to avoid detection and ensure redundancy. This also makes it harder for defenders to locate and shut down the attack infrastructure.

Tools: Utilize cloud-based hosting providers like AWS, DigitalOcean, or Linode for distributed infrastructure.

Encrypted C2 Traffic:

Ensure that all communications between the compromised systems and the C2 infrastructure are encrypted. Encryption prevents traffic from being intercepted by network monitoring tools, making it harder to detect communication with the C2 server.

Tools: Use SSL/TLS for encrypting communication, or utilize steganography to hide communication within innocuous files (e.g., image files).

Hiding in Plain Sight:

To evade detection by network monitoring tools, the C2 infrastructure can be disguised as legitimate traffic. This can be done by using common ports (like HTTP/HTTPS) or mimicking patterns associated with legitimate network traffic.

Example: Configure the C2 server to use Port 443 (HTTPS) to mask traffic as secure web browsing.

2. Secure Deployment of Red Team Tools

During a red team operation, various tools will be deployed to aid in reconnaissance, exploitation, post-exploitation, lateral movement, and exfiltration. Securing these tools and ensuring that their operation remains anonymous is critical for maintaining operational security.

Key Practices for Securing Red Team Tools:

Obfuscating Payloads and Exploits:

Payloads, exploits, and scripts should be obfuscated or encrypted to evade detection by endpoint security systems, antivirus software, and intrusion detection/prevention systems (IDS/IPS). Custom obfuscation can disguise the payload's signature and make it more difficult for defenders to identify.

Tools: Veil-Evasion, MSFVenom, shellter, or custom obfuscation scripts.

Secure Communication Channels:

The communication between red team tools and the C2 infrastructure must be secure. Instead of using unencrypted channels, leverage encrypted communication protocols, including HTTPS or DNS tunneling.

Tools: Cobalt Strike, Empire, and Metasploit all offer encrypted channels for communication. DNS tunneling tools like DnsCat2 can also help covertly exfiltrate data or maintain C2 communication.

Tactical DNS and HTTP Tunneling:

HTTP and DNS tunneling are useful techniques for bypassing network filters or firewalls by encoding traffic in DNS or HTTP requests. These techniques are often less detectable than traditional C2 channels.

Tools: DnsCat2, Iodine, HTTPort.

3. Maintaining Anonymity: Obfuscation and Traffic Analysis Resistance

Anonymity in a red team operation means ensuring that every aspect of the attack infrastructure is difficult to trace back to the operator. This is essential for avoiding counterattacks, legal risks, and detection by the target organization.

Techniques to Maintain Anonymity:

Use of VPNs and Proxies:

As with C2 infrastructure, the red team's own communication channels should be routed through anonymous VPNs or proxy servers. This ensures that their own IP addresses remain hidden and untraceable.

Tools: VPN providers (no-log policy), Tor, SOCKS5 proxies, Shadowsocks.

Operational Security (OpSec):

A crucial aspect of managing anonymity is practicing good operational security throughout the engagement. This includes using temporary email accounts, burner phone numbers, and false identities to avoid exposure during communication and coordination with external parties.

Examples: Temporary email services like ProtonMail, Tutanota, or Guerrilla Mail.

Use of Obfuscated or Decoy Domains:

Registering domains that appear legitimate, but are not directly tied to the red team operation, can help confuse defenders and delay detection. This is useful when setting up C2 infrastructure or phishing pages.

Techniques: Utilize domain names that appear harmless, such as setting up a blog or news website as a façade for malicious activity.

Tor and Other Anonymization Networks:

For an added layer of anonymity, Tor can be used to hide the red team's communications and traffic. Tor routes traffic through multiple volunteer-operated nodes, masking the origin of the connection. While this can sometimes impact performance, it offers a strong measure of privacy.

4. Resilience and Failover Mechanisms

In red teaming, resilience means ensuring that if the attack infrastructure is compromised or blocked, the red team can quickly recover and continue operations. Attackers may need to implement failover mechanisms to ensure uninterrupted access to compromised systems.

Key Resilience Practices:

Redundancy in C2 Servers:

Setting up multiple C2 servers across different locations or cloud providers ensures that if one server is blocked, the red team can quickly pivot to another server without losing access to the compromised systems.

Alternate Communication Channels:

Use multiple communication channels to ensure redundancy. If one channel (such as DNS tunneling) is blocked or detected, the red team can seamlessly switch to another (like HTTPS or SSH-based tunneling).

Tools: Tools like Cobalt Strike allow for easy switching between different communication methods, while Empire has built-in support for DNS and HTTP-based communication.

Backup Payloads and Tools:

Have multiple variations of payloads and tools ready for deployment. In case one payload is blocked or detected, a different version of the payload can be deployed to maintain persistence.

Decoy and Honeypot Infrastructure:

Red teamers can use decoy systems or honeypots as part of their infrastructure to divert attention away from the real attack infrastructure, distracting defenders and providing additional time for the red team to operate undetected.

Managing attack infrastructure with anonymity and security is a foundational aspect of successful red teaming. The combination of secure and anonymous command-and-control infrastructure, well-protected attack tools, and resilient failover mechanisms ensures that the red team can carry out operations effectively while avoiding detection. By adhering to best practices in anonymity, obfuscation, and infrastructure management, red teamers can simulate real-world adversaries and assess the resilience of an organization's defenses with the utmost stealth and professionalism. Maintaining operational security and ensuring continuity of operations throughout the engagement are the key factors that determine the success of any red team operation.

4. Initial Access Strategies

The first step in any red team engagement is gaining a foothold in the target environment, and achieving this requires a blend of creativity, precision, and technical expertise. This chapter focuses on advanced initial access strategies, including crafting effective phishing campaigns, exploiting vulnerabilities in web applications and software, and leveraging supply chain weaknesses. You'll also explore social engineering techniques and how to adapt your approach based on the target's security posture. By mastering these entry methods, you'll be equipped to breach defenses and establish the foundation for a successful operation.

4.1 Crafting Convincing Phishing Campaigns

Phishing is one of the most effective and widely used techniques in a red team engagement. It targets the human element of cybersecurity, leveraging social engineering to manipulate users into taking actions that compromise security. Whether the goal is to gain initial access to a network, exfiltrate sensitive information, or plant malicious software, phishing campaigns can provide the foothold needed for further exploitation.

In this chapter, we will explore the process of crafting convincing phishing campaigns designed to simulate real-world adversaries. We will delve into email-based phishing, spear-phishing, whaling, and phishing via other communication channels, providing best practices, tactics, and tools for creating highly effective social engineering attacks. This includes understanding the psychology behind phishing, using advanced techniques for crafting convincing bait, and evading detection by security tools and personnel.

The Psychology of Phishing

At the heart of any phishing campaign is an understanding of human behavior. Red teamers must tailor their campaigns to exploit psychological triggers that motivate users to engage with malicious content. Common triggers that phishing campaigns capitalize on include:

- **Urgency or Fear**: Messages that create a sense of urgency or fear can compel users to act impulsively. For example, an email claiming that an account will be suspended unless immediate action is taken.

- **Curiosity**: Phishing messages often prompt users with enticing offers, such as "Click here to see your surprise gift" or "You've been selected for an exclusive prize."
- **Trust**: Users are more likely to trust messages that appear to come from familiar sources, such as colleagues, bosses, or well-known brands. Crafting emails that mimic these trusted sources is key to successful phishing.
- **Lack of Knowledge**: Many phishing attempts take advantage of users' lack of knowledge about security measures, such as email security, password hygiene, or identifying scam links.

By crafting emails that appeal to these psychological triggers, red teamers can maximize the chances of successful exploitation.

Types of Phishing Campaigns

Before crafting a phishing campaign, it is crucial to understand the different types of phishing attacks that can be launched. Some common types include:

1. Spear-Phishing

Spear-phishing is a highly targeted form of phishing where the attacker tailors the message specifically for an individual or organization. Unlike generic phishing emails, spear-phishing campaigns often involve thorough research on the victim to craft a more convincing message. This research can include gathering information about the victim's job role, recent activities, and personal interests.

Key Strategies for Spear-Phishing:

- Research the target thoroughly via OSINT (Open-Source Intelligence) tools and social media platforms like LinkedIn, Facebook, and Twitter.
- Mimic the writing style or tone of familiar colleagues, clients, or supervisors to increase trust.
- Use personal details (e.g., names, job titles, recent events) to make the email appear highly legitimate.

2. Whaling

Whaling is a form of spear-phishing that targets high-profile individuals within an organization, such as executives, CEOs, or other key decision-makers. The stakes are high, as successful whaling attacks can provide attackers with direct access to sensitive financial data, intellectual property, or executive communications.

Key Strategies for Whaling:

- Craft emails that are formal and professional, matching the typical communication style of the targeted executive.
- Use business-related language and references to create the illusion of a legitimate request, such as financial transactions or important business decisions.
- A successful whaling attack often requires exploiting a trusted business relationship to lure the target into taking action.

3. Standard Phishing

This is the most common form of phishing, where attackers send out large numbers of generic emails in the hopes of catching a few victims. These emails might impersonate well-known brands or organizations, like banks, service providers, or government agencies.

Key Strategies for Standard Phishing:

- Leverage social engineering tactics, such as creating a fake "Account Suspended" notice from a bank or credit card company.
- Craft subject lines that invoke curiosity or urgency to compel the target to click the link or open an attachment (e.g., "Immediate Action Required on Your Account").
- Focus on making the email appear authentic and professional, even though it may be sent in bulk.

4. Vishing (Voice Phishing)

Vishing involves phishing attempts conducted over the phone, where attackers impersonate legitimate organizations, such as tech support or financial institutions, to steal sensitive information or install malware.

Key Strategies for Vishing:

- Craft a story that makes the phone call appear urgent, such as claiming that the target's account has been compromised or that they need to update their security credentials.

- Use caller ID spoofing tools to make the call appear to come from a trusted number (e.g., from a bank or service provider).
- Ask for personal information or direct the victim to visit a website where they can enter sensitive details.

Crafting the Phishing Email

Once you've decided on the type of phishing campaign, the next step is to create the phishing email itself. Crafting an email that is convincing requires attention to detail and an understanding of how to manipulate the victim's decision-making process.

1. Email Subject Line

The subject line is the first thing a target will see, so it needs to grab their attention. The subject line should create a sense of urgency, curiosity, or importance. Here are some examples:

- "Your account has been compromised – urgent action required"
- "Suspicious activity detected in your account"
- "You have a new message from your HR department"
- "Verify your identity to continue using your account"

The subject line must be concise, impactful, and relevant to the target's role or responsibilities.

2. Crafting the Message Body

The body of the email is where the bulk of the social engineering takes place. To craft a convincing message:

- **Personalization**: Include the victim's name, job title, or department to make the email feel more legitimate. Avoid generic greetings like "Dear Customer."
- **The Bait**: Provide a clear call to action, such as a link to reset a password, verify account information, or access an important document. This is where the attacker will often insert a malicious link or attachment.
- **Authority and Urgency**: The email should invoke a sense of urgency (e.g., "Your account will be locked in 24 hours unless you respond") and create authority (e.g., "This message is from IT security").

- **Fake Links**: Mask the real destination URL by embedding it behind a hyperlinked phrase like "Click here to resolve this issue." Use URL shorteners or misspelled domains that closely resemble legitimate ones to avoid suspicion.
- **Attachments**: Phishing emails often contain attachments, such as Word or Excel documents with embedded macros that run malicious code when opened. Always include a justification for why the recipient needs to open the attachment (e.g., "Invoice attached for your review").

3. Mimicking Legitimate Domains

One of the most critical steps in a phishing campaign is to create a domain name or email address that looks very similar to the legitimate source. For example:

- Use slight variations in domain names (e.g., "bankofamerica.com" vs. "bank0famerica.com").
- Implement domain spoofing or impersonation to make it appear as if the email is from an internal company email address.

Evading Detection: Anti-Phishing Techniques

While phishing is a highly effective method of attack, it is also one of the most commonly targeted methods by security tools and personnel. To avoid detection:

- **Obfuscate Links**: Use URL shorteners, such as Bit.ly, to mask malicious links and prevent easy identification of the destination.
- **Avoid Common Spam Triggers**: Phishing emails often trigger spam filters due to common characteristics, such as certain keywords ("Congratulations!" or "Action Required"). Red teamers should avoid these triggers and focus on creating legitimate-sounding messages.
- **Email Header Spoofing**: Spoofing the "From" header to mimic a trusted source can help bypass basic email filtering.
- **Test in Staging Environments**: Before sending phishing emails in a live engagement, test them against simulated security environments to assess their effectiveness and ensure they do not trigger any security mechanisms.

Tools for Crafting Phishing Campaigns

There are various tools available to assist in creating and managing phishing campaigns:

- **Social-Engineer Toolkit (SET):** A powerful tool that automates the creation of phishing emails and the launching of social engineering attacks. SET can simulate email-based phishing, SMS phishing (smishing), and more.
- **Gophish**: An open-source phishing framework designed to assist in running phishing campaigns, from creating emails to tracking results.
- **King Phisher**: A tool for testing and simulating real-world phishing attacks, with features for email campaign management, tracking, and analytics.
- **Evilginx2**: A man-in-the-middle phishing framework that allows attackers to intercept login credentials through phishing and provides advanced techniques such as session hijacking and two-factor authentication bypass.

Crafting convincing phishing campaigns is both an art and a science. Successful phishing attacks require a deep understanding of human psychology, advanced technical knowledge of email spoofing and obfuscation, and meticulous attention to detail. By mastering the tactics outlined in this chapter, red teamers can simulate realistic adversary behavior, gain initial access to target networks, and provide valuable insights into the vulnerabilities of an organization's human defenses. As the first line of defense in cybersecurity, human vulnerability is often the weakest link, and phishing remains one of the most effective methods of exploiting this weakness.

4.2 Exploiting Misconfigurations in Common Systems

Misconfigurations in systems are one of the most common and often overlooked vulnerabilities in cybersecurity. They can occur across all levels of an organization's infrastructure, from software applications to network configurations, cloud services, and server setups. For red teamers, exploiting these misconfigurations is a critical component of penetration testing and adversary simulation exercises, as they can provide a quick and reliable entry point into otherwise secure systems.

In this chapter, we will explore how red teamers can identify and exploit misconfigurations in some of the most commonly used systems in modern IT environments. We will cover the most frequently misconfigured systems, the impact these misconfigurations can have on security, and specific exploitation techniques that can be used to gain unauthorized access or escalate privileges within an organization.

What is a Misconfiguration?

A misconfiguration occurs when a system, service, or software is improperly set up, leaving it vulnerable to exploitation. Misconfigurations are typically the result of human error, rushed deployments, or a lack of proper security controls and oversight. This can include:

- Weak or default credentials
- Excessive permissions granted to users or services
- Insecure network settings or open ports
- Poorly configured security controls (e.g., firewalls, logging, or access controls)
- Lack of patching or outdated software
- Incomplete security policies or incorrect application settings

Misconfigurations can lead to unintended access to sensitive data, unauthorized system access, or the ability to execute arbitrary code. Red teamers can take advantage of these vulnerabilities to simulate real-world adversaries and identify gaps in an organization's defense posture.

1. Exploiting Misconfigurations in Web Servers

Web servers are one of the most common entry points for attackers. Misconfigured web servers can expose sensitive information, leave ports open, or allow attackers to bypass security mechanisms. Common misconfigurations in web servers like Apache, Nginx, and IIS include:

1.1 Exposing Sensitive Information Through Error Messages

Many web servers are configured to display detailed error messages when something goes wrong, such as a 404 error or an internal server error. These error messages can provide valuable insight into the structure of the web application, the underlying technology stack, and potential attack vectors.

- **Exploitation**: By triggering error conditions (e.g., through malformed URLs or requests), attackers can gather information such as database configurations, file paths, or even stack traces that point to vulnerable components.
- **Mitigation**: Configure the web server to display generic error messages and log detailed errors in a secure location (not publicly accessible).

1.2 Open or Misconfigured Directories

Web servers often host multiple directories, some of which may be misconfigured or improperly secured. If directories are not properly secured, an attacker may gain access to sensitive files such as configuration files, backups, or source code.

- **Exploitation**: By browsing the server's directory structure or using tools like DirBuster or Gobuster, an attacker can locate and exfiltrate these sensitive files.
- **Mitigation**: Ensure directory listings are disabled and sensitive files are properly protected with authentication mechanisms or encryption.

1.3 Weak Permissions on Web Directories

Incorrect file and directory permissions can allow attackers to modify or upload files to the web server. Common misconfigurations include granting write access to directories that should only be read-only, or setting weak permissions on configuration files.

- **Exploitation**: If an attacker can upload a malicious script (such as a PHP or ASPX file) to a writable directory, they could execute arbitrary code on the server.
- **Mitigation**: Regularly audit file and directory permissions and enforce the principle of least privilege.

2. Misconfigured Network and Firewalls

Networks and firewalls are designed to protect systems from external threats by controlling traffic. Misconfigurations, however, can inadvertently expose systems or services to attackers, providing a potential attack surface.

2.1 Open Ports and Services

In many environments, firewalls may be configured to allow inbound and outbound traffic on ports that should be restricted. This could include allowing all traffic to ports commonly used by remote services like SSH (Port 22), RDP (Port 3389), or HTTP/HTTPS (Ports 80/443).

- **Exploitation**: By scanning for open ports using tools like Nmap or Masscan, red teamers can identify exposed services. For example, open RDP ports could be leveraged to brute force login credentials or exploit known vulnerabilities in remote desktop services.
- **Mitigation**: Restrict unnecessary ports and services, and ensure that only authorized IP addresses have access to critical systems.

2. Misconfigured VPNs

Misconfigurations in VPNs can lead to unauthorized access to internal systems. For example, allowing remote users to access internal networks without proper authentication or encryption could expose sensitive data.

- **Exploitation**: Misconfigured VPNs might allow attackers to connect to internal networks without adequate protection or authentication, giving them access to critical resources.
- **Mitigation**: Ensure that VPN configurations enforce strong authentication (e.g., multi-factor authentication) and proper encryption protocols.

2. Overly Permissive Security Groups in Cloud Environments

In cloud environments like AWS, Azure, or GCP, security groups are often used to control traffic to instances. A common misconfiguration is allowing inbound traffic from any IP address (0.0.0.0/0) to services like SSH, RDP, or databases.

- **Exploitation**: If SSH or database ports are open to the public internet, attackers can easily attempt brute-force attacks or exploit known vulnerabilities to gain access to the system.
- **Mitigation**: Apply the principle of least privilege to security group rules by restricting access to trusted IP addresses and using secure access methods like VPNs or bastion hosts.

3. Misconfigured Cloud Storage and Databases

Cloud services have become a primary storage solution for many organizations, but misconfigurations in cloud storage buckets or databases can expose sensitive information. Services like Amazon S3, Google Cloud Storage, and Azure Blob Storage are often misconfigured to allow public read or write access.

3.1 Misconfigured S3 Buckets

Publicly accessible S3 buckets can contain confidential data, including financial records, private customer information, or source code. If not properly secured, these buckets can be easily accessed by attackers.

- **Exploitation**: Tools like Bucket Finder or S3Scanner can identify publicly accessible buckets, allowing attackers to download or modify files stored in them.

- **Mitigation**: Ensure that S3 buckets are private by default and enforce strict access control policies (e.g., use of IAM roles and policies). Use tools like AWS IAM to enforce least privilege on users and services.

3.2 Database Misconfigurations

Misconfigured database instances in cloud environments may be exposed to the public internet without proper authentication. This can lead to data leakage, modification, or even full control of the database.

- **Exploitation**: Attackers can scan for exposed databases using tools like Shodan and attempt to exploit common vulnerabilities or weak credentials.
- **Mitigation**: Use firewalls and VPNs to restrict access to databases, apply encryption, and ensure strong authentication practices (e.g., multi-factor authentication for database access).

4. Misconfigured Identity and Access Management (IAM) Systems

Proper identity and access management are critical for ensuring that only authorized individuals can access sensitive systems. Misconfigurations in IAM systems can grant excessive privileges to users, allowing them to escalate their access or perform unauthorized actions.

4.1 Excessive Permissions

Users and services should have the minimum permissions necessary to perform their jobs. Misconfigurations, such as granting unnecessary admin privileges or leaving unused accounts active, can lead to privilege escalation.

- **Exploitation**: Red teamers can leverage excessive permissions to escalate their access within the network, take control of critical systems, or exfiltrate sensitive data.
- **Mitigation**: Regularly audit user accounts and permissions, implementing least privilege policies and ensuring that users only have the access they need to perform their duties.

4.2 Weak Multi-Factor Authentication (MFA) Configurations

MFA is an important security measure, but misconfigurations can render it ineffective. For example, if backup codes are stored insecurely or the MFA challenge is too weak (e.g., SMS-based MFA), attackers may bypass MFA protections.

- **Exploitation**: Attackers can exploit weak MFA configurations to bypass access controls and gain unauthorized access to critical systems.
- **Mitigation**: Use strong MFA methods (e.g., app-based authentication or hardware tokens) and securely store backup codes. Regularly test MFA configurations to ensure they cannot be easily bypassed.

Exploiting misconfigurations is a powerful technique in red teaming, as these vulnerabilities often provide attackers with easy entry points into an organization's infrastructure. Misconfigurations can occur across a wide range of systems, including web servers, networks, cloud services, databases, and identity management systems. By understanding the common misconfigurations and knowing how to exploit them, red teamers can simulate real-world attacks that reveal critical gaps in an organization's security posture. The key to successfully exploiting misconfigurations lies in thorough system auditing, staying updated on best practices, and continuously improving security configurations to ensure they align with the principle of least privilege and minimize exposure to attack.

4.3 Breaking into Web Applications and APIs

Web applications and their associated APIs (Application Programming Interfaces) are core components of modern business infrastructure. These systems are often exposed to the internet and, therefore, present a significant attack surface for adversaries. As part of a red teaming engagement, breaking into web applications and APIs requires a deep understanding of their architecture, security vulnerabilities, and common attack vectors. This chapter delves into the techniques and methodologies used by red teamers to identify, exploit, and compromise web applications and APIs.

Web application security flaws can be exploited to gain unauthorized access to sensitive data, compromise user accounts, and even execute arbitrary code. In parallel, APIs—often acting as the communication bridge between different systems—also present significant vulnerabilities if they are not secured properly. This chapter will provide the tools and knowledge needed to exploit these weaknesses effectively.

1. Understanding Web Application Architectures

Before attacking web applications and APIs, it's essential to understand their typical architecture and components. Most modern web applications are built on three key components:

1.1 Frontend (Client-Side)

The frontend is what users interact with directly, typically built with HTML, JavaScript, CSS, and other client-side technologies. Vulnerabilities in frontend code can lead to security issues such as cross-site scripting (XSS), improper input validation, or insecure client-side storage.

1.2 Backend (Server-Side)

The backend processes requests from the frontend and typically interacts with a database or other services. Common server-side vulnerabilities include SQL injection, command injection, and improper access controls.

1.3 APIs

APIs serve as a bridge between the frontend and backend or between external services. Poor API design, improper authentication, and lack of rate limiting can expose sensitive data or lead to unauthorized actions.

To break into these systems, attackers must target weaknesses in each layer, as each part of the application can contain vulnerabilities that allow attackers to escalate their privileges or access sensitive information.

2. Identifying Common Web Application Vulnerabilities

2.1 Cross-Site Scripting (XSS)

XSS vulnerabilities occur when an attacker is able to inject malicious scripts into a trusted website. When users interact with the website, their browser unknowingly executes the malicious script, allowing attackers to steal cookies, session tokens, or perform actions on behalf of the user.

- **Exploitation**: Red teamers can exploit reflected, stored, or DOM-based XSS vulnerabilities to inject JavaScript payloads into web applications, often leading to session hijacking or credential theft.

- **Tools for Exploitation**: Tools like Burp Suite (for testing for XSS), XSSer, and BeEf (Browser Exploitation Framework) can help automate and exploit XSS vulnerabilities.
- **Mitigation**: Web developers should use proper input sanitization, output encoding, and implement a Content Security Policy (CSP) to mitigate XSS attacks.

2.2 SQL Injection (SQLi)

SQL injection is a common web application vulnerability where attackers inject malicious SQL queries into input fields, allowing them to manipulate the database. This can result in unauthorized access to sensitive data, database corruption, or even full system compromise.

- **Exploitation**: By inputting specially crafted SQL queries into form fields or URL parameters, attackers can gain access to data stored in a database. In some cases, attackers may be able to escalate their attack to command execution on the server.
- **Tools for Exploitation**: Tools like SQLmap, Burp Suite, or manual testing with Union-based or Error-based injection methods can be used to identify and exploit SQLi vulnerabilities.
- **Mitigation**: The best defense is to use parameterized queries, prepared statements, and ORM frameworks to prevent direct interaction with SQL queries. Proper input validation is crucial.

2.3 Cross-Site Request Forgery (CSRF)

CSRF attacks occur when an attacker tricks a user into performing an unintended action on a website where they are authenticated, such as changing account settings or transferring funds. The attacker does this by embedding malicious requests within a page that the victim unknowingly interacts with.

- **Exploitation**: Red teamers can craft malicious requests (e.g., submitting a password change or transferring funds) by exploiting the trust that a web application has in the user's session.
- **Tools for Exploitation**: Tools such as CSRFTester or Burp Suite can help detect and manipulate CSRF vulnerabilities.
- **Mitigation**: To prevent CSRF attacks, use anti-CSRF tokens in form submissions and require re-authentication for sensitive actions. SameSite cookie attributes can also help prevent these attacks.

2.4 Insecure Direct Object References (IDOR)

IDOR vulnerabilities occur when an application allows users to access resources (such as files, user records, or database entries) that they should not be able to access. This typically happens when resources are identified by user-controlled inputs like URLs or form parameters.

- **Exploitation**: An attacker can modify a parameter (such as a user ID or file name) to access or modify data that belongs to another user, potentially exposing sensitive information or compromising the application's integrity.
- **Tools for Exploitation**: Tools like Burp Suite and OWASP ZAP can help identify insecure object references through parameter manipulation.
- **Mitigation**: Implement proper access control checks to verify that the user has permission to access the requested resource. Ensure sensitive resources are not exposed through easily guessable identifiers.

3. API Security Vulnerabilities

APIs are often designed to enable communication between different services, but if improperly secured, they can become a major attack vector. Many modern web applications rely heavily on APIs for functions like user authentication, data retrieval, and communication with other services.

3.1 Insecure API Endpoints

Many APIs expose endpoints that provide access to sensitive data or functionality without proper authentication or authorization checks. An insecure endpoint could allow attackers to manipulate or retrieve data without being authorized.

- **Exploitation**: By inspecting the API's documentation, inspecting web traffic, or reverse engineering the mobile application or frontend, an attacker can identify insecure endpoints and exploit them.
- **Tools for Exploitation**: Tools like Postman, Burp Suite, and OWASP ZAP can be used to test and interact with exposed API endpoints, searching for vulnerabilities like improper authentication or access control.
- **Mitigation**: Ensure that all API endpoints require proper authentication (e.g., OAuth, API keys) and authorization checks to restrict access to sensitive resources.

3.2 Weak Authentication and Authorization

Many APIs use weak or improper authentication mechanisms, making them vulnerable to abuse. This includes relying on weak API keys, missing authentication headers, or improper access controls.

- **Exploitation**: If an API endpoint uses weak authentication or lacks proper authorization checks, an attacker can impersonate users, escalate privileges, or exfiltrate sensitive data.
- **Tools for Exploitation**: Tools such as JWT.io (for analyzing JSON Web Tokens) or Burp Suite can help exploit weak authentication or token handling mechanisms in API calls.
- **Mitigation**: Use secure authentication methods such as OAuth 2.0, API tokens, and strong encryption for sensitive data. Implement strict access control to limit users' ability to access API resources.

3.3 Lack of Rate Limiting

Many APIs do not implement rate limiting or fail to enforce strict request limits. This can make them susceptible to brute-force attacks, where an attacker tries to guess valid credentials or API tokens by sending numerous requests.

- **Exploitation**: Without proper rate limiting, an attacker can flood the API with requests, testing different combinations of tokens or credentials until they find a valid one.
- **Tools for Exploitation**: Hydra, Burp Suite, or Dirbuster can be used to automate brute-force attacks on APIs if rate limiting is not in place.
- **Mitigation**: Implement rate limiting and account lockout mechanisms to prevent brute-force attacks. Additionally, use CAPTCHAs for login or sensitive actions to mitigate automated attacks.

4. Tools for Web Application and API Exploitation

Several tools are available for identifying and exploiting vulnerabilities in web applications and APIs. Some commonly used tools include:

- **Burp Suite**: A comprehensive suite for web vulnerability scanning, including tools for intercepting traffic, scanning for vulnerabilities, and exploiting flaws like XSS, SQLi, and CSRF.
- **OWASP ZAP**: An open-source web application security scanner that can automate the detection of common vulnerabilities.

- **Nikto**: A web server scanner that identifies common vulnerabilities in web servers and applications.
- **Postman**: Used for interacting with and testing APIs, including crafting API requests, analyzing responses, and performing vulnerability testing.
- **SQLmap**: An automated tool for detecting and exploiting SQL injection flaws in web applications.
- **Burp Suite's Intruder**: For automated brute-forcing or fuzzing web application input points.

Breaking into web applications and APIs requires a deep understanding of common vulnerabilities, attack vectors, and exploitation techniques. Red teamers must focus on identifying weaknesses in both the frontend and backend of web applications, as well as in the APIs that connect them. By leveraging the appropriate tools, performing thorough testing, and using a combination of manual and automated techniques, red teamers can successfully exploit misconfigurations, weak authentication mechanisms, and other flaws to simulate real-world attacks and provide valuable insights to improve an organization's security posture. Proper mitigation measures, such as secure coding practices, strong authentication, and regular vulnerability assessments, can help reduce the risk of these critical vulnerabilities being exploited in a real attack scenario.

4.4 Gaining Initial Access via Third-Party and Supply Chain Attacks

In today's interconnected world, security is no longer limited to an organization's internal network. The growing reliance on third-party vendors, contractors, and suppliers—along with the complex web of interconnected software and services—has created new vectors for attackers to exploit. These external partnerships, often seen as a trust relationship, can present significant security risks if not properly managed. For red teamers, gaining initial access through third-party and supply chain attacks is a critical strategy that can bypass traditional security measures, as the attackers target not just the organization itself, but its suppliers, contractors, and service providers.

In this chapter, we will explore the methods and tactics red teamers can use to gain initial access via third-party and supply chain attacks. We'll also examine the risks these attacks pose, real-world case studies, and the steps organizations can take to defend against them.

1. Understanding Third-Party and Supply Chain Risks

1.1 The Importance of Third-Party Relationships

Many organizations rely heavily on third-party vendors, contractors, and service providers for services such as cloud storage, software development, accounting, and IT support. While these external relationships are essential to business operations, they also expand the organization's attack surface. If one of these vendors is compromised, an attacker can leverage this trust relationship to gain unauthorized access to the organization's systems or data.

1.2 Types of Third-Party Risks

- **Third-Party Vendors**: These include cloud service providers, software vendors, and outsourced services (e.g., IT support, payroll). If a third party is compromised, attackers can access sensitive systems, accounts, or data.
- **Supply Chain Attacks**: Supply chain attacks refer to any exploitation of vulnerabilities in the delivery chain, where attackers compromise software, hardware, or services before they reach the intended organization. This can include tampering with software updates, compromising hardware components, or injecting malicious code into software provided by a trusted vendor.

Both these vectors exploit trust relationships and can lead to severe security breaches, making them attractive to sophisticated adversaries.

2. Techniques for Gaining Access via Third-Party Vendors

2.1 Compromising Third-Party Vendor Systems

One of the most straightforward ways to gain initial access is by targeting third-party vendors who may have less stringent security protocols than the primary organization. For example, if a vendor has access to the organization's systems, compromising their internal network could provide attackers with access credentials, backdoors, or direct access to the organization's sensitive data.

- **Exploitation**: Attackers may target a third-party vendor using traditional attack vectors such as phishing, malware, or exploiting software vulnerabilities within the vendor's infrastructure. Once inside the vendor's network, attackers can search for ways to pivot to the primary organization's environment, such as by obtaining access credentials, installing malware, or exploiting trust relationships.

- **Real-World Example**: In the 2020 SolarWinds attack, attackers targeted the software supply chain by compromising the Orion software update mechanism. This allowed them to inject malicious code into updates that were later deployed to thousands of SolarWinds' customers, including government agencies and large corporations.
- **Mitigation**: Organizations should ensure that third-party vendors follow strict security policies, conduct regular security assessments, and use tools like multi-factor authentication (MFA) and least privilege access. Additionally, segmenting access to critical systems can help mitigate risks.

2.2 Phishing and Social Engineering via Third-Party Employees

Attackers may also target third-party employees with social engineering tactics, such as spear-phishing attacks. By impersonating trusted parties or leveraging publicly available information, attackers can trick third-party employees into divulging sensitive access credentials, installing malware, or executing unauthorized actions.

- **Exploitation**: A red team could craft a highly targeted phishing email that appears to come from a legitimate source (e.g., a manager or IT support) and direct the third-party employee to a fake login page or a malicious attachment. Once the employee interacts with the phishing attempt, the attacker gains access to the third-party's internal systems and potentially the organization's network.
- **Real-World Example**: In 2013, the Target breach was a result of an attacker compromising a third-party vendor (a HVAC company) that had access to Target's network. Attackers used stolen credentials from the vendor to infiltrate Target's system and steal over 40 million credit card details.
- **Mitigation**: Organizations should provide ongoing security training to employees and vendors, especially regarding social engineering and phishing threats. Additionally, ensuring third-party access is limited and closely monitored can reduce the impact of a successful attack.

3. Techniques for Gaining Access via Supply Chain Attacks

Supply chain attacks involve the exploitation of vulnerabilities in the manufacturing, shipping, or software distribution process, leading to malicious code being introduced into products or services before they reach the end user. These attacks often exploit the trust an organization places in its supply chain and can be more difficult to detect since the attack is initiated earlier in the process.

3.1 Injecting Malicious Code into Software or Updates

Malicious code can be inserted into a piece of software during development or in the update process. If an attacker gains access to a software vendor's build environment or update pipeline, they can inject malware or backdoors into software packages that are distributed to customers. When customers download and install these updates, they unknowingly introduce the malicious code into their systems.

- **Exploitation**: The attacker compromises the vendor's software development or distribution environment. This may involve hacking into a vendor's network, leveraging weak security practices, or compromising the update server. Once the malicious update is deployed to the primary organization, it could provide a backdoor into their infrastructure.
- **Real-World Example**: The SolarWinds attack (mentioned earlier) is a prime example of a supply chain attack where attackers compromised the software update system for the Orion platform, allowing them to infect thousands of organizations globally.
- **Mitigation**: To reduce the risk of supply chain attacks, organizations should implement robust software integrity checks, including using cryptographic signatures for software updates, maintaining an internal software bill of materials (SBOM), and performing security audits of software vendors and updates.

3.2 Compromising Hardware or Firmware

Supply chain attacks also target the physical supply chain by compromising hardware or firmware before it reaches the target organization. This type of attack can involve tampering with the hardware of devices or compromising firmware that runs on devices like routers, servers, or storage units.

- **Exploitation**: By introducing modified or counterfeit hardware components into the supply chain, attackers can compromise an organization's internal network. Once the hardware is installed, attackers can manipulate firmware to introduce persistent backdoors or monitoring mechanisms that allow ongoing access to the network.
- **Real-World Example**: In 2018, Supermicro hardware was allegedly compromised during the manufacturing process. Malicious chips were inserted into server motherboards that were later shipped to clients, including major tech companies and government entities.
- **Mitigation**: Organizations should prioritize purchasing hardware from reputable vendors with a demonstrated commitment to security. Conducting regular hardware audits and monitoring for unusual behavior in connected devices can help identify compromised systems.

3.3 Compromising External APIs or Services

In the case of third-party services or APIs, attackers can compromise an external API that the organization depends on for its business processes. Once compromised, the attacker can exploit weaknesses in the API or service to escalate privileges, access sensitive data, or disrupt operations.

- **Exploitation**: Red teamers can probe the third-party service for vulnerabilities or flaws in authentication mechanisms, such as weak API keys, improperly configured endpoints, or insufficient rate limiting. Once access is gained, the attacker can either gain insight into the organization's operations or inject malicious commands into the data pipeline.
- **Real-World Example**: The Capital One data breach in 2019 occurred when a former employee of a third-party vendor discovered and exploited a misconfigured firewall, allowing access to sensitive customer data through an API. The breach affected over 100 million customers.
- **Mitigation**: Organizations should ensure third-party APIs are properly secured, employ authentication mechanisms such as OAuth, and regularly audit third-party services for vulnerabilities.

4. Defending Against Third-Party and Supply Chain Attacks

4.1 Implement Strong Vendor Security Assessments

Organizations should conduct thorough security assessments of third-party vendors and ensure that they adhere to security best practices. This includes reviewing vendor security policies, performing regular security audits, and ensuring that vendors have robust access control mechanisms in place.

4.2 Limit Third-Party Access to Critical Systems

Only allow third-party vendors or contractors access to the systems and data they absolutely need to perform their tasks. Use granular access controls, and ensure that sensitive areas of the network are segmented from general access. Where possible, use zero trust architectures that minimize trust and control all access.

4.3 Monitor and Audit Third-Party Activity

Regularly monitor and audit third-party activities within your organization's systems. Any abnormal behavior, such as unusual access patterns or unexpected software installations, should trigger an immediate investigation.

4.4 Build a Robust Incident Response Plan

Having a well-documented and practiced incident response plan (IRP) is critical for managing the fallout of a third-party or supply chain attack. This should include specific procedures for identifying, containing, and mitigating third-party compromises.

Third-party and supply chain attacks are among the most sophisticated and damaging threats facing organizations today. By exploiting the trust relationships between organizations and their vendors, contractors, or software providers, attackers can bypass traditional security defenses and gain initial access to sensitive systems. Red teamers can simulate these attacks by targeting vulnerabilities in third-party relationships, APIs, and software supply chains to test an organization's resilience to these growing threats. For organizations, maintaining a proactive approach to vendor management, securing supply chains, and establishing comprehensive security protocols is essential to defend against these increasingly prevalent attack vectors.

5. Exploitation Techniques

Exploitation is where vulnerabilities are turned into actionable opportunities, enabling you to move deeper into the target environment. This chapter dives into advanced exploitation techniques, teaching you how to chain multiple vulnerabilities, bypass modern security controls, and leverage zero-day exploits when available. You'll learn to exploit logic flaws, craft custom payloads, and execute attacks with precision. By understanding the intricacies of exploitation, you'll not only enhance your technical skillset but also increase the realism and effectiveness of your red team engagements.

5.1 Vulnerability Chaining and Multi-Step Exploitation

In the world of penetration testing and red teaming, vulnerability chaining and multi-step exploitation are critical strategies used to escalate privileges, pivot across networks, and eventually gain full control of target systems. Vulnerability chaining involves linking multiple vulnerabilities, often across different layers of a system, to create an attack path that allows an adversary to bypass defenses and achieve their ultimate objectives. Multi-step exploitation, on the other hand, refers to the sequential execution of multiple exploits in stages, each step building on the previous one, to achieve the final goal—whether that is privilege escalation, lateral movement, or exfiltration of sensitive data.

This chapter explores how red teamers use vulnerability chaining and multi-step exploitation techniques to simulate advanced attacks that mimic the tactics of real-world adversaries. By understanding these methods, defenders can strengthen their defenses against sophisticated attack strategies.

1. Understanding Vulnerability Chaining

1.1 What is Vulnerability Chaining?

Vulnerability chaining refers to the process of exploiting a series of vulnerabilities in sequence to achieve a complex attack objective. In most cases, no single vulnerability by itself allows an attacker to fully compromise a target system. Instead, the attacker must exploit multiple vulnerabilities, each helping to mitigate the shortcomings of the previous one, to achieve their goal. Vulnerability chaining may involve a combination of:

- **Local Exploits**: These are typically vulnerabilities within the same system or device, such as privilege escalation flaws or bugs in system configurations.

- **Network Exploits**: These vulnerabilities allow the attacker to move across different systems within the target network, often involving flaws in network protocols or misconfigurations in firewalls or routers.
- **Application Exploits**: These target software weaknesses in applications, often exploiting flaws in user input validation, authentication mechanisms, or communication protocols.

By combining vulnerabilities from multiple sources—whether different software applications, system configurations, or network layers—red teamers can create a chain of attacks that eventually lead to a successful compromise.

1.2 How Vulnerability Chaining Works

To chain vulnerabilities effectively, an attacker needs to understand the interconnectedness of systems and their components. An attack may start with a relatively harmless vulnerability that enables limited access or creates an entry point into a system. The attacker then exploits another vulnerability that escalates privileges or provides access to a more critical area of the target network.

For example, a common vulnerability chain could look like this:

- **Initial Exploit**: The attacker gains access through a low-severity vulnerability, such as an unauthenticated remote file inclusion (RFI) vulnerability in a web application.
- **Privilege Escalation**: The attacker then exploits a local privilege escalation vulnerability to escalate from a regular user to an administrative user on the compromised system.
- **Lateral Movement**: Next, the attacker uses the administrative access to exploit an unpatched vulnerability in a networked service, enabling them to pivot to a new target system.
- **Full System Compromise**: Once on the new system, the attacker may exploit another vulnerability to escalate privileges again or gain access to sensitive data or credentials.

1.3 Benefits and Challenges of Vulnerability Chaining

- **Benefits**: Vulnerability chaining enables attackers to work around security defenses that may be effective against isolated vulnerabilities. By combining multiple attack vectors, red teamers can simulate realistic multi-stage attacks, helping organizations identify weaknesses in their layered security strategies.

- **Challenges**: Chaining vulnerabilities requires extensive reconnaissance, deep knowledge of the target environment, and the ability to quickly pivot from one attack vector to the next. Additionally, some vulnerabilities may only be exploitable under certain conditions, which requires a highly adaptive approach.

2. Multi-Step Exploitation: The Process of Sequential Attacks

2.1 What is Multi-Step Exploitation?

Multi-step exploitation is the process of using several sequential attack steps to gain access to a target system, escalate privileges, or achieve other attack objectives. This often involves chaining together vulnerabilities, social engineering tactics, and various exploitation techniques. Multi-step exploitation is common in sophisticated red team engagements because it mirrors the techniques used by advanced persistent threats (APTs) and other malicious actors.

In multi-step exploitation, each step of the attack builds upon the success of the previous one, gradually expanding the attacker's control over the environment. These steps can include initial access, lateral movement, privilege escalation, persistence, and data exfiltration.

2.2 Example of Multi-Step Exploitation

Let's walk through an example of a multi-step exploitation process:

- **Initial Access**: The red team initiates the attack with a social engineering campaign—perhaps a spear-phishing email with a malicious attachment that exploits a vulnerability in the target's email client, allowing remote code execution.
- **Initial Compromise**: Once the victim opens the malicious attachment, a reverse shell is triggered, giving the attacker low-level access to the victim's machine.
- **Privilege Escalation**: Using this foothold, the red team searches for privilege escalation vulnerabilities, such as misconfigured permissions or kernel vulnerabilities. By exploiting a vulnerability in the Windows kernel, they escalate their privileges to system administrator level.
- **Lateral Movement**: With administrator access, the red team uses tools like PsExec or WinRM to move laterally across the network, compromising additional systems and mapping out the environment.
- **Persistence**: To maintain access to the network, the red team installs a backdoor or creates a new user with administrative privileges that will persist even if the initial access vector is patched.

- **Data Exfiltration**: Finally, after navigating through the network and identifying sensitive data, the red team exfiltrates files via encrypted channels or by exploiting a flaw in the file-sharing system to bypass data-loss prevention (DLP) controls.

Each step in the chain requires careful planning, execution, and a solid understanding of the target system's architecture and defenses.

2.3 Tools for Multi-Step Exploitation

Red teamers employ a variety of tools to facilitate multi-step exploitation, including:

- **Metasploit**: A popular framework for testing vulnerabilities and exploiting systems. It includes exploits, payloads, and auxiliary modules to automate parts of the exploitation process.
- **Cobalt Strike**: A versatile post-exploitation tool used for lateral movement, privilege escalation, and persistence. It provides tools for evading detection and maintaining access.
- **PowerShell Empire**: A post-exploitation framework used for executing commands on Windows machines remotely, with extensive support for lateral movement and persistence.
- **Mimikatz**: A powerful tool for extracting credentials from memory and performing Kerberos ticket extraction, which is invaluable for lateral movement and privilege escalation in Windows environments.

3. Combining Vulnerability Chaining with Multi-Step Exploitation

3.1 Building Complex Attack Paths

While vulnerability chaining involves the exploitation of multiple flaws in sequence, multi-step exploitation relies on attackers progressing through a sequence of stages, where each stage could involve chaining multiple vulnerabilities. When combined, these methods provide red teamers with powerful capabilities for testing defense mechanisms against complex, multi-faceted attack scenarios.

For instance, a red team engagement could involve multiple layers of vulnerability chaining within each exploitation step. The team could exploit a web application vulnerability (like SQL injection) to gain initial access, escalate privileges by exploiting a system misconfiguration, then use lateral movement techniques to compromise other systems before exfiltrating data.

3.2 Targeting Multiple Layers of Defense

Multi-step exploitation often targets different layers of an organization's security defenses, including:

- **Perimeter Defenses**: The initial access phase often bypasses firewalls, intrusion detection systems (IDS), and email security solutions.
- **Network Defenses**: Exploiting internal network vulnerabilities or misconfigurations to gain lateral access to other systems or networks.
- **Application Defenses**: Leveraging flaws in business-critical applications or web services that are not properly hardened or monitored.
- **Endpoint Defenses**: Exploiting misconfigurations or weaknesses in endpoint security solutions (such as antivirus, endpoint detection and response (EDR) tools) to maintain persistence.

By targeting and chaining vulnerabilities across these layers, red teamers can simulate real-world attacks that combine various tactics and techniques, reflecting the persistence and sophistication of modern cyber adversaries.

4. Mitigation and Defending Against Vulnerability Chaining and Multi-Step Exploitation

4.1 Defense-in-Depth

Organizations should implement defense-in-depth strategies that layer multiple security mechanisms to prevent an attacker from chaining vulnerabilities successfully. Each security layer—whether at the network, application, or endpoint level—should be designed to catch and stop an attack at different stages of the exploitation process.

4.2 Patch Management and Vulnerability Scanning

Regular patching and vulnerability scanning are essential to identifying and mitigating the risks of chaining known vulnerabilities. Automated tools like Nessus, Qualys, and OpenVAS can help identify known flaws in systems, while static and dynamic application security testing (SAST/DAST) tools can help find vulnerabilities in software before attackers do.

4.3 Endpoint Detection and Response (EDR)

An effective EDR solution can detect and prevent exploitation attempts at the endpoint level, including tracking suspicious activity and identifying abnormal behavior. EDR solutions should be configured to look for evidence of exploitation, privilege escalation, and lateral movement.

4.4 Red Team and Blue Team Collaboration

Collaboration between red teams (offensive) and blue teams (defensive) is vital for improving overall security posture. Red team engagements can simulate complex attack chains to identify gaps in security controls, while blue teams can learn from these engagements to improve detection, containment, and response.

Vulnerability chaining and multi-step exploitation are powerful techniques used by red teamers to simulate sophisticated cyber-attacks. By combining multiple vulnerabilities and stages of exploitation, red teamers can bypass multiple layers of defenses and compromise critical systems in a manner that mimics advanced persistent threats. Understanding these methods is crucial for both attackers and defenders, as it enables organizations to build stronger security defenses, identify vulnerabilities, and protect against increasingly complex and multi-faceted cyber threats.

5.2 Exploiting Logic Flaws in Applications

Logic flaws in applications are vulnerabilities that arise when the application's intended behavior does not match its actual behavior due to incorrect assumptions or flaws in the system design. These flaws can be particularly dangerous because they often do not arise from direct technical weaknesses like buffer overflows or code injection, but from errors in the logic that controls how the application processes inputs, decisions, and user actions. Exploiting logic flaws typically requires an understanding of the business logic, application flow, and how users interact with the system in unintended ways. As a result, attacks targeting logic flaws can be more difficult to detect and mitigate, making them an attractive avenue for advanced attackers.

This section explores how red teamers exploit logic flaws in applications, providing a deeper understanding of the tactics, techniques, and tools involved in identifying and taking advantage of these vulnerabilities.

1. What Are Logic Flaws?

Logic flaws occur when an application fails to enforce its intended security policies due to incorrect logic, assumptions, or design flaws. These flaws can be exploited in various ways, often bypassing traditional security mechanisms such as input validation, authentication, and authorization.

Common examples of logic flaws include:

- **Broken Authentication Logic**: Flaws that allow attackers to bypass authentication mechanisms or gain unauthorized access to user accounts by manipulating the logic controlling session management.
- **Insecure Business Logic**: When business rules are improperly enforced, attackers can manipulate transactions or processes in their favor (e.g., purchasing items at a discount, modifying account balances, etc.).
- **Race Conditions**: Conditions that arise when the behavior of an application depends on the timing of events or user actions. Attackers can exploit race conditions by manipulating the order of operations, leading to unexpected or insecure behavior.

Unlike traditional vulnerabilities like SQL injection or cross-site scripting (XSS), logic flaws are harder to detect through automated vulnerability scanners because they usually don't leave behind exploitable signatures in code. Instead, they stem from the way a system is designed or behaves in certain situations.

2. Types of Logic Flaws

2.1 Authentication and Authorization Bypass

One of the most dangerous types of logic flaws is when an application fails to properly check whether a user has the correct privileges to perform a specific action. This can lead to attackers bypassing authentication mechanisms, gaining unauthorized access, or performing actions that they should not be able to.

Example: In an online banking application, an attacker could manipulate the parameters in a transaction request to alter the amount being transferred from one account to another, despite being logged in as a regular user without administrative privileges.

Exploitation: To exploit this flaw, attackers often use manual testing techniques to try bypassing or manipulating the authentication checks. This can involve modifying URLs, HTTP headers, or session tokens, or leveraging flaws in multi-factor authentication (MFA) mechanisms.

2.2 Insecure Business Logic

Insecure business logic flaws occur when an application's design does not properly enforce its intended business rules. This can result in attackers exploiting these weaknesses to perform unintended actions, such as modifying account balances, executing transactions outside of authorized limits, or accessing restricted data.

Example: In an e-commerce application, a flaw in the logic that calculates discounts could allow an attacker to exploit the system by applying a massive discount to products in their shopping cart, essentially bypassing the intended price calculation logic.

Exploitation: Exploiting this type of flaw typically involves identifying areas where the business logic can be manipulated. This can include testing edge cases, manipulating input data (e.g., modifying parameters or values submitted via forms or APIs), and analyzing the application's responses to find unexpected results.

2.3 Race Conditions and Time-of-Check to Time-of-Use (TOCTOU)

Race conditions and TOCTOU vulnerabilities arise when an attacker is able to manipulate the timing of an application's behavior to gain an advantage. These types of flaws occur when there is a discrepancy between when a check is made (time of check) and when the action is performed (time of use).

Example: In an online auction application, a race condition could occur if two users are allowed to place bids on an item at the same time. If the application doesn't properly synchronize bid updates, a user could exploit the flaw to place a bid higher than their authorized limit.

Exploitation: Attackers may trigger specific actions in quick succession to exploit race conditions, using tools like Burp Suite or custom scripts to simulate rapid, simultaneous requests or modify data in ways that the system doesn't expect.

2.4 Improper Input Handling in Logic Flaws

Input validation is a key area where logic flaws can arise. If an application does not properly validate the data input by users, attackers can manipulate those inputs to influence the behavior of the application in malicious ways. While input validation vulnerabilities are typically classified as technical flaws, improper input handling in the context of business logic can also cause serious issues.

Example: A web application that allows users to update their account details might incorrectly handle input validation for the "address" field. An attacker could inject specially crafted data into this field to trigger unexpected behavior, such as bypassing address verification or injecting hidden fields that alter the internal logic.

Exploitation: Exploiting this flaw often involves manipulating input fields, either via the web interface or API calls, to test how the system handles unexpected values or attempts to bypass validation logic.

3. Identifying and Exploiting Logic Flaws

Red teamers use a variety of techniques to identify and exploit logic flaws in applications. The following steps outline a typical approach to uncovering and exploiting these vulnerabilities:

3.1 Mapping the Application Flow

Before exploiting logic flaws, red teamers must map out the application's flow, understanding the different user roles, actions, and business logic. This process typically involves:

- Reviewing the application's source code (if available).
- Analyzing how different components interact with each other.
- Identifying areas where security checks and user input validation are applied.

Tools like Burp Suite and OWASP ZAP can be used to intercept and modify requests to test how the application responds to unexpected or manipulated data.

3.2 Manual Testing and Fuzzing

While automated vulnerability scanners can find some common flaws like SQL injection or XSS, identifying logic flaws usually requires manual testing. This involves interacting with the application, understanding its workflow, and looking for areas where the logic can be bypassed.

Fuzzing, or sending random or unexpected input to the application, can also help identify how the system handles unusual conditions and whether any logic errors or security flaws are triggered by specific inputs.

3.3 Crafting Attack Scenarios

To exploit a logic flaw, red teamers craft attack scenarios that manipulate the application's intended behavior. For example, they might attempt to bypass authentication by replaying old session tokens or exploit a business logic flaw to gain unauthorized access to resources by modifying input values.

A common approach is to:

- Identify sensitive actions in the application that are controlled by business logic.
- Try manipulating inputs or sequencing requests in ways that alter the outcome of a transaction.
- Use timing-based attacks to exploit race conditions or TOCTOU vulnerabilities.

3.4 Using Automated Tools

Certain tools can aid red teamers in identifying logic flaws by testing for edge cases and unusual inputs. Some tools to consider include:

- **Burp Suite**: Useful for intercepting and manipulating HTTP requests, allowing red teamers to modify inputs and test for logic flaws in real-time.
- **OWASP ZAP**: Another web application security testing tool that helps in identifying vulnerabilities related to business logic flaws by analyzing application behavior and intercepting HTTP requests.
- **Fuzzing tools**: Tools like AFL (American Fuzzy Lop) or Peach Fuzzer can be used to send malformed or randomized input data to applications, potentially revealing unexpected behaviors or flaws in logic.

4. Mitigating Logic Flaws

Defending against logic flaws requires robust testing, thorough understanding of application workflows, and comprehensive security policies. Some key mitigation strategies include:

- **Secure Software Development Lifecycle (SDLC):** Security should be integrated into the application's development lifecycle. Regular code reviews, automated testing, and static code analysis can help identify logic flaws early in the development process.

- **Comprehensive Input Validation**: All user inputs should be validated and sanitized, especially when they affect critical operations like financial transactions or account management. This ensures that only valid data is accepted.
- **Business Logic Testing**: Conduct manual and automated testing for business logic vulnerabilities, particularly for applications that handle sensitive or financial data.
- **Regular Penetration Testing**: Red team exercises and regular penetration testing should simulate sophisticated attacks, including those that target business logic flaws. This helps identify potential weaknesses in application workflows and business processes.
- **User Behavior Monitoring**: Implement monitoring to track abnormal user behavior that could indicate exploitation of a logic flaw (e.g., unusual transaction sizes, access to unauthorized areas).

Exploiting logic flaws in applications is a sophisticated and subtle form of attack that often evades traditional vulnerability scanning tools. By understanding how applications are supposed to function and identifying where the logic can be manipulated, red teamers can simulate realistic and complex attack scenarios. Defending against these vulnerabilities requires a deep understanding of business processes, regular security testing, and comprehensive defenses that go beyond technical vulnerabilities.

5.3 Zero-Day Exploitation: Finding and Leveraging Unknown Vulnerabilities

Zero-day vulnerabilities are security flaws that are unknown to the vendor or the public, meaning no patch or fix has been released to mitigate the issue. These vulnerabilities present an enormous risk to organizations because attackers can exploit them with little to no defense, leaving systems vulnerable to compromise. The term "zero-day" refers to the fact that the vendor has had zero days to fix the vulnerability before it is discovered and exploited.

Exploiting zero-day vulnerabilities is one of the most sophisticated and dangerous techniques in a red teamer's arsenal. Red teamers and advanced persistent threats (APTs) often target zero-days to gain unauthorized access, escalate privileges, or bypass security controls without being detected. Finding and leveraging these vulnerabilities is a complex process that requires a deep understanding of system internals, application logic, and attack vectors that could be exploited.

This section explores the concept of zero-day exploitation, detailing how red teamers find, analyze, and leverage zero-day vulnerabilities for penetration testing and ethical hacking purposes.

1. What is a Zero-Day Vulnerability?

A zero-day vulnerability is a flaw in software, hardware, or firmware that is unknown to the vendor or security community. Because these vulnerabilities are not yet disclosed or patched, they are highly valuable to attackers, who can exploit them to compromise a system or network before a fix is made available.

Zero-day vulnerabilities are particularly dangerous because:

- **No Patches Available**: Since the vulnerability is unknown, there are no patches or updates to fix it.
- **Difficult to Detect**: Because these vulnerabilities are not publicly known, they can be challenging for security systems to detect.
- **Targeted by Sophisticated Attackers**: Zero-days are highly sought after by cybercriminals, state-sponsored actors, and advanced red teams because they allow attackers to infiltrate systems without triggering alarms.

Once a zero-day vulnerability is discovered, it becomes a high-value asset. Its exploitation can lead to significant damage, ranging from the theft of sensitive information to complete system compromise.

2. The Lifecycle of a Zero-Day Exploit

Understanding the lifecycle of a zero-day exploit is key to comprehending how it works and how it can be leveraged. This lifecycle typically includes several phases:

2.1 Discovery

The discovery phase is when a researcher, hacker, or red teamer identifies an unknown vulnerability in a system. The discovery could happen in many ways, such as:

- **Manual Code Review**: A red teamer might manually review the source code of an application or system to find flaws.
- **Fuzzing**: Automated tools like AFL (American Fuzzy Lop) or Peach Fuzzer can be used to test inputs and discover unexpected behaviors that may indicate vulnerabilities.

- **Reverse Engineering**: In some cases, red teamers reverse-engineer software to discover vulnerabilities in proprietary applications or even hardware-based systems.

When a researcher finds a zero-day vulnerability, it is typically kept private, either to exploit it themselves, sell it on the dark web, or use it for a targeted attack. Some researchers report their findings to vendors in a responsible manner, while others may use the knowledge for malicious purposes.

2.2 Weaponization

Once a zero-day vulnerability is discovered, attackers must turn the vulnerability into an exploit that can be used to achieve a specific attack goal. This process is known as weaponization and involves:

- **Developing an Exploit**: The zero-day is often used to create an exploit payload that takes advantage of the vulnerability. This may involve crafting a malicious input, a payload to execute, or a specific sequence of steps to trigger the vulnerability.
- **Bypassing Defenses**: Zero-day vulnerabilities are often used to bypass security mechanisms such as firewalls, anti-virus software, or intrusion detection systems (IDS). Weaponization may involve crafting exploits that avoid detection or leveraging known evasion techniques.
- **Payload Development**: The exploit is often accompanied by a payload, such as remote code execution, a reverse shell, or privilege escalation, allowing the attacker to take control of the system.

Weaponizing a zero-day is a time-consuming and technical process that requires specialized knowledge of the system being targeted, its security mechanisms, and how the vulnerability can be manipulated.

2.3 Delivery

Once the exploit has been weaponized, the next step is delivery, where the attacker delivers the exploit to the target system. Delivery methods can include:

- **Phishing**: Attackers often use phishing emails to deliver a zero-day exploit through malicious attachments or links. The email may entice the victim to open the file or click the link, triggering the exploit.

- **Web Application Attacks**: Exploiting vulnerabilities in web applications (e.g., server-side flaws, deserialization issues) to deliver an exploit through HTTP requests.
- **Malicious Software**: Attacks can be delivered by embedding zero-day exploits into malicious software or through software vulnerabilities that allow the attacker to execute arbitrary code.

In red team engagements, delivery often involves creative social engineering techniques, combined with the weaponized zero-day exploit, to bypass security defenses and gain access to the target system.

2.4 Exploitation

Exploitation is the process of triggering the zero-day vulnerability on the target system to execute the malicious payload. Exploitation might occur through various methods, such as:

- **Remote Code Execution**: A successful zero-day exploit might enable the attacker to run arbitrary code on the target system, often resulting in the establishment of a backdoor for persistence.
- **Privilege Escalation**: Some zero-day vulnerabilities allow attackers to escalate privileges, such as from a regular user to an administrator, providing greater control over the system or network.
- **Information Disclosure**: A zero-day vulnerability might allow attackers to extract sensitive data from a system, including passwords, encryption keys, or confidential documents.

Once the exploit is triggered, the red team gains the initial access or executes the desired operation, often creating persistence to maintain access.

2.5 Post-Exploitation and Persistence

After successfully exploiting a zero-day vulnerability, the attacker often moves into post-exploitation, maintaining access to the system and expanding the attack.

- **Lateral Movement**: Exploiting additional systems in the network by leveraging the initial foothold gained from the zero-day.
- **Privilege Escalation**: Further exploiting the system to gain higher levels of access or take over more critical infrastructure.

- **Data Exfiltration**: Extracting sensitive data or conducting espionage through the access achieved by the zero-day exploit.

Maintaining access after exploiting a zero-day often requires using other tools or techniques, including creating backdoors, planting malware, or using stolen credentials to escalate privileges further.

3. Tools and Techniques for Finding Zero-Day Vulnerabilities

Finding zero-day vulnerabilities is a highly specialized skill that requires a deep understanding of software, hardware, and security protocols. Some common tools and techniques for discovering zero-day vulnerabilities include:

3.1 Fuzzing Tools

Fuzzing is one of the most effective techniques for discovering zero-day vulnerabilities. It involves sending random or malformed inputs to a system to see how it behaves and where it fails. Common fuzzing tools include:

- **AFL (American Fuzzy Lop):** A powerful fuzzer for finding bugs in software by continuously sending random inputs.
- **Peach Fuzzer**: A commercial fuzzing platform that automates the testing of applications and network protocols.
- **Sulley**: A Python-based fuzzer used for fuzzing network protocols, file formats, and more.

Fuzzing tools can uncover unexpected behaviors in applications and help identify areas that may contain zero-day vulnerabilities.

3.2 Reverse Engineering

Reverse engineering involves analyzing compiled software to discover flaws in the underlying code. Tools like IDA Pro, Ghidra, or OllyDbg can be used to inspect the binary code, identify flaws in memory handling, and uncover vulnerabilities that are not obvious from the source code.

3.3 Static and Dynamic Analysis

Static analysis involves examining the code without running it, while dynamic analysis examines the behavior of the software during execution. Both techniques can uncover security flaws that could lead to zero-day discoveries. Tools like Radare2 and Binary Ninja provide insights into software behavior and help identify issues that may be exploited.

3.4 Code Audits and Security Testing

Code audits and manual review of source code can uncover logic flaws and security issues that might lead to zero-day vulnerabilities. Security experts examine the source code for improper input validation, insecure memory handling, and other flaws that could be exploited by attackers.

4. Ethical Considerations and Legal Implications

The discovery and exploitation of zero-day vulnerabilities come with significant ethical and legal considerations. While red teamers and security researchers may responsibly disclose zero-day vulnerabilities to the vendor, others may choose to sell the information to criminal organizations or use it for malicious purposes. The ethical handling of zero-day vulnerabilities requires careful judgment, and disclosure should always be done responsibly to avoid harming others.

- **Responsible Disclosure**: Involves notifying the vendor about the vulnerability so they can issue a patch before public disclosure.
- **Exploit Marketplaces**: Some individuals may attempt to sell zero-day vulnerabilities on dark web marketplaces, leading to malicious exploitation.
- **Legal Implications**: Depending on local laws, exploiting zero-day vulnerabilities without authorization can be illegal, even in red team scenarios. It is crucial to ensure that all activities are authorized and ethical.

Zero-day exploitation is one of the most powerful tactics available to red teamers and advanced attackers. These vulnerabilities allow for stealthy attacks that bypass traditional security defenses, and exploiting them requires skill, patience, and a deep understanding of system behavior. While the discovery and weaponization of zero-day vulnerabilities are complex, they offer valuable insight into how attackers operate and provide crucial lessons for strengthening defenses. Understanding the lifecycle, tools, and techniques for finding zero-day vulnerabilities is critical for both offensive and defensive cybersecurity efforts, ensuring that organizations can better prepare for the threats posed by these powerful exploits.

5.4 Breaking Modern Security Mechanisms: Sandboxes, ASLR, and DEP

Modern software systems have evolved to incorporate advanced security mechanisms designed to protect against common types of attacks, such as buffer overflows, code injection, and privilege escalation. These mechanisms aim to make exploitation more difficult and reduce the effectiveness of traditional attack vectors. However, no security measure is foolproof, and skilled red teamers are often tasked with bypassing or circumventing these defenses to simulate sophisticated, real-world attacks.

Three critical security mechanisms that are commonly found in modern operating systems and applications are sandboxes, Address Space Layout Randomization (ASLR), and Data Execution Prevention (DEP). While these techniques provide essential layers of defense, understanding their weaknesses and limitations is key to successfully exploiting them.

This section explores how red teamers break or bypass modern security mechanisms like sandboxes, ASLR, and DEP, detailing the techniques used and how attackers exploit these mechanisms for penetration testing and vulnerability research.

1. Sandboxing: What It Is and How It Works

A sandbox is a security mechanism used to isolate applications or processes from the rest of the system, preventing them from interacting with critical resources, files, or other parts of the operating system. Sandboxes are commonly used to contain potentially malicious applications, such as web browsers, email clients, or untrusted code, in a restricted environment where any exploits or vulnerabilities are less likely to cause harm.

- **Common Uses**: Sandboxing is used in web browsers (e.g., Chrome's sandboxing), mobile applications (e.g., Android's app sandbox), and virtualized environments (e.g., VMware or Docker containers).
- **Isolation**: Sandboxes typically limit access to the file system, networking, and process memory, making it difficult for attackers to break out and escalate privileges.
- **Goal**: The primary goal is to prevent an attacker who compromises a sandboxed application from gaining access to the underlying system or other applications.

Breaking Sandboxes

While sandboxes add significant protection, they are not infallible. Red teamers often attempt to bypass sandbox restrictions using various techniques:

Exploiting Inter-Process Communication (IPC): Attackers may try to exploit communication channels between processes that are running in the sandbox and processes outside of it. For instance, by abusing flaws in the sandbox's IPC mechanisms (e.g., sockets, pipes, shared memory), they can potentially send malicious commands or data to processes running outside the sandbox.

Escaping Through Vulnerabilities in the Host: If the sandbox is running on a specific operating system or virtual machine, vulnerabilities in the OS or the virtual environment can be exploited. For example, escape exploits target bugs in virtualization platforms (e.g., VMware, VirtualBox) or OS vulnerabilities that allow code to break free from its virtualized container.

Using Native API Calls: Some sandbox environments, particularly those in browsers or mobile apps, rely on allowing limited access to system resources via native APIs. If these APIs are not adequately secured, attackers can exploit them to gain further access or even break out of the sandbox.

Time-based and Side-channel Attacks: Attackers may also use time-based or side-channel attacks to detect sandbox behavior and adapt their strategy accordingly. By measuring execution times or resource consumption, attackers can detect when they are operating in a sandbox and adjust their exploit technique to bypass it.

2. Address Space Layout Randomization (ASLR)

Address Space Layout Randomization (ASLR) is a memory protection technique used to randomize the memory addresses where system components, such as libraries, heap, stack, and executable code, are loaded. ASLR makes it much harder for an attacker to predict the memory location of key components, thus preventing certain types of attacks like buffer overflows and return-oriented programming (ROP).

- **Purpose**: ASLR is designed to thwart attacks that rely on knowing the memory location of critical structures. By randomizing memory addresses on each program execution, it makes it far more difficult for an attacker to craft an exploit that targets specific locations in memory.
- **Impact**: Without knowing the location of code or buffers, an attacker cannot easily perform traditional attacks like buffer overflows or code injection.

Bypassing ASLR

While ASLR is an effective defense, skilled red teamers use a variety of techniques to bypass it:

Memory Disclosure Attacks: If an attacker can disclose a small portion of memory (for example, by exploiting a vulnerability such as format string vulnerabilities), they can learn the address of certain memory locations. From this, they can infer or calculate the locations of other critical structures, effectively bypassing ASLR.

Brute-forcing: Attackers can attempt brute-forcing techniques, where they repeatedly guess random memory addresses until they land on the correct one. This method, however, requires extensive time and resources and is only feasible under certain conditions.

Information Leaks: Certain vulnerabilities, such as buffer overflows, provide attackers with a small amount of information about memory layout. By exploiting these leaks, attackers can progressively narrow down the memory layout, gaining insight into the locations of key structures or functions.

Return-Oriented Programming (ROP): ROP is a technique used to execute code without the need for a single executable payload. Instead of injecting new code, ROP chains together existing pieces of code from the program itself. Even with ASLR, attackers can use gadgets (small code snippets) located in various parts of the memory to bypass ASLR and perform malicious actions.

3. Data Execution Prevention (DEP)

Data Execution Prevention (DEP) is a security feature that marks certain regions of memory (such as the stack, heap, and data segments) as non-executable. The goal of DEP is to prevent the execution of code from regions of memory that should not contain executable code, such as user-controlled buffers.

- **Purpose**: DEP helps prevent attacks that rely on executing malicious code from non-executable memory regions, such as buffer overflow attacks where shellcode is injected into a program's memory.
- **Impact**: With DEP enabled, attackers cannot execute injected shellcode directly from the stack or heap, making certain traditional attack methods ineffective.

Bypassing DEP

Although DEP is an essential protection mechanism, there are several techniques that red teamers use to bypass it:

Return-Oriented Programming (ROP): ROP, as mentioned earlier, is a technique that allows attackers to execute arbitrary code by chaining together existing executable code within a program. Since ROP doesn't require new code to be injected, it can bypass DEP by executing code that is already present in memory (e.g., code from system libraries or the application itself).

Heap Spraying: Heap spraying is a technique where attackers place a large number of known, executable code snippets into the heap. The goal is to overflow the heap buffer and force the application to execute one of the injected payloads. By combining heap spraying with other techniques like ROP or Return-to-libc, attackers can bypass DEP.

Code Reuse Attacks: In code reuse attacks, attackers use legitimate executable code, such as system calls or library functions, to perform their malicious actions. Since the code is already executed, DEP restrictions on new code injection are bypassed.

JIT (Just-In-Time) Spray Attacks: JIT compilers, used in environments such as Java or JavaScript, can sometimes be manipulated to generate executable code dynamically during runtime. Attackers can exploit this to bypass DEP by causing the JIT compiler to execute malicious code.

4. Combining Techniques to Bypass Multiple Defenses

The real challenge for attackers is breaking multiple layers of defense simultaneously. Sandboxes, ASLR, and DEP are often used together, making it increasingly difficult to compromise a system. Skilled red teamers typically use a combination of techniques to bypass multiple security mechanisms:

- **Bypassing Sandboxing and ASLR**: An attacker might use a memory disclosure vulnerability inside a sandboxed application to leak memory locations, followed by exploiting an ASLR-bypass technique like brute-forcing or ROP.
- **ASLR and DEP Combination**: By combining ROP chains with heap spraying or JIT spraying, attackers can bypass both ASLR and DEP in tandem.
- **Privilege Escalation**: Once an initial foothold is obtained through sandbox bypass or DEP exploitation, red teamers can use further exploits to escalate privileges and achieve their objectives, such as creating backdoors or accessing sensitive data.

The security mechanisms that modern operating systems and applications use—such as sandboxes, ASLR, and DEP—represent significant advances in defending against a wide range of attacks. However, as attackers continue to evolve their methods, these defenses are not foolproof. Red teamers and penetration testers need to understand the strengths and weaknesses of each of these security features and how to bypass or circumvent them.

By employing techniques like ROP, heap spraying, memory disclosure, and exploit chaining, red teamers can successfully bypass these protections and simulate real-world attacks, providing invaluable insights into how organizations can strengthen their defenses. While these mechanisms add layers of security, understanding how they work, and the techniques used to bypass them, is essential for both attackers and defenders in the ever-evolving world of cybersecurity.

6. Lateral Movement and Privilege Escalation

Once inside a target environment, moving undetected and escalating your privileges are critical for gaining deeper access and achieving your objectives. In this chapter, we explore advanced techniques for lateral movement across networks, from exploiting trust relationships and leveraging misconfigurations to abusing insecure protocols. You'll also learn sophisticated privilege escalation methods for both Windows and Linux environments, including exploiting weak permissions, insecure service configurations, and exploiting kernel vulnerabilities. By mastering these tactics, you'll be able to navigate complex networks and elevate your access without triggering alarms.

6.1 Leveraging Misconfigured Trust Relationships

In modern network environments, trust relationships play a crucial role in ensuring secure communication and proper access control between different systems, applications, and users. Trust relationships define the permissions and connections that allow entities to interact with one another, often involving shared access to sensitive data or services. These relationships are often established between different users, systems, services, or even organizations.

However, when these trust relationships are improperly configured or neglected, they can become a significant attack vector, providing an opportunity for red teamers and adversaries to escalate privileges, move laterally within a network, or bypass access controls. Misconfigured trust relationships can exist in many different forms, from improperly configured Active Directory settings to insecurely shared resources between domains.

In this section, we will explore how misconfigured trust relationships can be exploited to gain unauthorized access, escalate privileges, and move within an environment undetected.

1. What are Trust Relationships?

A trust relationship is the foundational connection that allows one entity (such as a user or computer) to access resources or services from another. Trust relationships are most commonly seen in networked environments, especially in Active Directory (AD) networks or multi-domain organizations, where entities trust one another to grant access to certain resources, files, or network services. Trusts help organizations manage access across multiple systems while avoiding the complexity of maintaining separate credentials for each user or system.

There are different types of trust relationships, including:

- **Domain Trusts**: In Active Directory, domain trusts enable users and resources in one domain to access those in another domain. These can be one-way or two-way, with varying degrees of access depending on the trust settings.
- **Federated Trusts**: In cloud environments or cross-organization scenarios, federated trust relationships are used to enable single sign-on (SSO) and access control between different organizations or systems.
- **Trusts Between Services**: Services or applications in an organization often trust each other for API calls or shared resources. Misconfigurations in these relationships can provide attackers with access to sensitive data or systems.

While trust relationships can enhance security and facilitate communication between systems, they also present risks if not configured properly. Misconfigurations in these relationships can result in elevated privileges, unauthorized access to critical systems, and lateral movement across the network.

2. Common Misconfigurations in Trust Relationships

Misconfigurations in trust relationships often arise from poor planning, lack of proper auditing, or misinterpretation of security policies. Some of the most common misconfigurations that red teamers exploit include:

2.1 Overly Permissive Domain Trusts

In a typical Active Directory setup, trust relationships are configured between domains (e.g., Domain A trusts Domain B). A one-way trust allows users from Domain A to access resources in Domain B, but not vice versa. If this trust is set up improperly—such as allowing overly broad access from Domain A to Domain B—it can provide attackers with an easy path to escalate privileges or access resources that should be restricted.

Exploit Technique:

Exploitation of Misconfigured Domain Trusts: Attackers may take advantage of overly permissive trusts to access sensitive systems or databases in other domains. If a trust relationship allows unauthenticated users from one domain to access resources in another, attackers can move laterally into that domain by simply impersonating a trusted entity.

2.2 Insecure Service Trusts

Many organizations rely on services (like web applications, database servers, or cloud services) that are configured to trust each other's identities. If these trust relationships are improperly configured, an attacker might be able to impersonate a legitimate service, allowing them to hijack services or access confidential data.

Exploit Technique:

Service Impersonation: If an attacker gains control over a service with broad trust permissions, they can masquerade as a legitimate service or user, granting them unauthorized access to systems or databases that they otherwise wouldn't be able to reach.

2.3 Kerberos Misconfigurations in Active Directory

Kerberos is a popular authentication protocol used in Active Directory environments. Misconfigurations in Kerberos settings, such as improperly set Service Principal Names (SPNs) or weak delegation, can create security gaps. These gaps may allow attackers to escalate their privileges or impersonate other users or services in a process known as Kerberos ticket abuse.

Exploit Technique:

Golden Ticket Attacks: Attackers can leverage Kerberos misconfigurations by obtaining or forging Kerberos tickets (e.g., Golden Tickets). With this forged ticket, they can impersonate any user or service in the domain and gain access to sensitive resources.

Silver Ticket Attacks: Similar to Golden Tickets, Silver Tickets grant access to a specific service by impersonating a user to that service alone. These attacks can be executed if the attacker can exploit misconfigurations in service trust or delegate permissions.

2.4 Improperly Configured External Trusts

External trusts are used to connect an organization's Active Directory environment to an external domain, often across different organizations. If these trusts are not configured with strict security settings (e.g., limiting permissions), attackers can leverage them to access external resources and potentially escalate privileges to other systems.

Exploit Technique:

Exploitation of External Trusts: Attackers may exploit an external trust that is not properly secured to move laterally between organizations. For example, if external trust relationships are set up with the wrong permissions, attackers could use this path to gain access to partner networks or even compromise external·entities' resources.

3. Exploitation Techniques for Leveraging Misconfigured Trusts

Once a red teamer identifies misconfigured trust relationships, the next step is to use them to gain unauthorized access or escalate privileges. The following are common exploitation techniques used in red team engagements to leverage these misconfigurations:

3.1 Pass-the-Ticket (PTT) Attacks

A Pass-the-Ticket (PTT) attack allows an attacker to use a valid Kerberos ticket to authenticate to a service or server. If the attacker can steal or forge a valid ticket—such as through a misconfigured trust or insecure service delegation—they can bypass the normal authentication flow and gain unauthorized access.

Exploit Example:

By exploiting an over-permissive service trust relationship, an attacker could steal a service ticket from one system and use it to access another system, effectively bypassing authentication and gaining privileged access.

3.2 Privilege Escalation through Trusts

Misconfigured trusts may allow attackers to escalate privileges to domain admin or other high-privilege accounts. For instance, an attacker who gains low-level access in one domain may exploit an insecure trust to access a higher-privileged domain.

Exploit Example:

If an attacker can abuse an incorrectly configured trust between two domains (e.g., a two-way trust between Domain A and Domain B), they may escalate their privileges to domain admin in Domain B, gaining full control of both networks.

3.3 Lateral Movement via Trust Exploitation

Lateral movement is a technique that attackers use to move from one compromised system to another within a network. Misconfigured trust relationships, such as over-permissive domain trusts, provide a quick way for attackers to jump from one domain to another, enabling the lateral movement of their attack.

Exploit Example:

By exploiting a trust misconfiguration, an attacker who has compromised a lower-privileged account in one domain can access resources in another domain without being detected, moving laterally within the network.

4. Mitigating the Risks of Misconfigured Trusts

Organizations must take several steps to properly configure and secure trust relationships to prevent exploitation. The following best practices can help mitigate the risks associated with misconfigured trusts:

4.1 Auditing and Monitoring

- Regularly audit trust relationships to ensure that they are configured with the least privilege principle in mind, ensuring that only necessary access is granted.
- Use tools like BloodHound to identify and map trust relationships and detect any misconfigurations.

4.2 Principle of Least Privilege

- Configure trust relationships with minimal access permissions. Ensure that entities and services can only access what they absolutely need.
- For instance, avoid granting unrestricted access across domains, and limit external trust relationships to the essential services.

4.3 Kerberos and SPN Auditing

- Regularly audit Service Principal Names (SPNs) and ensure they are properly configured to prevent Kerberos misconfigurations, which can lead to golden ticket and pass-the-ticket attacks.
- Implement strict controls around delegation settings, ensuring that only trusted services are allowed to impersonate other users.

4.4 Segmentation of Trust Relationships

- Segment and isolate sensitive systems to ensure that trust relationships do not span across different security zones unnecessarily.
- Employ network segmentation to contain and limit the impact of a compromised trust relationship.

Misconfigured trust relationships represent a significant vulnerability in modern enterprise environments. When improperly configured, they can provide adversaries with easy paths for lateral movement, privilege escalation, and unauthorized access to critical resources. Understanding how to identify and exploit these misconfigurations is crucial for red teamers in simulating real-world attack scenarios. By applying a combination of techniques, including pass-the-ticket attacks, privilege escalation, and lateral movement, attackers can exploit trust vulnerabilities to achieve their objectives.

At the same time, organizations must take proactive steps to secure trust relationships by auditing, segmenting, and applying the principle of least privilege to ensure these critical connections do not become an attack vector.

6.2 Credential Harvesting and Abuse Techniques

Credential harvesting is one of the most critical aspects of any red teaming or penetration testing operation. Gaining access to user credentials—especially those with high-level privileges—can be the key to breaching an organization's defenses and achieving broader access within its network. Credential harvesting is the process of obtaining valid credentials (usernames and passwords) through various techniques, which are then used to gain unauthorized access to systems and services.

Once credentials are harvested, adversaries often abuse them in several ways to escalate privileges, move laterally across the network, or steal sensitive data. The ability to effectively harvest and abuse credentials is fundamental for a red teamer, as it mimics common real-world attack methods, often employed in sophisticated cyberattacks.

In this section, we will explore credential harvesting techniques, the tools used to collect credentials, and the ways in which harvested credentials are abused to escalate access and compromise organizations.

1. Understanding Credential Harvesting

Credential harvesting can take many forms, ranging from basic tactics such as password guessing to more complex techniques like social engineering, phishing, or exploiting vulnerable services. The key objective of credential harvesting is to obtain a valid combination of a username and password that allows the attacker to authenticate to an organization's systems or services. Once the attacker possesses valid credentials, they can perform various actions depending on the privileges of the user account—such as moving laterally, accessing sensitive data, or escalating privileges.

There are various methods attackers use to collect credentials. Some of the most common methods include:

- **Phishing**: Trick users into revealing their usernames and passwords by impersonating legitimate services or platforms.
- **Keylogging**: Use malicious software to record keystrokes and capture credentials entered by users.
- **Credential Dumping**: Extract credentials from compromised systems, network protocols, or misconfigured systems.
- **Man-in-the-Middle (MitM) Attacks**: Intercept user credentials being transmitted over an insecure network connection.

Each of these methods targets different stages of credential acquisition, from direct user interaction to exploiting existing vulnerabilities in the environment.

2. Techniques for Credential Harvesting

Credential harvesting can be accomplished through multiple vectors, and red teamers often rely on a combination of social engineering, technical exploitation, and network-based attacks to collect credentials.

2.1 Phishing and Spear Phishing

Phishing is one of the most common methods for credential harvesting. It involves tricking users into providing their login information by impersonating a trusted entity, such as a bank, email provider, or organizational service. Phishing can take many forms, including:

Email Phishing: The attacker sends emails that appear legitimate, often containing links to fake login pages (e.g., a fake login page for Microsoft or Google). When the victim enters their credentials, the attacker captures them.

Spear Phishing: A more targeted form of phishing where attackers craft highly personalized messages tailored to specific individuals or organizations. The goal is to gain a higher success rate by making the message seem more trustworthy and relevant to the victim.

Exploitation: Once a user falls for a phishing attack, the attacker can harvest their credentials, often with the goal of accessing their email, cloud services, or internal applications.

2.2 Credential Dumping from Compromised Systems

Credential dumping refers to the process of extracting credentials from a compromised machine or system. Once a system has been compromised, an attacker can use various tools to dump stored credentials, which may include local login credentials, cached domain credentials, or password hashes. Some popular methods and tools for credential dumping include:

Mimikatz: One of the most well-known tools for credential dumping, Mimikatz can extract plaintext passwords, Kerberos tickets, and NTLM hashes from memory. It can also be used to escalate privileges and move laterally.

Windows Credential Store: Attackers may use tools like WCE (Windows Credential Editor) or Procdump to dump credentials stored in Windows' Credential Manager or other memory locations.

LSASS Dumping: The LSASS (Local Security Authority Subsystem Service) process stores sensitive authentication information like passwords and Kerberos tickets in memory. Attackers can dump the contents of LSASS to retrieve credentials.

Exploitation: By dumping credentials from a compromised system, attackers can harvest password hashes, which may be cracked offline or used in Pass-the-Hash attacks to impersonate users without needing to know the plaintext password.

2.3 Keylogging and Screen Capture

Keylogging involves the use of malware or a physical device that records keystrokes entered by a user. This method can be highly effective for credential harvesting, as it captures all user input—including usernames, passwords, and other sensitive information.

Software Keyloggers: Attackers often deploy keylogging software, either via phishing campaigns or exploiting vulnerabilities in the operating system. These keyloggers may capture keystrokes, screenshots, and even clipboard content.

Hardware Keyloggers: Physical devices connected to a computer (e.g., a USB keylogger) can capture keystrokes. These devices are often difficult to detect and can be used to harvest credentials even in environments where the network is secure.

Exploitation: Keyloggers are useful for harvesting credentials, especially when the attacker cannot directly obtain passwords through other means. The captured data can be sent back to the attacker, who can then use it to gain unauthorized access to systems.

2.4 Man-in-the-Middle (MitM) Attacks

Man-in-the-Middle (MitM) attacks involve intercepting and manipulating communications between two parties. In the context of credential harvesting, an attacker can use MitM techniques to intercept credentials as they are transmitted over an unsecured network. This type of attack is especially effective in environments where data is transmitted without encryption or on insecure networks (e.g., public Wi-Fi).

SSL Stripping: An attacker downgrades a secure HTTPS connection to an unencrypted HTTP connection, allowing them to intercept and capture login credentials sent in plain text.

DNS Spoofing: By poisoning a DNS server or manipulating the victim's DNS requests, an attacker can redirect the victim to a fake login page that looks like a legitimate site. When the victim enters their credentials, the attacker collects them.

Exploitation: MitM attacks are effective when users unknowingly submit their credentials over an insecure or manipulated channel. These stolen credentials can then be used for unauthorized access.

3. Abuse of Harvested Credentials

Once credentials are harvested, attackers often abuse them for various malicious activities, including privilege escalation, lateral movement, and unauthorized data access. Here are some common ways red teamers abuse stolen credentials:

3.1 Lateral Movement and Escalation

Once an attacker has harvested valid user credentials, they can attempt to use these credentials to move laterally across the network. Lateral movement allows attackers to escalate their access to more critical systems or services. Attackers can use tools like PsExec, WMI (Windows Management Instrumentation), or RDP (Remote Desktop Protocol) to remotely execute commands on other machines, using the harvested credentials.

Pass-the-Hash Attacks: Attackers can use the NTLM hash of a password (instead of the plaintext password) to authenticate as a user on other machines, bypassing the need to know the actual password.

Pass-the-Ticket Attacks: Using harvested Kerberos tickets, attackers can impersonate users or services and access systems or resources without needing the plaintext password.

3.2 Accessing Sensitive Data

Harvested credentials can be used to access sensitive data, such as customer records, intellectual property, or financial information. If the attacker obtains high-privilege credentials (such as domain admin or root), they can access entire databases, file systems, and other critical infrastructure.

Exploitation of Cloud Environments: In organizations using cloud infrastructure, harvested credentials may provide access to cloud services like AWS, Azure, or Google Cloud. With appropriate permissions, attackers can delete, exfiltrate, or modify critical data stored in the cloud.

3.3 Persistence and Backdoor Creation

Once the attacker has successfully gained unauthorized access to a system using the harvested credentials, they may set up backdoors or persistence mechanisms to maintain access in case the initial breach is discovered and remediated.

Adding New Users or Accounts: Attackers may create new accounts with elevated privileges (e.g., local admin or domain admin accounts) to maintain access even if the compromised user account is locked or deleted.

Deploying Malware or Remote Access Tools (RATs): Attackers may deploy malware, remote access Trojans (RATs), or other tools to establish a long-term foothold within the network.

4. Mitigating Credential Harvesting Risks

To defend against credential harvesting attacks, organizations should implement the following security measures:

- **Multi-Factor Authentication (MFA):** Require MFA for all critical systems and services to reduce the impact of credential theft.
- **Strong Password Policies**: Enforce strong, unique passwords for all users, and regularly rotate credentials, especially for administrative accounts.
- **Network Segmentation**: Implement strict access controls to limit the scope of damage that can be caused by a single set of compromised credentials.
- **Monitor for Suspicious Activity**: Use security monitoring tools to detect abnormal authentication patterns, lateral movement, or the use of compromised credentials.
- **Encryption and Secure Protocols**: Ensure that sensitive communications are encrypted (e.g., using TLS) to prevent interception of credentials during transmission.

Credential harvesting is a critical technique used by red teamers to gain access to an organization's systems and resources. By using methods like phishing, keylogging, credential dumping, and man-in-the-middle attacks, attackers can obtain valid credentials that allow them to escalate privileges, move laterally, and compromise sensitive data. Understanding how these techniques work and how to abuse harvested credentials is essential for simulating real-world attacks. However, organizations can defend against these threats by enforcing strong security practices, including multi-factor authentication, password policies, and robust monitoring.

6.3 Advanced Privilege Escalation on Windows and Linux

Privilege escalation is a critical phase in the lifecycle of a penetration test or red team engagement. It refers to the process of elevating one's access privileges to gain higher levels of control over a system. For red teamers, the goal is often to escalate from a low-privileged user (such as a standard user) to an administrator or root-level account, which allows full control over the system and greater freedom to carry out additional actions.

Privilege escalation attacks exploit vulnerabilities in the operating system (OS), applications, and misconfigurations. The techniques and tools used for privilege escalation on Windows and Linux vary considerably due to differences in OS architectures, security models, and privilege management. In this section, we will explore advanced privilege escalation techniques on both platforms, highlighting common and more sophisticated methods that red teamers may employ.

1. Privilege Escalation on Windows

Windows privilege escalation typically involves exploiting security flaws, misconfigured system settings, or weak permissions to gain elevated privileges. There are several techniques to escalate privileges on a Windows machine, some of which are simple, while others take advantage of deeper vulnerabilities in the OS.

1.1 Exploiting Weak Permissions and Misconfigurations

Windows has complex permission structures for both users and files. Misconfigured permissions can provide a path to privilege escalation:

Unrestricted File Access: If an attacker has read/write access to sensitive files such as system configuration files, registry entries, or executables that require elevated privileges, they can modify these files to gain higher privileges. For example, modifying system startup scripts (e.g., boot.ini or services registry key) can give the attacker administrative privileges when the system restarts.

Insecure Service Permissions: Windows services run under the context of an account, and if the permissions of the service are misconfigured, an attacker can potentially replace a service binary with their own malicious executable. This allows for execution with elevated privileges, as the service often runs with system-level privileges.

Example: If a service binary is stored in a directory where a low-privileged user has write access, the attacker could replace the binary with their own malicious code. Upon restarting the service, the attacker's code would execute with system privileges.

1.2 Token Impersonation and Pass-the-Hash

Windows OS maintains various types of security tokens that represent a user's identity and permissions. These tokens can be exploited for privilege escalation through techniques like token impersonation and pass-the-hash:

Token Impersonation: If a low-privileged user gains access to a process running under a high-privileged account (such as SYSTEM or Administrator), they can use the Token Impersonation technique to assume the identity of the high-privileged user. Tools like Mimikatz allow attackers to interact with process tokens and impersonate higher-privileged users.

Pass-the-Hash: Rather than needing the plaintext password of a user, attackers can use a captured NTLM hash (a hashed password value) to impersonate the user on other systems. This allows attackers to escalate their privileges without needing to crack the password.

Example: Using Mimikatz, attackers can dump the hashes of users in a compromised machine's memory, then use those hashes to authenticate as high-privileged users on other systems.

1.3 Exploiting Windows Kernel Vulnerabilities

Kernel-level vulnerabilities can provide a critical route for privilege escalation. The kernel has full control over the system, and any vulnerability in it can allow an attacker to execute arbitrary code with the highest possible privileges. Some examples include:

Local Privilege Escalation (LPE): Windows kernel vulnerabilities can be exploited using tools like CVE-2019-0841 (a privilege escalation flaw in the Windows kernel) or CVE-2020-0601 (which allows for spoofing of cryptographic certificates). These vulnerabilities enable an attacker to gain SYSTEM privileges, even if they initially only had access as a standard user.

Exploiting Vulnerable Drivers: Some device drivers in Windows may contain vulnerabilities that can be leveraged for privilege escalation. For example, exploiting a buggy driver might allow an attacker to execute arbitrary code in kernel space, enabling them to escalate their privileges.

Example: Using an exploit for a known vulnerability, an attacker can execute code that allows them to obtain SYSTEM-level access to the machine, bypassing normal privilege boundaries.

1.4 Exploiting Insecure Deserialization and DLL Hijacking

Another avenue for privilege escalation on Windows comes from exploiting insecure deserialization and DLL hijacking:

DLL Hijacking: When an application loads a dynamic link library (DLL), it looks for the DLL in predefined locations. If these locations are writable by a lower-privileged user, the attacker can place a malicious DLL in these directories. When the application runs, it loads the attacker's DLL, executing code with the privileges of the application.

Insecure Deserialization: If an application accepts serialized objects without proper validation, an attacker can craft malicious input that will cause the application to execute arbitrary code during the deserialization process.

Example: An attacker can place a malicious DLL in a folder that an application looks at when it starts up, causing the application to load the malicious DLL and execute code with the application's privileges.

2. Privilege Escalation on Linux

Linux privilege escalation techniques tend to differ from Windows due to its Unix-based architecture, but many of the same principles apply: exploiting weak configurations, vulnerable services, and incorrect file permissions. Advanced privilege escalation on Linux requires an in-depth understanding of how Linux manages users, permissions, and system services.

2.1 Sudo Misconfigurations

One of the most common and impactful privilege escalation techniques on Linux involves misconfigured sudoers files. The sudoers file controls who can execute commands with root (administrator) privileges, and misconfigurations can allow unauthorized users to execute privileged commands. Some scenarios include:

Command Path Override: If the sudoers file allows a user to run a specific command as root but does not specify the full path (e.g., allowing sudo someprogram but not specifying /usr/bin/someprogram), the attacker may be able to place a malicious executable in a directory that is included in the system's $PATH and run it with root privileges.

Allowing Unrestricted Commands: If the sudoers file allows a user to run all commands without a password prompt (e.g., username ALL=(ALL) NOPASSWD: ALL), an attacker can easily escalate privileges by running commands that they otherwise wouldn't have access to.

Example: If a user can run sudo /usr/bin/python3, they can abuse the fact that Python is a powerful interpreter capable of executing arbitrary code. By invoking sudo python3 -c 'import os; os.setuid(0); os.system("/bin/bash")', they could spawn a root shell.

2.2 Exploiting Setuid Binaries

Linux provides setuid functionality, which allows users to execute files with the privileges of the file's owner (usually root). If an attacker has access to a setuid binary that has flaws, they may be able to exploit it to escalate their privileges. Setuid binaries are often exploited because they are executed with the privileges of the binary's owner, which is typically root.

Exploiting Misconfigured Binaries: Attackers can identify vulnerable setuid binaries by scanning for files with the setuid bit enabled. If these binaries are vulnerable to buffer overflows or other flaws, they can be exploited to execute arbitrary code with root privileges.

Example: Using a tool like find to locate setuid binaries (find / -perm -4000 -type f -exec ls -l {} \;), an attacker can identify a vulnerable setuid binary and attempt to exploit it.

2.3 Kernel Exploits

As with Windows, the Linux kernel is a critical part of the system. Exploiting vulnerabilities in the kernel can allow an attacker to escalate privileges to root. Kernel exploits often involve complex bugs or vulnerabilities in the kernel's code that allow an attacker to execute arbitrary code with kernel-level privileges.

Privilege Escalation via CVEs: Specific kernel vulnerabilities, such as CVE-2016-5195 (a privilege escalation flaw in the Linux kernel), can be exploited to gain root access.

Example: An attacker might use a known privilege escalation exploit for the Linux kernel to break out of the restricted environment and gain root access.

2.4 Exploiting Cron Jobs and Scheduled Tasks

Linux uses cron jobs to schedule tasks that run periodically. If a cron job is misconfigured (for instance, if it runs a script that is writable by a low-privileged user), an attacker can exploit the cron job to execute malicious code with higher privileges.

Abusing Cron Jobs: An attacker can modify scripts that are part of scheduled tasks to run their own code with elevated privileges.

Example: If a cron job runs a script owned by root but is writable by a low-privileged user, the attacker can modify the script to run malicious commands when the cron job executes.

Privilege escalation techniques on both Windows and Linux are integral to the success of red team engagements, as they allow attackers to break through user-level barriers and assume full control of systems. Whether exploiting weak permissions, kernel vulnerabilities, or service misconfigurations, privilege escalation enables attackers to access more sensitive parts of an organization's infrastructure, setting the stage for further exploitation or data exfiltration. Understanding these advanced techniques equips red teamers with the knowledge needed to simulate real-world adversarial tactics and helps defenders strengthen their defenses against these common attack vectors.

6.4 Cross-Environment Lateral Movement: On-Premises to Cloud

Lateral movement refers to the technique of expanding an attacker's access to different systems, networks, or environments within an organization after gaining initial foothold access. While traditional lateral movement typically occurs within a single environment— such as moving between servers and workstations on a corporate network—modern adversaries often seek to extend their reach beyond on-premises systems and into cloud environments. This ability to traverse the gap between on-premises and cloud infrastructures is a complex challenge, but one that is increasingly critical in red team operations.

In today's hybrid IT environments, which consist of both on-premises and cloud systems (public or private clouds), attackers need to understand how to move seamlessly across these environments to simulate sophisticated real-world attacks. This chapter will explore how adversaries achieve cross-environment lateral movement, focusing on the strategies, tools, and techniques used to bridge the gap between on-premises networks and cloud environments. By understanding these tactics, red teamers can better evaluate the resilience of their client's infrastructure and provide detailed recommendations on how to strengthen cloud and on-premises defenses.

1. Understanding the Hybrid Environment and Its Challenges

Organizations today typically have a mix of on-premises systems (including physical and virtualized servers, workstations, and network devices) and cloud systems (usually public cloud environments like AWS, Azure, or Google Cloud). These systems may be interconnected through a variety of mechanisms, such as VPNs, Direct Connect, or hybrid cloud setups. This hybrid IT architecture, while offering flexibility and scalability, can also introduce new attack surfaces for lateral movement.

In such environments, lateral movement from on-premises to cloud systems requires attackers to exploit specific misconfigurations or weak points in the network, authentication, and access control policies between the two. The complexity of the hybrid architecture presents challenges for defenders who must secure both environments in unison. Cross-environment lateral movement techniques thus focus on exploiting vulnerabilities or weaknesses in both infrastructures, often through common access mechanisms like identity management, federated access, or cloud-native tools.

2. Identifying Key Attack Vectors for Cross-Environment Movement

Successful lateral movement between on-premises and cloud environments typically involves understanding how an organization connects the two, and which tools and processes are in place to facilitate communication and resource access across environments. The following are key attack vectors that an attacker may exploit to bridge the gap between on-premises systems and the cloud.

2.1 Misconfigured Identity Federation and Single Sign-On (SSO)

Modern organizations often use identity federation and Single Sign-On (SSO) solutions to manage authentication across on-premises and cloud services. Tools like Active Directory Federation Services (ADFS), Azure AD, and other identity management systems (e.g., Okta, AWS SSO) can create single authentication points for users to access both internal and cloud resources. However, misconfigurations in these identity systems can create significant attack vectors for cross-environment lateral movement.

Exploiting Weak or Misconfigured SSO: If an attacker gains access to an on-premises user account that has federated access to cloud services, they can leverage the existing authentication to move into the cloud environment. For example, an attacker can use

Kerberos tickets, tokens, or stolen credentials to authenticate and access cloud resources.

Privilege Escalation through Federated Identity: In a federated environment, weak permissions on the federated identity provider can allow an attacker to escalate privileges in both the on-premises and cloud environments. By manipulating roles or tokens, an attacker could gain administrator access to both networks.

Example: An attacker who compromises a low-privileged user's credentials in the on-premises network may find that this user has federated SSO access to AWS or Azure. By exploiting weak session management or token caching, the attacker may escalate privileges within the cloud environment.

2.2 Exploiting Cloud Storage and File Sharing Misconfigurations

Organizations may use cloud storage solutions (such as Amazon S3, Google Cloud Storage, or Azure Blob Storage) to store backups, logs, or other critical data. If these cloud storage buckets are not properly secured with access controls or if default access permissions are left wide open (e.g., publicly accessible buckets), attackers can potentially move from on-premises systems to the cloud by exploiting these misconfigurations.

Accessing Cloud Storage from On-Premises: Attackers can use publicly accessible cloud storage as a means of exfiltrating data from the on-premises environment or as a stepping stone to compromise further systems. Once attackers gain access to cloud storage, they may find sensitive information, such as cloud credentials, that allows them to escalate their access within the cloud environment.

Exploiting Shared File Systems: Cloud services that allow file sharing, such as AWS EFS (Elastic File System) or Azure File Shares, may be misconfigured to allow access from outside the corporate network. An attacker with access to the on-premises network could move laterally to these resources, gaining access to cloud-based data or services.

Example: An attacker who has compromised a machine within the corporate network may discover that an S3 bucket used for backups is misconfigured and accessible from the corporate network. By accessing this bucket, the attacker can extract sensitive information, including cloud access keys or other data that could enable further lateral movement into the cloud environment.

2.3 Exploiting Cloud-Native Access Points and APIs

Cloud environments provide many access points and services that allow for programmatic interaction with infrastructure. If an organization has not properly secured these points, an attacker could exploit them to gain access to cloud resources.

Misconfigured Cloud IAM Roles: Poorly configured cloud Identity and Access Management (IAM) roles or permissions can allow attackers to gain excessive privileges. For example, if a user or service account in the on-premises network has a federated role that grants excessive permissions to cloud services, an attacker can use this access to create new users or elevate privileges in the cloud environment.

Abusing Cloud APIs: Many organizations use APIs to interact with cloud resources, often relying on keys or tokens for authentication. If these API keys or tokens are improperly stored, shared, or accessible in code repositories (e.g., GitHub), an attacker could capture them and use them to authenticate with the cloud environment.

Example: If an attacker compromises an API key for a cloud service (e.g., AWS or Azure), they could use this key to interact with cloud resources, potentially gaining access to critical data, launching instances, or even modifying security configurations within the cloud.

3. Techniques for Moving from On-Premises to Cloud Systems

Successful lateral movement across environments often requires several different techniques. Here are some common approaches that red teamers can use when attempting to traverse from on-premises systems to cloud environments:

3.1 Pivoting via VPNs or Direct Connect

Organizations with hybrid cloud infrastructures often rely on Virtual Private Networks (VPNs) or dedicated connections like AWS Direct Connect or Azure ExpressRoute to link on-premises environments with cloud services. Attackers can leverage these connections to pivot between networks.

Exploiting Misconfigured VPNs: If VPN access is poorly configured or if users have VPN access to cloud resources without proper segmentation or monitoring, attackers can easily use the VPN tunnel to extend their reach into the cloud.

Leveraging Direct Connect to Pivot: Attackers who gain access to on-premises VPNs or network connections can pivot to cloud environments by exploiting these direct connections to internal cloud systems.

3.2 Using Remote Desktop Protocol (RDP) or SSH to Access Cloud Instances

In many cloud environments, users may deploy virtual machines (VMs) or instances that allow remote access through protocols like RDP (on Windows) or SSH (on Linux). If these instances are misconfigured, attackers can use compromised credentials from on-premises environments to access cloud instances directly.

RDP Exploitation: Compromised RDP credentials from the on-premises environment can be used to access virtual machines in the cloud if proper access control mechanisms are not in place.

Abusing SSH Keys: If SSH keys are not properly managed or secured, attackers can leverage compromised keys from on-premises systems to gain access to cloud-based Linux instances.

Example: After compromising an internal Windows machine with RDP access to cloud VMs, an attacker can use these credentials to move into the cloud network, escalating privileges or performing reconnaissance on cloud-hosted infrastructure.

Cross-environment lateral movement from on-premises systems to cloud environments represents a significant challenge for both attackers and defenders. It requires a sophisticated understanding of hybrid cloud architectures, misconfigurations in identity federation, improper access control, and cloud-native security mechanisms. Red teamers who can successfully simulate these kinds of attacks will provide invaluable insights into the resilience of an organization's security posture and assist in strengthening defenses against these increasingly common attack vectors. Organizations must recognize the potential for cross-environment attacks and invest in securing both on-premises and cloud environments in a unified manner to mitigate these risks.

7. Post-Exploitation Tactics

After successfully breaching a target, the true challenge lies in maintaining access, gathering valuable data, and ensuring that your presence remains undetected. This chapter delves into post-exploitation strategies, focusing on techniques for data exfiltration, establishing persistent access, and enhancing command-and-control infrastructure. You'll learn how to move stealthily within the system, avoiding detection while extracting high-value intelligence and preparing for long-term access. Whether it's by exploiting Windows and Linux persistence mechanisms or using advanced C2 methods, this chapter arms you with the tools to extend your engagement and maximize impact.

7.1 Analyzing and Exfiltrating High-Value Data

The goal of red teaming is not just to test the security of systems but to mimic the strategies and tactics of real-world adversaries. A key aspect of this involves identifying and exfiltrating high-value data from an organization's network. This chapter explores the methods and techniques used by red teamers to extract sensitive information, with a focus on the strategies employed to avoid detection and the tools leveraged to achieve success.

In many cases, high-value data can be anything that an organization values highly enough to take measures to protect. This might include intellectual property, financial records, customer information, trade secrets, or any other data critical to the organization's operations. The analysis and exfiltration of this data are often the final steps in a red team engagement, intended to demonstrate how attackers can move from gaining access to a system to extracting useful information.

1. Understanding High-Value Data and Its Importance

High-value data is critical to an organization's operations, reputation, and strategic goals. When conducting a red team assessment, identifying high-value data can guide the attacker to the most sensitive parts of the network and expose vulnerabilities that need to be addressed. High-value data can be found in various forms, including:

- **Financial Information**: Such as bank records, payment information, and financial statements that are critical to the company's operations and are targets for theft or fraud.

- **Intellectual Property**: Including patents, trademarks, proprietary technologies, source code, designs, and other assets that give a company a competitive advantage.
- **Customer Data**: Personal information such as names, addresses, contact information, and transaction histories that can be exploited for identity theft or fraud.
- **Confidential Documents**: Legal documents, contracts, non-disclosure agreements, and other sensitive paperwork that, if exposed, could cause significant harm to the organization.

Understanding where high-value data is stored and how it is accessed helps red teamers in planning their exfiltration strategy. This information can be stored on file shares, databases, cloud services, or proprietary systems, and may be accessed via various protocols and methods.

2. Techniques for Analyzing High-Value Data

Analyzing high-value data involves understanding what constitutes valuable information to the organization and how it is stored and protected. This process often involves the following steps:

2.1 Identifying Sensitive Data Locations

A key step in data analysis is locating where sensitive information resides. Red teamers use a variety of methods to identify these locations:

- **Network Mapping**: Using network scanning tools like Nmap, Cobalt Strike, or Recon-ng to discover file shares, databases, or storage solutions that contain critical data.
- **Active Directory Enumeration**: In Windows environments, leveraging tools like BloodHound can help identify sensitive data shares and roles that can access these resources.
- **Cloud Service Discovery**: Using cloud-specific reconnaissance tools such as CloudMapper or ScoutSuite to find sensitive data in cloud storage services (e.g., S3 buckets, Azure Blob Storage).
- **Example**: A red team might run network scans to find open file shares that contain sensitive documents, or use Active Directory enumeration to identify group memberships that have access to payroll information.

2.2 Data Classification and Analysis Tools

Once high-value data locations are identified, red teamers often use specialized tools to analyze and extract relevant information:

- **Data Digger Tools**: Tools like Metagoofil can be used to extract metadata from files (e.g., Word, PDF) to find sensitive data such as author names, document versions, and organizational names.
- **Data Extraction Scripts**: Custom scripts can be written to automate the extraction of specific types of data (e.g., credit card numbers, Social Security numbers) from documents or databases.
- **Log Analysis Tools**: Tools like Kansa or Osquery can be used to analyze logs and identify usage patterns that might indicate where data is being transferred or accessed.
- **Example**: By running a script to extract Excel files from a specific directory, a red teamer can search for financial data, such as transaction logs or client lists, which are likely to be of high value to the organization.

2.3 Social Engineering for Data Discovery

In some cases, red teamers may also use social engineering tactics to obtain high-value data indirectly. This could involve:

- **Phishing Campaigns**: Crafting targeted phishing emails to employees with access to sensitive data, convincing them to click on malicious links or download files.
- **Pretexting**: Creating a scenario where the red teamer poses as a trusted source (e.g., technical support) to obtain information about where high-value data is stored or how it can be accessed.
- **Tailgating**: Gaining physical access to offices or secure areas to see where important documents are stored or accessed, such as looking for documents left unattended on desks or printers.
- **Example**: A red teamer could send a phishing email to a user working in HR, containing a link to a malicious site that appears to be a file storage service. The user may unknowingly upload sensitive files to this site, which the attacker can later exfiltrate.

3. Exfiltrating High-Value Data

Exfiltrating high-value data is often the culmination of a red team engagement and requires stealth and technical expertise to avoid detection. The methods used for exfiltration can vary based on the type of data and the security measures in place, but generally involve the following techniques:

3.1 Data Encryption and Compression

To avoid detection during exfiltration, red teamers often encrypt and compress the data before transmitting it:

- **Encryption Tools**: Using tools like GPG or OpenSSL to encrypt the data, making it unreadable without the correct decryption key. This helps in masking the data's content and prevents it from being intercepted and understood if captured.
- **Compression**: Compressing files before encryption can further reduce the size of the data, making it easier to transfer without triggering alert thresholds set by network monitoring systems.
- **Example**: An attacker might use tar to compress and openssl to encrypt a batch of sensitive documents, then upload the compressed and encrypted files to an external server.

3.2 Data Exfiltration Techniques

There are several methods that red teamers use to exfiltrate data:

- **Command and Control Channels**: Setting up covert channels (e.g., using DNS tunneling, HTTP/HTTPS POST requests, or DNS over HTTPS) to transmit data out of the organization. These channels can be set up to blend in with normal network traffic and avoid suspicion.
- **File Transfer Protocols**: Transferring data using protocols like FTP, SFTP, or WebDAV over HTTPS, where the data is transmitted in a secure and encrypted manner, making it less likely to be intercepted.
- **Cloud Storage Services**: Uploading exfiltrated data to cloud storage services (e.g., Dropbox, Google Drive, AWS S3) that are not well monitored, allowing for direct access from external locations.
- **Example**: An attacker might use a reverse shell to create an encrypted connection back to a server under their control, through which they can upload stolen files. Alternatively, they could use a cloud storage service that allows uploading large files without detailed inspection.

3.3 Automating the Exfiltration Process

To maximize efficiency and reduce the risk of detection, red teamers often automate the exfiltration process:

- **Automated Scripts**: Writing scripts to automate the exfiltration of data, such as using rsync to copy files to an external server or using curl to upload files to a web server.
- **Scheduled Exfiltration**: Setting up the exfiltration process to run on a schedule that aligns with low-activity periods in the network, reducing the chance of detection.
- **Use of Stealthy Protocols**: Utilizing stealthy protocols or ports (e.g., port 80 or 443 for HTTP/HTTPS) to conceal the exfiltration traffic and blend it into normal web traffic.
- **Example**: A red teamer could schedule a script to regularly check for high-value files, compress and encrypt them, and upload them to a remote server using HTTPS over port 443, thus bypassing network security measures that might be monitoring standard data exfiltration ports.

Analyzing and exfiltrating high-value data is a critical component of red teaming. It not only demonstrates the effectiveness of an organization's security measures but also reveals the vulnerabilities that need to be addressed. By understanding the techniques and tools used by attackers to extract sensitive information, organizations can enhance their defenses to prevent real-world data breaches. This includes securing high-value data locations, implementing stronger access controls, using data encryption and compression, and monitoring for anomalous network activities that might indicate an ongoing exfiltration attempt.

7.2 Persistence Techniques: Maintaining Access Long-Term

In the realm of red teaming, persistence refers to the ability of an attacker to maintain access to compromised systems or networks over extended periods. Achieving persistence allows an adversary to retain control over their target, even after the initial access point is discovered or patched. Persistence techniques are a critical part of an attacker's toolbox because they provide long-term access for data exfiltration, espionage, or further exploitation, often without triggering immediate detection by the target organization.

This chapter delves into the various methods red teamers use to maintain access to a compromised network, discussing the tools, tactics, and techniques employed to evade detection and ensure continued access to critical systems. The persistence mechanisms described in this chapter are based on real-world attack strategies that mimic advanced persistent threats (APTs) and other sophisticated adversaries. By understanding these techniques, defenders can better prepare their environments to detect and mitigate such efforts.

1. The Need for Persistence in Red Teaming

While an attacker may initially gain access to a network, it is often necessary to maintain that access for weeks, months, or even longer in order to simulate a persistent threat scenario. Persistence is valuable because:

- **Continued Exploitation**: An attacker can continue to gather intelligence, exfiltrate data, or deploy additional attacks over time without the need for repeated compromises.
- **Evasion of Detection**: Persistence allows the attacker to remain unnoticed, even as the network or system undergoes routine security monitoring, updates, or audits.
- **Backup Access**: Even if the initial entry point is closed or patched, maintaining persistence ensures that the attacker has a backup method to re-enter the network.

Because of its strategic importance, maintaining access for long periods is a key goal for red teamers who seek to test an organization's resilience against highly advanced attackers.

2. Common Persistence Techniques in Red Teaming

There are several ways red teamers can ensure that their access remains intact, despite efforts by defenders to detect and remove their foothold. These methods range from simple backdoors to complex mechanisms designed to blend seamlessly into normal operations and avoid detection.

2.1 Backdoor Accounts and Privileged Access

One of the simplest and most effective ways to maintain access is by creating backdoor accounts or escalating privileges to gain administrative control over a system. Red teamers often:

- **Create Hidden User Accounts**: Using tools like net user on Windows or useradd on Linux, attackers can create hidden, privileged user accounts that are not listed in the normal user directories.
- **Add Accounts to Sensitive Groups**: Attackers can add themselves to local administrator groups or Active Directory privileged groups (such as Domain Admins) to retain high-level access.

These backdoor accounts can be configured to be non-obvious, such as using obfuscated usernames or disguised account attributes, making them harder for defenders to spot. Often, these accounts are set with a strong password, and may be further protected by multi-factor authentication (MFA), if required.

Example: An attacker compromises a server and creates an admin account with a username that looks like a legitimate service account. This account is then added to the Domain Admins group, providing the attacker with full administrative access to the entire network.

2.2 Scheduled Tasks and Cron Jobs

Attackers often create scheduled tasks or cron jobs to maintain access to compromised systems by executing malicious code at regular intervals. These scheduled jobs can run scripts, load backdoors, or even re-establish access if the attacker is disconnected.

- **Windows Task Scheduler**: Attackers can use Windows Task Scheduler to run malicious scripts at a predefined time, or after a system reboots, ensuring persistent access even if the original compromise is discovered and remediated.
- **Linux Cron Jobs**: On Linux, cron jobs can be used to execute malicious commands or scripts periodically, keeping the attacker's access persistent.

By hiding these tasks in obscure locations or using legitimate system processes (e.g., using a scheduled task that mimics a normal update process), attackers can avoid detection by basic monitoring tools.

Example: After compromising a server, an attacker creates a Windows task that runs every hour and connects back to a command-and-control (C2) server, maintaining access to the system even if the initial backdoor is detected and removed.

2.3 Registry Modifications (Windows)

In Windows environments, attackers often modify the system registry to ensure that malicious software or scripts execute automatically upon system boot or login. These modifications allow attackers to retain access even after a system reboot.

- **Persistence via Registry Keys**: Attackers can insert malicious code into specific registry keys, such as HKCU\Software\Microsoft\Windows\CurrentVersion\Run, which ensures that the malware or backdoor will execute each time the user logs into the system.
- **Boot-time Persistence**: Attackers can also add registry values to start their backdoor at boot time, even before the user logs in.

This form of persistence is often hard to detect because registry keys used for persistence are often associated with legitimate applications or services.

Example: A red teamer might add a backdoor script to the registry key that launches every time the system boots, ensuring that the malware is executed even if the attacker's initial exploit is discovered and removed.

2.4 Rootkits and Kernel-Level Persistence

A rootkit is a highly sophisticated form of malware designed to hide its presence at the kernel level. It can be used to maintain long-term access to a system by modifying or replacing system files and drivers to evade detection by antivirus software and other security measures.

- **Kernel Rootkits**: By modifying the system's kernel, an attacker can hide processes, files, or network connections from both the user and security software, thus making the malicious presence invisible to most detection mechanisms.
- **Bootkits**: A bootkit is a type of rootkit that infects the Master Boot Record (MBR) or the boot loader, ensuring that it is executed every time the machine starts, even before the operating system loads.

Rootkits are difficult to detect and remove, making them a powerful tool for maintaining persistence on a compromised machine.

Example: An attacker might install a rootkit to modify system processes so that their backdoor service is not visible in task managers or process lists, even if security software is running on the target machine.

3. Advanced Persistence: Living off the Land

Red teamers can also rely on living off the land (LOTL) techniques, where they use existing tools and resources in the environment to maintain access, making detection even more difficult.

3.1 Leveraging Existing Administrative Tools

Many administrative tools and scripts that are already present in the environment (like PowerShell, Windows Management Instrumentation (WMI), and PsExec) can be weaponized to maintain persistence.

- **PowerShell**: Attackers can create PowerShell scripts that run hidden, using native Windows tools to maintain access without needing to install external malware.
- **WMI**: Using WMI, attackers can create scheduled tasks that run on target machines, making it difficult for defenders to differentiate between legitimate administrative actions and malicious activity.

These techniques can be especially difficult to detect because they rely on built-in tools that are commonly used for normal administration purposes.

Example: An attacker creates a PowerShell script that runs a malicious payload every time a user logs in, using legitimate PowerShell commands and without installing any new software.

Persistence techniques are an essential part of any advanced red team engagement, allowing attackers to maintain access for prolonged periods without detection. By understanding the various methods red teamers use to ensure long-term access, organizations can better prepare their defenses, employing advanced monitoring systems, stricter access controls, and continuous auditing to detect and eliminate persistent threats. Effective defense against persistence requires an integrated approach to system monitoring, response, and continuous improvement to detect hidden backdoors, scheduled tasks, or kernel-level modifications. Ultimately, maintaining access is one of the most important goals for an adversary, and understanding how it is achieved is critical for both offensive and defensive cybersecurity strategies.

7.3 Advanced Command and Control (C2) Strategies

In the context of red teaming, Command and Control (C2) refers to the infrastructure and methods that attackers use to communicate with compromised systems and execute commands remotely. The goal of a C2 strategy is to maintain a reliable, covert, and often redundant communication channel with a target system, allowing the attacker to issue commands, exfiltrate data, or propagate further attacks without being detected.

Effective C2 strategies are vital to a red team engagement, as they allow adversaries to simulate real-world cyber-attacks by using sophisticated, stealthy, and resilient methods to interact with compromised systems. The following chapter explores advanced C2 techniques, including evasion tactics, covert channels, redundancy, and the use of modern tools and frameworks that are designed to blend seamlessly into legitimate network traffic, making detection more difficult.

1. The Importance of Command and Control in Red Teaming

In real-world attacks, adversaries typically aim to establish persistent and stealthy C2 channels to control compromised systems. In red teaming, emulating advanced C2 strategies allows teams to:

- **Mimic Advanced Threat Actors**: Many advanced persistent threats (APTs) rely on sophisticated C2 strategies to maintain long-term access and undetected activity in target networks.
- **Maintain Access and Flexibility**: By leveraging reliable C2 infrastructure, red teamers can execute commands at will, pivot between systems, and carry out further exploitation without being disrupted by network monitoring or defensive measures.
- **Test Defenses**: By simulating various C2 techniques, red teams can test how well a target's defense mechanisms (such as firewalls, intrusion detection systems, and endpoint monitoring) respond to covert or encrypted communication channels.

Advanced C2 strategies typically focus on bypassing network defenses, evading detection, and maintaining access across diverse environments, including corporate networks, cloud infrastructure, and even physical systems.

2. Core Components of Advanced Command and Control

To execute an effective C2 strategy, attackers rely on several core components, each designed to ensure continuous and reliable communication with the compromised system.

2.1 Command and Control Servers

The C2 server is the central hub that allows the attacker to issue commands to compromised systems. This server may be hosted on external infrastructure or concealed within trusted environments to avoid detection.

- **Obfuscation**: C2 servers often use domain generation algorithms (DGAs), encryption, or polymorphism to obfuscate their location and avoid being blocked by threat intelligence or firewalls.
- **Redundancy**: To ensure reliability, red teamers will often configure multiple backup C2 servers. If one server is discovered and blocked, the attacker can quickly switch to another.
- **Example**: In an engagement simulating a sophisticated threat actor, a red team might deploy a C2 server behind a legitimate service, such as a content delivery network (CDN), to blend in with regular web traffic.

2.2 Beaconing and Polling

After the initial compromise, the target system must periodically "phone home" to the C2 server to receive new commands or upload stolen data. This communication often occurs in the form of beacons (short, periodic pings to the C2 server) or polling (where the compromised system asks the C2 server if there is anything new to process).

- **Low and Slow**: Red teamers often configure beaconing intervals to be very long (e.g., 5-10 minutes) to avoid detection by monitoring systems that look for rapid communication.
- **Exfiltration via Beaconing**: Some red teamers use beaconing to exfiltrate data by encoding it into the beaconing request. This allows data to be transferred in small, inconspicuous chunks, reducing the likelihood of triggering network traffic alarms.
- **Example**: A compromised host might be configured to send a small HTTP GET request every 10 minutes to a C2 server. The request might contain an encoded exfiltration payload that can be decoded on the server side for further analysis.

2.3 Protocols and Ports Used for Communication

Advanced C2 channels often utilize non-standard communication protocols or regular, trusted ports to avoid detection by intrusion detection systems (IDS) and firewalls.

- **Common Protocols**: Traditional C2 communication occurs over well-known protocols like HTTP/HTTPS, DNS, SMTP, and ICMP. These protocols are commonly used for legitimate network traffic, so they are less likely to be blocked or flagged as suspicious.

- **Custom Protocols**: Some attackers develop custom protocols that allow for low-latency, encrypted communication that is harder to detect by automated traffic analysis systems.
- **Example**: An attacker might use DNS tunneling to send C2 commands. By encoding data within DNS requests, they avoid detection because DNS is often whitelisted by network firewalls.

3. Advanced C2 Techniques

While basic C2 methods rely on straightforward communication channels, advanced C2 strategies are designed to evade detection by increasingly sophisticated network security tools. Below are several advanced techniques used by red teamers to enhance the stealth, reliability, and redundancy of their C2 infrastructure.

3.1 DNS Tunneling and Covert Channels

DNS tunneling is a technique used to encode data in DNS queries and responses, effectively hiding C2 communication within otherwise legitimate DNS traffic. This can be an incredibly effective method for bypassing firewalls, proxy servers, and network filters that might block other ports or protocols.

- **Tunneling Tools**: Tools like Iodine, dns2tcp, and DNScat2 allow attackers to create a covert C2 channel over DNS, facilitating bi-directional communication between the attacker and the compromised system.
- **Stealth and Obfuscation**: DNS tunneling can be used to send data that looks like a typical DNS request. In some cases, attackers can even use publicly available DNS servers to avoid detection and reduce the likelihood of their infrastructure being traced.
- **Example**: An attacker uses DNS tunneling to exfiltrate sensitive data from a compromised server. Data is split into small packets and sent through DNS requests, making it almost impossible to distinguish from legitimate DNS traffic.

3.2 HTTPS and SSL/TLS Encryption

While standard HTTP traffic is often monitored and filtered by security solutions, HTTPS (encrypted HTTP) is more difficult to intercept. This makes HTTPS a popular choice for C2 communication in red team engagements.

- **SSL/TLS Certificates**: Red teamers may use valid SSL/TLS certificates to encrypt C2 communications, making them appear as regular, secure traffic to web servers and network security tools.
- **Obfuscation**: Attackers can obfuscate their traffic within normal-looking HTTPS requests, using steganography techniques to hide malicious payloads within encrypted communication streams.
- **Example**: A red team uses an HTTPS channel to issue commands to a compromised system, ensuring that the communication is encrypted and blends in with legitimate traffic passing through corporate web proxies.

3.3 Reverse Shells and Reverse Proxy Chains

A reverse shell occurs when the compromised system initiates a connection back to the attacker's server. By using reverse shells, red teamers can bypass firewall restrictions, as most firewalls block inbound traffic but allow outbound connections.

- **Reverse HTTP/Shells**: Attackers may use reverse HTTP or HTTPS connections to establish a C2 channel over web traffic.
- **Proxy Chains**: Attackers use proxy chains to make their C2 connections appear as if they are originating from legitimate sources. This makes the attacker's infrastructure harder to trace.
- **Example**: A reverse shell is set up to connect back to an attacker's server over a secure HTTPS connection, passing through several proxy servers to hide the true source of the communication.

4. Maintaining C2 Reliability and Redundancy

Redundancy and reliability are key components of an advanced C2 strategy. Attackers often prepare multiple layers of fallback options in case their primary C2 channel is disrupted or detected.

4.1 Domain Generation Algorithms (DGAs)

Domain Generation Algorithms (DGAs) are used to generate a large number of domain names that are randomly or pseudorandomly created. This allows attackers to continuously update their C2 server address without needing to rely on a static domain name.

- **Dynamic DNS**: DGAs are commonly paired with dynamic DNS services to provide real-time DNS resolution updates, ensuring attackers can always reach their compromised systems, even if their primary domain is blocked or blacklisted.
- **Example**: A red teamer's C2 server dynamically generates new domain names at regular intervals, allowing them to control a network of compromised systems even if DNS filtering is applied.

4.2 Fast Flux and Proxy Networks

Fast Flux involves rapidly changing the IP addresses associated with a particular domain, making it harder for defenders to block the C2 server's infrastructure. Similarly, proxy networks are used to hide the attacker's location and make the C2 communication appear to originate from multiple geographic regions.

- **Botnet-Driven Infrastructure**: Many advanced C2 setups use botnet-driven infrastructures, making the attacker's C2 network more resilient to takedowns and detection.
- **Example**: Using fast flux, an attacker's C2 domain resolves to a rotating pool of IP addresses, making it difficult for defenders to block the server without affecting legitimate services.

Advanced C2 strategies are integral to the success of a red team engagement, as they simulate the methods employed by sophisticated attackers. By understanding how adversaries use encryption, tunneling, reverse connections, and redundancy techniques, red teamers can better test the resilience of an organization's defenses. For defenders, it is critical to implement robust monitoring, traffic analysis, and anomaly detection to identify and mitigate covert C2 communications. Red teams and defenders alike must continuously evolve their tactics and tools to stay one step ahead in the ever-changing landscape of cybersecurity.

7.4 Cleaning Up and Covering Tracks to Avoid Detection

In the world of red teaming, covering tracks and cleaning up after an engagement is a crucial aspect of simulating a highly sophisticated attack. Once access has been achieved, the ultimate goal is to maintain that access for as long as possible without detection. However, an effective red team exercise is not just about gaining initial access or exploiting vulnerabilities but also about understanding the adversary's full lifecycle, which includes how to clean up evidence of compromise and avoid leaving traces that could lead to detection.

This chapter explores the various techniques used by red teamers to cover their tracks, remove traces of their activities, and clean up artifacts that could otherwise alert defenders to the presence of malicious activity. These tactics are designed to mimic the strategies employed by real-world advanced persistent threats (APTs) and other high-level attackers, who routinely seek to erase all traces of their presence from compromised systems and networks.

1. The Importance of Cleaning Up and Covering Tracks

Just as attackers take deliberate steps to gain unauthorized access, they also go to great lengths to ensure their activity remains undetected. The ability to cover tracks and erase evidence is one of the key traits that differentiates a true advanced persistent threat (APT) from a less sophisticated cybercriminal group. Red teamers must simulate these same tactics to effectively test an organization's ability to detect and respond to real-world threats.

The importance of cleaning up and covering tracks stems from several factors:

- **Evading Detection**: By removing evidence of their presence, red teamers reduce the likelihood of being detected by defensive measures such as endpoint detection and response (EDR) systems, SIEM (Security Information and Event Management) platforms, and forensic investigations.
- **Mimicking Real-World Attacks**: In real-world attacks, APTs and sophisticated attackers often spend long periods within a network, exfiltrating sensitive data and carrying out their objectives. Successful red teams simulate these behaviors to test the organization's ability to identify, contain, and eliminate the threat.
- **Escalating the Test**: In the context of red teaming, covering tracks allows the simulation of a more realistic, long-term engagement. This helps the organization understand how it would react to a highly stealthy adversary.

This chapter will explore techniques commonly employed by attackers to clean up traces, ensuring the red team exercise is as realistic as possible.

2. Key Methods for Cleaning Up and Covering Tracks

2.1 Erasing Log Files and Artifacts

Logs are one of the first places defenders look when investigating an incident. During red team operations, cleaning up log files is an essential part of covering tracks. Successful attackers know how to manipulate, delete, or hide logs to prevent defenders from gaining insight into their activities.

Log Tampering: Red teamers can delete or modify system and application logs, making it difficult for investigators to reconstruct their activities. This can involve erasing login records, deletion events, or network connections.

- **Windows Event Logs**: In Windows environments, red teamers may use tools like EventLogZ or wevtutil to clear event logs or modify event timestamps, making it harder to correlate activities over time.
- **Linux Logs**: In Linux systems, attackers often delete or modify logs in directories like /var/log/ using commands like logrotate, journalctl, or custom scripts.

Time Stomping: Time-stomping is the practice of altering file or log timestamps to make it appear as though malicious activity occurred during a legitimate timeframe. This helps to avoid raising suspicion regarding the timeline of the attack.

Example: After establishing a foothold on a target system, a red team may delete all successful login entries from the Security Event Log and erase network connection records from the System Event Log to prevent investigators from seeing traces of lateral movement or initial access.

2.2 Removing Tools and Payloads

One of the most crucial elements of cleaning up after a red team engagement is ensuring that any tools, payloads, or malicious software used during the operation are removed from compromised systems. This is essential to prevent defenders from identifying signatures or artifacts associated with known attack techniques.

- **Tools and Exploit Frameworks**: Red teamers often use tools like Metasploit, Cobalt Strike, or Empire during engagements. After the engagement, they will remove any remaining binaries, scripts, or payloads that could be tied back to their activities.
- **Fileless Malware**: Tools like PowerShell or WMI can be used to execute malicious code in memory, leaving minimal or no traces on disk. Removing memory artifacts is more challenging but can still be done by clearing cached artifacts or terminating malicious processes.
- **Custom Payloads**: After deploying a custom exploit or backdoor, red teamers will delete or overwrite files on disk to avoid leaving any indicators that could be linked to their activities.

- **Example**: After performing privilege escalation via an exploit, the red teamer removes the custom payload executable from disk and deletes any temporary files left behind to reduce the likelihood of detection.

2.3 Overwriting Evidence and Clearing History

The more evidence an attacker leaves behind, the more likely they are to be detected. Red teamers often use a variety of methods to overwrite evidence, making it more difficult for defenders to gather forensic data.

- **Clearing Browser History**: Attackers may clear browser histories, cookies, and cache files that could provide evidence of command-and-control activity, site access, or web-based attacks.
- **Overwriting Files**: Red teamers may overwrite files or directories on a compromised system to eliminate traces of the files they used or modified during their operations. This can involve wiping temporary files, deleting created user accounts, or removing tools.
- **Eraser Tools**: Specialized eraser tools, such as SDelete (for Windows) or shred (for Linux), can be used to securely delete files and overwrite disk sectors, making file recovery nearly impossible.
- **Example**: A red team might clear the command history in a compromised system's shell to prevent investigators from seeing the commands used for lateral movement, credential harvesting, or privilege escalation.

2.4 Covering Tracks in Active Directory and Network Infrastructure

In corporate environments, Active Directory (AD) is often the backbone of authentication and user management. As red teamers move through a network, they may interact with AD to escalate privileges or establish persistence. Covering tracks within AD and network infrastructure is crucial to avoid detection by defenders.

- **AD Cleanup**: Red teamers will delete or modify service accounts they create, removing any lingering credentials that could raise suspicion. They may also delete or modify Group Policy Objects (GPOs) or scheduled tasks set up to maintain access.
- **Stealthy Credential Harvesting**: Credentials obtained from password dumping or keylogging can be erased from memory or deleted from stored files, leaving no evidence of theft.

- **Example**: After creating a backdoor account in the Domain Admins group in Active Directory, a red teamer deletes the account from AD, ensuring no traces of their activities remain.

3. Advanced Techniques for Evasion and Cleanup

Red teamers must continuously evolve their tactics to evade detection and cover tracks in environments that are well-monitored and have advanced security mechanisms.

3.1 Anti-Forensics and Obfuscation Tools

To cover tracks more effectively, red teamers may leverage anti-forensics and obfuscation tools that are designed to help attackers erase evidence and avoid detection. These tools can be used to:

- Modify timestamps, logs, and file attributes to prevent forensic investigators from identifying the attacker's activities.
- Mask malicious activity, such as tool execution or system modifications, so that they blend into normal system operations.
- **Example**: A red teamer might use a rootkit to hide files, processes, or registry entries from being detected by antivirus software or system administrators, essentially erasing all traces of the attack.

3.2 Using Encrypted and Hidden Channels for Communication

Instead of using traditional methods to communicate with compromised systems, attackers often employ encrypted and hidden channels to avoid detection. This might include:

- DNS Tunneling: As mentioned earlier, red teamers can use DNS tunneling to covertly send C2 commands and exfiltrate data, all while evading traditional detection methods.
- HTTPS/SSL Encryption: Leveraging SSL/TLS encryption to disguise C2 traffic as regular HTTPS traffic, making it harder for intrusion detection systems to flag suspicious behavior.
- **Example**: A red teamer uses an encrypted HTTPS tunnel to communicate with a compromised system. The traffic appears normal to network monitoring systems, reducing the risk of detection.

In red teaming, covering tracks and cleaning up evidence is an essential component of a successful engagement, mimicking the techniques used by real-world adversaries. By understanding and executing advanced evasion and cleanup strategies, red teams can ensure their operations remain undetected and more closely resemble actual attack scenarios. For organizations, testing defenses against these techniques can help improve their detection capabilities, enabling them to identify and mitigate advanced threats more effectively. Ultimately, mastering the art of cleaning up and covering tracks ensures that a red team engagement is both realistic and effective in strengthening an organization's overall cybersecurity posture.

8. Advanced Evasion Techniques

To remain undetected while executing sophisticated attacks, red teamers must master evasion techniques that bypass security measures like endpoint detection and response (EDR), intrusion detection systems (IDS), and firewalls. This chapter explores advanced methods to evade detection, including obfuscating network traffic, manipulating logs, and bypassing antivirus and EDR solutions. You'll also learn how to exploit gaps in security monitoring, using anti-forensics tactics to erase traces of your presence and maintain stealth. With these advanced evasion strategies, you'll be able to conduct operations under the radar and avoid triggering defensive countermeasures.

8.1 Techniques to Evade EDR and Antivirus Detection

In the ever-evolving landscape of cybersecurity, Endpoint Detection and Response (EDR) systems and antivirus (AV) software are critical components in defending against malicious activities. They are designed to detect, analyze, and respond to security incidents, often relying on signature-based detection, behavioral analysis, and heuristic methods to identify suspicious activities. However, as red teamers and advanced persistent threats (APTs) know all too well, these defensive tools are not impenetrable. The ability to evade EDR and AV detection is paramount for simulating real-world cyberattacks and testing the robustness of an organization's defense mechanisms.

This chapter explores a variety of advanced techniques used by red teamers to bypass EDR and antivirus defenses, ultimately demonstrating how attackers might exploit weaknesses in detection mechanisms and maintain a stealthy presence on compromised systems.

1. Living Off the Land (LotL) Techniques

One of the most effective ways to evade EDR and antivirus detection is by utilizing Living Off the Land (LotL) techniques. This strategy involves leveraging tools and capabilities that are already present in the target system to carry out malicious activities. Since these tools are often signed and trusted by the operating system, they are less likely to be flagged by antivirus or EDR software.

1.1 PowerShell and Windows Management Instrumentation (WMI)

PowerShell is an extremely powerful scripting language built into Windows that administrators often use for automation and management tasks. Unfortunately, its versatility makes it a prime target for attackers. Red teamers can use PowerShell for tasks such as:

- **Payload delivery**: Running payloads directly from memory rather than executing them from disk, bypassing traditional file-based AV/EDR detections.
- **Command and Control (C2):** PowerShell can be used to establish covert communication channels back to the attacker.
- **Exfiltration**: Attackers can use PowerShell to send stolen data or execute system commands without leaving any files behind that could be detected.
- WMI is another tool that attackers often exploit to execute commands remotely or persist on systems. Because WMI is a legitimate system management tool, malicious WMI commands often evade detection by AV/EDR tools, particularly when executed in a way that mimics regular administrative activities.
- **Example**: A red team might use PowerShell Empire or Covenant to inject a payload into PowerShell and execute it directly from memory, avoiding disk-based detection mechanisms used by AV/EDR systems.

1.2 Scheduled Tasks and Registry Keys

Another powerful LotL technique involves abusing Scheduled Tasks and Windows Registry Keys for persistence. By creating tasks or modifying registry entries to run malicious scripts or binaries at regular intervals, red teamers can evade detection by staying under the radar. Since scheduled tasks and registry entries are commonly used by system administrators, malicious activity performed through these means is more likely to go unnoticed.

Example: A red team might create a new Task Scheduler entry that runs a malicious script every time the system reboots. The script could be an obfuscated PowerShell script or a fileless exploit that leaves no trace in traditional disk scans.

2. Fileless Malware Techniques

Fileless malware is a class of malware that operates entirely in memory, avoiding traditional disk-based detection mechanisms. Since fileless malware does not rely on creating files on the system's hard drive, it can bypass many antivirus solutions that focus on scanning files for known signatures.

2.1 In-Memory Execution of Malicious Code

Instead of relying on executables or scripts that must be saved to disk, fileless malware runs directly from the system's memory. It can be delivered through techniques such as PowerShell injection, DLL injection, or exploitation of legitimate tools.

This approach allows the attacker to remain undetected for much longer, as no malicious files are written to disk that could trigger antivirus or EDR alerts. Additionally, fileless malware often lives in the Windows Registry, Windows Management Instrumentation (WMI), or even in kernel memory, which makes it extremely hard for traditional antivirus programs to detect.

Example: A red team might use a tool like PowerShell Empire to run malicious code directly from memory. Rather than saving the payload as a file, they inject it into a legitimate process, avoiding file-based detection methods altogether.

2.2 Exploiting Trust Relationships

Fileless malware often exploits trusted processes to bypass security controls. For example, an attacker might inject malicious code into a trusted system process such as svchost.exe or explorer.exe. Because these processes are whitelisted and trusted by AV/EDR systems, their use for malicious purposes can often go undetected.

Example: A red team could exploit the PowerShell process to execute their malicious payload in memory, using a living-off-the-land method, ensuring that no suspicious files are written to disk and avoiding antivirus detection.

3. Obfuscation and Encryption Techniques

To avoid detection by signature-based detection engines, attackers often use obfuscation and encryption to conceal their payloads. This makes it more difficult for antivirus software and EDR systems to identify the malware based on known patterns or signatures.

3.1 Obfuscating Code

Obfuscation is the process of transforming malicious code to make it difficult for security software to understand its purpose. This can include:

- String encoding: Encoding strings that might be flagged as malicious, such as URLs or command-and-control (C2) addresses, in an unreadable format.

- Control flow obfuscation: Altering the flow of a script or program to make it more difficult for detection algorithms to follow its execution.
- **Example**: A red team might use Obfuscator-LLVM or other obfuscation tools to modify the appearance of their payloads, making them look like benign or benign-looking scripts.

3.2 Encrypting Payloads

Another method of evading AV/EDR detection is to encrypt the payload until it is needed, decrypting it only at runtime. Since antivirus tools typically rely on signature-based detection methods, encrypted payloads are often overlooked until the malware has already executed.

Example: The red team may use AES encryption or other advanced encryption methods to encrypt a payload before transferring it to a target system. Once transferred, the encrypted payload is decrypted and executed in memory, further bypassing detection.

4. Anti-Analysis Techniques

In addition to evasion, red teamers often employ anti-analysis techniques to thwart automated analysis systems or security professionals who attempt to analyze or reverse-engineer their payloads.

4.1 Polymorphism and Metamorphism

- Polymorphic malware changes its code with every iteration, making it difficult for signature-based detection tools to identify. Each time the malware executes, it alters itself, which forces security software to continually update its detection techniques to account for new variations.
- Metamorphic malware goes a step further by completely rewriting its code each time it executes. This makes the malware appear entirely different on each run, complicating detection by even the most advanced security systems.
- **Example**: A red team might use Cobalt Strike or a custom tool to create polymorphic payloads that constantly change their appearance, rendering signature-based detection ineffective.

4.2 Anti-Sandbox and Anti-VM Techniques

Red teamers may also include anti-sandbox and anti-VM (virtual machine) techniques in their payloads to avoid detection during automated analysis. Many security companies use sandboxes or VMs to detonate suspicious files and observe their behavior. By detecting these environments, malware can alter its behavior to avoid executing or revealing its true nature in these contexts.

Example: A red team payload might check for the presence of common virtualization markers (like VMware or VirtualBox) or sandboxing software, and if detected, it will refrain from executing or will produce benign output to avoid triggering alarms.

The ability to evade EDR and antivirus detection is a critical skill for red teamers seeking to simulate realistic, sophisticated adversaries. By leveraging techniques such as Living Off the Land (LotL), fileless malware, obfuscation, and anti-analysis, red teamers can effectively bypass modern detection mechanisms and mimic the stealthy tactics used by real-world cybercriminals and APT groups.

Ultimately, these techniques are designed not only to test and challenge an organization's defenses but also to improve the detection capabilities of security teams, helping them to strengthen their defenses against increasingly advanced threats. As security tools evolve, so too must the tactics and techniques employed by red teamers to ensure that they remain one step ahead in the ongoing cybersecurity arms race.

8.2 Network Traffic Obfuscation and Encryption

Modern cybersecurity defenses rely heavily on network traffic analysis to identify suspicious or malicious activities. Tools such as Intrusion Detection Systems (IDS), Intrusion Prevention Systems (IPS), and Security Information and Event Management (SIEM) platforms analyze network patterns, payloads, and metadata to detect anomalies. For attackers, the ability to obfuscate and encrypt their network traffic is critical for evading detection. This chapter explores techniques and tools used by red teamers to obfuscate and encrypt network traffic, ensuring stealthy communication during an engagement.

1. Why Obfuscation and Encryption Matter

Effective network traffic obfuscation and encryption techniques serve multiple purposes during a red team engagement:

- **Avoid Detection by Security Systems**: Signature-based IDS/IPS tools can flag known malicious payloads or communication patterns. Obfuscation disguises these indicators, while encryption prevents content inspection.

- **Prevent Reverse Engineering**: Encrypted payloads and communications make it difficult for defenders to analyze red team tools and techniques.
- **Mimic Advanced Threats**: Many sophisticated attackers use obfuscation and encryption to bypass defenses. Emulating these tactics provides organizations with a realistic assessment of their detection capabilities.

Attackers employ several strategies to evade network monitoring, ranging from basic encryption to advanced tunneling and traffic obfuscation.

2. Common Techniques for Network Traffic Obfuscation

2.1 Protocol Abuse and Covert Channels

Attackers often disguise malicious traffic by embedding it within legitimate protocols or channels. These covert channels allow malicious traffic to blend into normal network operations, making detection more difficult.

DNS Tunneling: DNS is often allowed through firewalls and rarely monitored in depth. Attackers use DNS queries and responses to exfiltrate data or communicate with command-and-control (C2) servers.

Example: Encoding malicious data in DNS TXT records and using frequent queries to covertly exfiltrate information or receive commands.

HTTP/S and HTTPS Tunneling: By disguising malicious traffic as legitimate web requests over HTTP/S, attackers can blend in with normal web traffic.

Example: Sending C2 commands embedded in seemingly harmless HTTP headers or encrypted HTTPS POST requests.

ICMP Tunneling: Internet Control Message Protocol (ICMP), commonly used for diagnostic tools like ping, can be repurposed to carry data. Since ICMP is often ignored by firewalls, this method can go unnoticed.

Example: Using ICMP packets to encode exfiltrated data, with each packet representing a piece of the payload.

2.2 Packet Manipulation and Fragmentation

Manipulating the structure of network packets can help attackers evade detection by signature-based systems.

Packet Fragmentation: Attackers can split malicious payloads into smaller packet fragments. These fragments bypass signature detection because the full payload is not reassembled until it reaches its destination.

Example: Splitting a malware payload into multiple TCP segments to avoid detection by IDS/IPS systems that inspect individual packets.

Traffic Padding and Randomization: Attackers may add random data or timing delays to network communications, making it harder to identify patterns.

Example: Adding random bytes to every packet or introducing delays between packets to disrupt timing-based anomaly detection.

2.3 Obfuscating Indicators of Compromise (IoCs)

IoCs such as IP addresses, domain names, and URLs are often monitored by security tools. Attackers can obfuscate these indicators to evade detection.

Domain Generation Algorithms (DGAs): DGAs generate large numbers of domain names, making it difficult for defenders to blacklist specific C2 servers.

Example: A malware sample might generate hundreds of domains per day and connect only to one, forcing defenders to track all possibilities.

Dynamic DNS (DDNS): Using DDNS services to frequently change the IP address associated with a C2 domain.

Example: A red team might configure their C2 infrastructure to rotate IPs every hour, preventing static IoC detection.

3. Advanced Encryption for Stealthy Communication

Encryption not only protects the content of network traffic but also helps attackers hide the fact that communication is occurring at all. Modern encryption techniques are essential for red teamers aiming to evade deep packet inspection (DPI) tools.

3.1 SSL/TLS Encryption

Using HTTPS for C2 Channels: Attackers frequently establish C2 communication over HTTPS, taking advantage of the encryption to hide payloads and commands from inspection.

Example: A red team might use tools like Cobalt Strike or Metasploit to communicate with C2 servers over HTTPS, blending in with normal web traffic.

Certificate Pinning: To avoid SSL inspection by corporate proxies, attackers may use custom SSL certificates and pinning techniques.

Example: A red team could generate self-signed certificates for their C2 server and pin them in their payload, ensuring secure and uninspectable communication.

3.2 Encrypted Tunneling

SSH Tunnels: By establishing SSH tunnels, attackers can create encrypted channels that bypass most network monitoring.

Example: A red teamer might set up an SSH reverse tunnel to exfiltrate data securely from the target environment.

VPNs and Proxy Chains: Virtual Private Networks (VPNs) and proxy tools like Tor provide an additional layer of anonymity and encryption.

Example: A red team might route all their traffic through a VPN service and chain it with Tor nodes to obfuscate their origin.

3.3 Custom Encryption Protocols

Attackers may use proprietary or customized encryption protocols to evade detection, as these are less likely to have existing signatures or detection methods.

Custom XOR Encryption: Simple XOR-based encryption can disguise payloads in transit.

Example: A red team might XOR-encode their payloads before sending them over the network, ensuring that no plaintext data is visible.

Steganography in Network Traffic: Hiding malicious data within innocuous-looking traffic, such as image or video files transmitted over HTTP/S.

Example: Encoding commands in the pixel values of an image file and transmitting it as part of an HTTP response.

4. Tools for Traffic Obfuscation and Encryption

Several tools are commonly used by attackers and red teamers to implement traffic obfuscation and encryption:

- **Cobalt Strike**: A popular red teaming framework that supports encrypted C2 communication over HTTPS and customizable profiles for traffic obfuscation.
- **Metasploit**: Offers modules for encrypted communication and tunneling.
- **Ncat**: A networking utility that supports SSL/TLS encryption for secure communication.
- **PowerShell Empire**: Provides encrypted communication channels and supports payload delivery over HTTPS.
- **Chisel**: A fast TCP/UDP tunnel that works over HTTP, ideal for bypassing firewalls and network monitoring systems.

5. Countermeasures and Blue Team Insights

While traffic obfuscation and encryption are powerful techniques, defenders have tools and strategies to detect and mitigate these threats:

- **Behavioral Analysis**: Monitoring anomalies in network traffic, such as unusual packet sizes, irregular DNS queries, or traffic patterns inconsistent with normal behavior.
- **Certificate Validation**: Inspecting SSL/TLS certificates to identify self-signed or suspicious certificates used in encrypted C2 communication.
- **DNS Monitoring**: Detecting unusual DNS activity, such as high volumes of DNS queries or domains with random names.
- **Deep Packet Inspection (DPI):** While encryption limits the effectiveness of DPI, it can still identify suspicious patterns, such as high volumes of encrypted traffic to unknown endpoints.

Network traffic obfuscation and encryption are essential tactics for red teamers seeking to evade detection during engagements. By blending malicious traffic with legitimate activity and using advanced encryption techniques, attackers can stay one step ahead of modern defenses. Understanding these tactics not only equips red teams to emulate sophisticated adversaries but also challenges blue teams to enhance their detection and response capabilities, fostering a more resilient security posture.

8.3 Anti-Forensics: Disabling and Deceiving Logging Systems

Logs are an organization's critical source of evidence for detecting, analyzing, and responding to cyberattacks. They capture everything from login attempts and process execution to network activity and system changes. For red teamers simulating advanced threats, understanding and manipulating logging systems is essential to maintain stealth and demonstrate the organization's detection limitations. This chapter delves into anti-forensic techniques that disable, deceive, or manipulate logging systems, ensuring attackers remain undetected for as long as possible.

1. Why Attack Logging Systems?

Logging systems are indispensable to defenders, serving as their eyes and ears in the fight against cyber threats. By targeting these systems, red teamers can:

- **Evade Detection**: Concealing malicious activities by eliminating or altering log entries.
- **Delay Incident Response**: Without logs, defenders struggle to reconstruct events, delaying containment and remediation.
- **Simulate Advanced Threats**: Sophisticated attackers often prioritize disrupting logging mechanisms to maintain operational security.

Anti-forensics techniques can target various stages of the logging process, from disabling log generation to corrupting stored logs or misdirecting analysts with deceptive entries.

2. Disabling or Modifying Logging on Endpoints

2.1 Targeting Native Logging Mechanisms

Operating systems like Windows and Linux rely on native logging services that attackers can manipulate:

Windows Event Logs:

Disable logging by stopping the Windows Event Log service:

net stop EventLog

This halts all log generation until the service is restarted, leaving defenders blind.

Selectively clear logs using PowerShell:

Clear-EventLog -LogName Security

This removes existing entries in a specific log, concealing past activities.

Linux System Logs:

Disable logging by stopping the syslog or rsyslog service:

sudo systemctl stop rsyslog

Attackers can also modify log configurations in /etc/rsyslog.conf to exclude certain events from being recorded.

2.2 Log Tampering

Instead of outright disabling logs, attackers may choose to tamper with existing entries to conceal malicious actions:

- **Editing Logs Directly**: Attackers with elevated privileges can edit raw log files (e.g., /var/log/auth.log on Linux or .evtx files on Windows) to remove traces of unauthorized access or lateral movement.
- **Time Manipulation**: Changing system time before executing malicious actions can cause logs to have misleading timestamps, confusing investigators.
- **Example**: A red teamer might alter the timestamps of login events in /var/log/auth.log to make unauthorized access appear to occur outside of regular working hours, misdirecting forensic analysis.

3. Disabling Security and Monitoring Tools

Modern organizations rely on third-party security solutions to monitor and centralize logs. Red teamers often target these tools to disrupt log collection and analysis.

3.1 Endpoint Detection and Response (EDR) Evasion

Disabling EDR Logging: Many EDR systems provide process monitoring and behavioral analysis. Attackers with sufficient privileges can stop EDR agents, disable features, or kill processes:

taskkill /IM edr_agent.exe /F

Tools like Defender Control can temporarily disable Microsoft Defender, limiting visibility during exploitation.

Bypassing Monitoring Features: Some EDR tools rely on kernel drivers for monitoring. Attackers can unload these drivers using tools like AVKill or directly via system commands.

3.2 Log Aggregation Tools

Centralized logging tools like Splunk, ELK Stack (Elasticsearch, Logstash, Kibana), or SIEM platforms collect and analyze logs across systems. Disrupting these tools can sever defenders' access to critical telemetry:

- **Overloading Log Systems**: Flooding logs with excessive entries (log flooding) can cause storage issues, make relevant logs harder to find, or even crash the logging system.
- **Example**: A red teamer might script repeated invalid login attempts to generate an overwhelming volume of authentication logs.

Tampering with Forwarding Configurations:

On Linux, editing /etc/rsyslog.conf can redirect logs to an inaccessible location or a remote server controlled by the attacker.

4. Deception Techniques: Poisoning Logs

Rather than simply erasing or disabling logs, attackers may choose to inject misleading entries to confuse or misdirect defenders.

4.1 False Log Entries

Creating false logs can divert attention from real attack vectors:

Windows Example: Use tools like eventcreate.exe to generate fake event logs:

eventcreate /T WARNING /ID 1234 /L APPLICATION /D "Fake malware detection log."

Linux Example: Append fake login attempts to /var/log/auth.log:

echo "Nov 19 23:59:59 localhost sshd[12345]: Failed password for root from 192.168.1.100" >> /var/log/auth.log

4.2 Misleading Indicators of Compromise (IoCs)

Injecting fake IoCs into logs can lead defenders down the wrong path:

Example: Modifying network logs to show traffic to well-known threat actor domains, making defenders believe they are under attack by a sophisticated adversary.

4.3 Staging Fake Persistence Techniques

Red teamers can create decoy persistence mechanisms (e.g., registry keys or scheduled tasks) and log their execution to distract defenders from real backdoors.

5. Advanced Tools and Frameworks for Anti-Forensics

Red teamers can leverage various tools to automate anti-forensics activities:

- **Invoke-Phant0m**: A PowerShell script that selectively disables Windows Event Logs without stopping the Event Log service entirely, maintaining operational stealth.
- **Auditpol**: A native Windows tool to configure and disable auditing policies. Attackers can use it to turn off specific logging categories:

auditpol /set /subcategory:"Logon/Logoff" /success:disable /failure:disable

Meterpreter: A post-exploitation framework that includes modules for clearing logs on compromised systems:

meterpreter > clearev

LogKill: A tool designed to remove specific log entries from Windows Event Logs, targeting high-value entries while leaving others intact.

6. Countermeasures: Blue Team Defenses

Defenders can implement various strategies to detect and mitigate anti-forensics techniques:

- **Logging Integrity**: Use tamper-proof logging mechanisms, such as write-once, read-many (WORM) storage or cloud-based logging solutions, to prevent attackers from modifying logs.
- **Endpoint Hardening**: Protect logging services by restricting administrative privileges and monitoring changes to logging configurations.
- **Anomaly Detection**: Flag sudden decreases in log volume, unusual timestamps, or the absence of expected logs as potential indicators of tampering.
- **Decoy Logs**: Deploy fake logging systems to lure attackers into revealing anti-forensic techniques without disrupting critical telemetry.

Disabling and deceiving logging systems is a core capability for advanced red teamers, enabling them to operate undetected and mimic real-world adversaries. These anti-forensics techniques challenge blue teams to enhance their monitoring and incident response strategies, reinforcing the importance of robust, tamper-resistant logging practices. By understanding these tactics, organizations can proactively defend against sophisticated threats, turning the lessons of red teaming into actionable security improvements.

8.4 Exploiting Gaps in SIEM and IDS Configurations

Security Information and Event Management (SIEM) systems and Intrusion Detection Systems (IDS) are critical components of an organization's defense strategy. They collect, analyze, and correlate logs, events, and network traffic to detect potential threats. However, these systems are only as strong as their configurations, and misconfigurations or blind spots often create exploitable gaps. For red teamers, understanding how to identify and leverage these gaps is essential to simulate real-world advanced adversaries effectively. This chapter explores common weaknesses in SIEM and IDS setups and strategies for exploiting them.

1. Why SIEM and IDS Gaps Matter

SIEM and IDS platforms depend on comprehensive configuration, including rules, policies, and data sources. Misconfigurations or omissions can result in:

- **Blind Spots**: Activities or systems that are not monitored, providing undetected attack vectors.
- **False Negatives**: Malicious actions that fail to trigger alerts due to weak or missing detection rules.
- **Performance Trade-offs**: Limited processing capacity leads to selective monitoring or delayed analysis, creating opportunities for stealthy attacks.

By exploiting these gaps, red teamers can bypass detection, demonstrate real-world risks, and help organizations improve their defensive posture.

2. Identifying SIEM Configuration Gaps

2.1 Insufficient Data Sources

SIEM platforms rely on log ingestion from various sources such as endpoints, network devices, applications, and cloud services. Missing or misconfigured data sources result in gaps in visibility:

Endpoint Monitoring:

- Systems lacking endpoint monitoring tools (e.g., EDR) are blind to local activity such as privilege escalation, file tampering, or process injections.
- **Example**: If logs from Linux servers are not forwarded to the SIEM, attackers can operate on those servers without triggering alerts.

Cloud Services:

- Gaps in logging for cloud environments (e.g., AWS, Azure, Google Cloud) are common due to improper configuration of native logging services like CloudTrail, Azure Monitor, or GCP Audit Logs.
- **Example**: Missing logs for IAM changes in AWS can hide an attacker's privilege escalation efforts.

2.2 Weak Correlation Rules

SIEM systems use correlation rules to link related events and identify threats. Weak or overly generic rules often fail to detect sophisticated attacks:

Over-Reliance on Default Rules:

- Many organizations use out-of-the-box rules that fail to account for their specific environments.
- **Example**: Default rules may trigger alerts for failed login attempts but fail to detect password spraying attacks with low and slow techniques.

Ignoring Low-Priority Events:

- Rules often prioritize high-severity events, ignoring low-priority ones. Attackers can chain multiple low-priority actions to evade detection.
- **Example**: An attacker might create a new low-privilege user account (low-priority event) and gradually escalate its privileges without triggering alerts.

2.3 Delayed or Incomplete Event Processing

SIEM platforms often struggle to process large volumes of logs in real time. Delays or incomplete ingestion create windows of opportunity:

Latency in Alerting:

- High log volumes can result in delays between event occurrence and alert generation.
- **Example**: An attacker may execute a privilege escalation exploit and exfiltrate data before the SIEM generates an alert.

Dropped Events:

- Overloaded SIEMs may drop low-priority events or fail to process logs from secondary sources.
- **Example**: Low-priority logs from non-critical systems like printers or IoT devices can harbor entry points but are ignored due to resource constraints.

3. Exploiting IDS Configurations

3.1 Avoiding Signature-Based Detection

IDS platforms often rely on predefined signatures to detect known threats. Attackers can modify their techniques to avoid detection:

Payload Obfuscation:

- Encrypting or encoding payloads can bypass signature detection.
- **Example**: Using Base64 encoding or XOR encryption to disguise malware delivered via HTTP.

Custom Malware:

- Deploying bespoke malware ensures no existing signature matches.
- **Example**: Modifying known exploits (e.g., MS17-010) with custom shellcode.

3.2 Exploiting Threshold-Based Detection

IDS often uses threshold rules to detect abnormal behavior, such as a specific number of failed login attempts. Attackers can exploit these thresholds:

Low and Slow Attacks:

- Spreading attack attempts over time avoids triggering thresholds.
- **Example**: Attempting one password every hour to avoid detection by a brute-force rule.

Randomized Behavior:

- IDS systems may flag repeated attempts with identical patterns but fail to detect randomized behavior.
- **Example**: Using randomized payloads or varying source IPs to evade detection.

3.3 Traffic Analysis Gaps

Network IDS (NIDS) platforms analyze traffic to detect anomalies. Improper configurations can leave critical areas unmonitored:

Encrypted Traffic:

- NIDS cannot inspect encrypted HTTPS traffic without SSL/TLS decryption capabilities.
- **Example**: Attackers may use HTTPS-based C2 channels, bypassing inspection.

Blind Spots in Network Segments:

- IDS often lacks visibility into traffic within isolated VLANs or between hosts on the same subnet.
- **Example**: Red teamers can perform lateral movement within a subnet, bypassing NIDS monitoring.

4. Tactics for Exploiting SIEM and IDS Gaps

4.1 Exploiting Logging Gaps

- Identify unmonitored endpoints or devices, such as development servers, IoT devices, or legacy systems, and use them as entry points.
- Leverage cloud misconfigurations to perform undetected actions, such as creating new user accounts without triggering alerts.

4.2 Bypassing Correlation Rules

- Chain low-priority actions to execute a larger attack without triggering high-severity alerts.
- Perform lateral movement between systems that are monitored but not correlated in SIEM rules, such as using SMB traffic to move laterally between Windows hosts.

4.3 Timing Attacks

- Conduct activities during SIEM maintenance windows or peak log ingestion times when processing delays are likely.
- Exploit delayed alerts to achieve objectives before defenders react.

5. Defensive Strategies for SIEM and IDS Gaps

5.1 Comprehensive Data Ingestion

- Ensure that all critical data sources are integrated with the SIEM, including endpoints, cloud services, and third-party tools.
- Regularly audit data sources to identify gaps in coverage or improperly configured log forwarding.

5.2 Tuning Correlation Rules

- Develop custom correlation rules tailored to the organization's environment, including rules for low-and-slow attacks and lateral movement patterns.
- Regularly test and validate rules using red team exercises and attack simulations.

5.3 Enhancing IDS Visibility

- Deploy SSL/TLS decryption to monitor encrypted traffic while maintaining privacy compliance.
- Use network segmentation and ensure IDS coverage for all critical network segments, including internal and isolated environments.

Exploiting gaps in SIEM and IDS configurations demonstrates the importance of thorough configuration and regular validation of monitoring systems. By understanding these gaps, red teamers can emulate advanced adversaries effectively, providing actionable insights to improve organizational defenses. For defenders, proactive tuning, continuous audits, and ongoing collaboration with red teams are key to closing these gaps and building resilient detection and response capabilities.

9. Red Teaming in the Cloud

As more organizations migrate to the cloud, understanding how to conduct red team operations in cloud environments has become essential. This chapter focuses on the unique challenges and opportunities presented by cloud infrastructures such as AWS, Azure, and Google Cloud. You'll learn how to identify and exploit misconfigurations in cloud access management (IAM), leverage cloud-specific attack vectors, and perform lateral movement within hybrid cloud environments. We'll also cover the nuances of red teaming in multi-tenant environments and how to exploit vulnerabilities across both on-premises and cloud infrastructure. By mastering cloud-specific tactics, you'll be prepared to simulate modern, cloud-based threats with precision and impact.

9.1 Assessing Cloud Security Postures (AWS, Azure, GCP)

Cloud platforms such as Amazon Web Services (AWS), Microsoft Azure, and Google Cloud Platform (GCP) have become the backbone of modern IT infrastructure, offering scalability, flexibility, and powerful tools for businesses. However, with these benefits come unique security challenges. Assessing the security posture of cloud environments is critical for identifying misconfigurations, vulnerabilities, and potential attack vectors that adversaries might exploit. This chapter provides a structured approach to evaluating cloud security postures and understanding the nuances of each major platform.

1. The Importance of Cloud Security Posture Assessment

As organizations migrate to the cloud, the shared responsibility model dictates that while cloud providers manage the infrastructure, customers are responsible for securing their workloads, configurations, and data. Misconfigurations and a lack of visibility often lead to:

- **Unauthorized Access**: Weak permissions or improperly configured Identity and Access Management (IAM) policies.
- **Data Exposure**: Publicly accessible storage buckets or unsecured databases.
- **Misused Services**: Compromised resources used for malicious purposes, such as cryptocurrency mining or malware distribution.

Assessing cloud security postures ensures that these vulnerabilities are identified and mitigated before attackers can exploit them.

2. Key Areas of Assessment

2.1 Identity and Access Management (IAM)

IAM is central to securing cloud environments, as it governs user access and permissions.

AWS:

- Evaluate IAM policies for overly permissive roles (e.g., *:* permissions).
- Ensure the use of multi-factor authentication (MFA) for root and privileged accounts.
- Check for orphaned keys or unused access keys.

Azure:

- Analyze role assignments in Azure Active Directory (AAD) to identify roles with excessive privileges.
- Review conditional access policies for gaps.

GCP:

- Inspect IAM bindings to ensure the principle of least privilege is enforced.
- Identify service accounts with unrestricted access to sensitive resources.

2.2 Storage and Data Protection

Cloud environments offer multiple storage options, each with its own potential risks.

AWS S3:

- Check for publicly accessible S3 buckets and objects.
- Verify encryption settings (e.g., SSE-S3, SSE-KMS) for data at rest.

Azure Blob Storage:

- Ensure private access is enforced and shared access signatures (SAS) are restricted by IP and time.

GCP Cloud Storage:

- Audit bucket permissions for public exposure and encryption compliance.
- Review logging and versioning configurations.

2.3 Networking and Perimeter Security

Cloud networking configurations determine exposure to external and internal threats.

AWS:

- Assess VPC configurations for open security group rules (e.g., 0.0.0.0/0 for inbound traffic).
- Validate the use of network ACLs and subnets to segment resources appropriately.

Azure:

- Check Network Security Groups (NSGs) for overly permissive rules.
- Analyze Azure Firewall configurations and ensure logging is enabled.

GCP:

- Review firewall rules for permissive ingress and egress settings.
- Inspect VPC peering and hybrid cloud connections for security controls.

2.4 Logging and Monitoring

Visibility into cloud activities is essential for detecting and responding to threats.

AWS:

- Verify that CloudTrail is enabled and configured to log to a secure S3 bucket.
- Ensure AWS Config is monitoring resource compliance.

Azure:

- Check that Azure Monitor and Log Analytics are collecting and storing security logs.
- Validate the configuration of Azure Security Center.

GCP:

- Confirm that Audit Logs are enabled for all resources.
- Review the configuration of the Security Command Center for threat monitoring.

3. Tools and Techniques for Assessment

3.1 Native Cloud Security Tools

- **AWS**: AWS Security Hub, Trusted Advisor, and Config provide insights into misconfigurations and compliance.
- **Azure**: Azure Security Center and Defender for Cloud offer security recommendations.
- **GCP**: Security Command Center provides a centralized view of security risks.

3.2 Third-Party Tools

Cloud Security Posture Management (CSPM) Tools:

- Platforms like Prisma Cloud, Orca Security, and Lacework offer automated assessments and insights across multi-cloud environments.

Open-Source Tools:

- **Pacu**: AWS exploitation framework for assessing IAM and other configurations.
- **ScoutSuite**: Multi-cloud auditing tool for identifying misconfigurations.
- **Cloudsploit**: Open-source tool for continuous monitoring of cloud environments.

3.3 Manual Techniques

API Analysis:

- Use CLI tools (awscli, az, gcloud) to list and analyze resources and policies.
- Query resource configurations using SDKs or APIs.

Misconfiguration Hunting:

- Simulate attacker behavior by searching for public resources or over-permissive roles.
- Review logging gaps or unmonitored services.

4. Assessing Misconfigurations with Practical Examples

4.1 Public Storage Buckets

AWS: Identify buckets with public read or write access:

```
aws s3api list-buckets --query "Buckets[].Name"
aws s3api get-bucket-acl --bucket <bucket-name>
```

Azure: Use Azure CLI to check for public access:

```
az storage container list --account-name <account-name> --query
"[].properties.publicAccess"
```

GCP: Validate bucket permissions using the gsutil tool:

```
gsutil ls -L -b gs://<bucket-name>
```

4.2 Weak IAM Policies

AWS: Query for policies with wildcard permissions:

```
aws iam list-policies --query "Policies[].PolicyName"
aws iam get-policy --policy-arn <policy-arn>
```

Azure: List role assignments with privileged access:

```
az role assignment list --all
```

GCP: Use gcloud to inspect IAM roles:

```
gcloud projects get-iam-policy <project-id>
```

4.3 Open Firewall Rules

AWS: Detect security groups with overly permissive rules:

```
aws ec2 describe-security-groups
```

Azure: Audit NSG rules for unrestricted access:

az network nsg list --query "[].securityRules"

GCP: Inspect firewall rules:

gcloud compute firewall-rules list

5. Remediation Recommendations

IAM Hardening:

- Implement the principle of least privilege for all roles and accounts.
- Regularly rotate and deactivate unused credentials.

Storage Security:

- Enforce encryption by default for all storage resources.
- Use access logging to monitor interactions with sensitive data.

Network Controls:

- Restrict inbound and outbound traffic using tightly scoped rules.
- Enable and review network flow logs for anomaly detection.

Logging and Monitoring:

- Centralize logs in secure storage for long-term analysis.
- Regularly test alerting configurations to ensure they cover critical resources.

Assessing the security posture of cloud environments requires a deep understanding of platform-specific configurations and common pitfalls. By leveraging both manual and automated techniques, red teamers can identify gaps that adversaries might exploit. This assessment not only helps organizations strengthen their defenses but also fosters proactive collaboration between red and blue teams, ensuring cloud environments remain resilient against evolving threats.

9.2 Exploiting Misconfigured IAM Roles and Policies

Identity and Access Management (IAM) is the backbone of cloud security, controlling access to resources and services in environments like AWS, Azure, and GCP.

Misconfigured IAM roles and policies are among the most common cloud vulnerabilities, often leading to privilege escalation, resource abuse, and data exfiltration. For red teamers, understanding how to identify and exploit these misconfigurations is crucial to simulating real-world adversary behavior. This chapter dives into the techniques and tools used to identify and exploit misconfigured IAM roles and policies across the major cloud platforms.

1. The Role of IAM in Cloud Security

IAM governs the access rights for users, services, and applications within a cloud environment. It is structured around:

- **Users**: Individual accounts assigned to human operators.
- **Roles**: Temporary, assumable identities for services or users to interact with cloud resources.
- **Policies**: Rules that define permissions for users, roles, or groups.

Misconfigurations often occur due to over-permissive policies, weak role definitions, or a lack of monitoring, leading to:

- Unauthorized access to sensitive resources.
- Privilege escalation by exploiting trust relationships.

Service abuse, such as turning cloud resources into cryptocurrency miners.

2. Common Misconfigurations in IAM

2.1 Overly Permissive Policies

Wildcard Permissions:

- IAM policies allowing actions like *:* (all actions on all resources) grant unrestricted access.
- **Example**: An attacker could delete critical resources or exfiltrate sensitive data.

Lack of Resource Constraints:

- Policies that do not restrict access to specific resources allow attackers to interact with unintended services.

- **Example**: A policy permitting s3:ListBucket without specifying a bucket ARN exposes all S3 buckets.

2.2 Misconfigured Trust Relationships

AWS: Trust policies for roles often allow excessive permissions for external accounts.

Example: A role with a trust policy allowing any account to assume it can be exploited for lateral movement.

Azure: Misconfigured app registrations or managed identities may grant unauthorized access.

GCP: Service accounts may be misconfigured to permit external users or applications to impersonate them.

2.3 Unused or Orphaned Credentials

Access keys or service accounts left unmonitored can become entry points for attackers.

Example: Access keys for an unused user are compromised, allowing attackers to operate undetected.

2.4 Role Chaining Vulnerabilities

- **AWS**: Attackers can chain roles by exploiting over-permissive sts:AssumeRole policies.
- **Azure**: Role assignments in Azure AD may allow privilege escalation through lateral moves.
- **GCP**: Service accounts with high privileges can be exploited to impersonate other roles.

3. Exploiting IAM Misconfigurations

3.1 Identifying Over-Permissive Policies

AWS: Use aws iam get-policy to identify policies with wildcards.

aws iam list-policies --query "Policies[].PolicyName"
aws iam get-policy --policy-arn <policy-arn>

Azure: Query role assignments for over-privileged roles.

az role assignment list --query "[?roleDefinitionName=='Contributor']"

GCP: Inspect IAM bindings for wildcard permissions.

gcloud projects get-iam-policy <project-id>

3.2 Exploiting Trust Policies

AWS:

Identify roles with permissive trust policies using tools like Pacu or manual inspection.

aws iam list-roles --query "Roles[].AssumeRolePolicyDocument"

Exploit trust policies to assume roles and escalate privileges:

aws sts assume-role --role-arn <role-arn> --role-session-name exploit-session

Azure:

- Exploit misconfigured app registrations or managed identities to gain unauthorized access.
- **Example**: Use the Microsoft Graph API to list service principals and identify misconfigurations.

GCP:

Exploit service account impersonation:

gcloud auth activate-service-account --key-file=<keyfile.json>
gcloud auth print-access-token

3.3 Privilege Escalation via Role Chaining

AWS: Use tools like Cloudsploit or Pacu to identify and chain roles.

Example:

- Assume a role with limited privileges.
- Use its permissions to assume a higher-privilege role.

aws sts assume-role --role-arn <privileged-role> --role-session-name escalated-session

Azure: Identify opportunities for lateral movement via role assignments or resource permissions.

GCP: Exploit IAM role bindings to escalate privileges across projects.

3.4 Abusing Unused or Orphaned Credentials

- Scan for unused keys or service accounts using cloud-native tools or scripts.
- Exploit these credentials to operate under the radar:

AWS: Use access_key to interact with the cloud environment.

export AWS_ACCESS_KEY_ID=<key_id>
export AWS_SECRET_ACCESS_KEY=<secret_key>
aws s3 ls

GCP: Exploit service account tokens for lateral movement.

4. Tools for IAM Exploitation

4.1 AWS Tools

- **Pacu**: AWS exploitation framework for identifying and exploiting IAM vulnerabilities.
- **ScoutSuite**: Multi-cloud auditing tool for identifying over-permissive policies.

4.2 Azure Tools

- **ROADTools**: Azure AD exploration framework for identifying privilege escalation paths.
- **StormSpotter**: Maps Azure configurations to identify potential attack paths.

4.3 GCP Tools

- **G-Scout**: GCP security assessment tool for identifying IAM misconfigurations.
- **Forseti Security**: Open-source tool for auditing GCP environments.

4.4 Multi-Cloud Tools

- **Cloudsploit**: Audits configurations and permissions across AWS, Azure, and GCP.
- **Steampipe**: A query-based tool for analyzing cloud security postures.

5. Defensive Measures Against IAM Exploitation

5.1 Implement the Principle of Least Privilege

- Limit permissions to the minimum required for users, roles, and services.
- Regularly audit and prune unused permissions.

5.2 Enforce Strong Trust Policies

- Restrict trust relationships to specific accounts, services, or users.
- Use conditions like source IP, MFA, or time-based access restrictions.

5.3 Rotate and Monitor Credentials

- Regularly rotate access keys, tokens, and passwords.
- Implement logging and alerting for all IAM activity.

5.4 Continuous Monitoring and Assessment

- Use CSPM tools to automatically identify misconfigurations.
- Conduct regular penetration testing to validate IAM policies and roles.

IAM roles and policies are central to cloud security but also represent a significant attack surface if misconfigured. For red teamers, exploiting these misconfigurations demonstrates the critical importance of strong access controls and regular policy reviews. By identifying weaknesses, red teams provide valuable insights into securing IAM configurations, reducing the risk of exploitation by malicious actors, and ensuring robust cloud security postures.

9.3 Cross-Account Exploitation in Cloud Environments

Modern cloud environments often span multiple accounts and subscriptions to facilitate resource management, enhance security, or align with business units. While this segmentation is designed to increase isolation, misconfigurations or overly permissive trust relationships can allow adversaries to breach one account and leverage it as a launchpad to compromise others. Cross-account exploitation presents a critical challenge in cloud security, and mastering these attack techniques is essential for red teamers simulating advanced threat actors.

This chapter explores cross-account exploitation strategies, including identifying vulnerabilities, leveraging trust relationships, and escalating privileges across accounts in platforms like AWS, Azure, and GCP.

1. Understanding Cross-Account Relationships

Cloud platforms offer features to enable collaboration and integration between accounts or tenants. Examples include:

- **AWS**: Cross-account access via IAM roles, resource sharing, and account-level trust policies.
- **Azure**: Azure Active Directory (AAD) tenant relationships, such as guest access or B2B collaboration.
- **GCP**: Service accounts with permissions that extend to external projects or organizations.

Misconfigurations in these trust mechanisms can lead to:

- **Privilege Escalation**: Exploiting access to gain higher privileges in the target account.
- **Data Breaches**: Accessing sensitive resources in another account.
- **Service Misuse**: Using another account's resources for malicious activities, such as deploying cryptominers.

2. Common Cross-Account Exploitation Scenarios

2.1 Misconfigured Trust Relationships

AWS: Overly permissive IAM trust policies can allow attackers to assume roles in other accounts.

Example: A trust policy allows all principals in another account to assume a role without conditions.

Exploitation: Use sts:AssumeRole to gain access to the target account.

Azure: Poorly configured guest access can lead to lateral movement across tenants.

Example: A guest user retains access to sensitive resources due to mismanaged roles.

GCP: Service accounts with permissions to interact with external projects can be abused.

Example: A misconfigured service account in Project A has write access to Project B's resources.

2.2 Over-Permissive Shared Resources

Shared services such as S3 buckets, Azure Blob storage, or GCP Cloud Storage are often misconfigured, exposing sensitive data or allowing unauthorized actions.

- **AWS**: Cross-account S3 bucket access with overly permissive ACLs or bucket policies.
- **Azure**: Misconfigured access to shared resources like Azure Files or Azure Storage.
- **GCP**: Public or external access granted to critical storage buckets.

2.3 Exploiting External Identity Providers (IdPs)

Cloud platforms often integrate with external IdPs (e.g., Okta, AAD, or custom SAML providers). Misconfigurations in these integrations can be exploited to impersonate users across accounts.

2.4 Credential Sharing Across Accounts

- Shared credentials (e.g., API keys, tokens) between accounts or services can inadvertently grant unauthorized cross-account access.
- **Example**: A leaked API key for Account A can be used to access resources in Account B due to shared credentials.

3. Cross-Account Exploitation Techniques

3.1 Exploiting AWS Cross-Account Trust Policies

Enumerating Roles:

Identify roles in other accounts that allow cross-account access:

aws iam list-roles --query "Roles[].AssumeRolePolicyDocument"

Look for overly permissive policies like:

```
"Principal": {
    "AWS": "*"
}
```

Assuming a Role:

Use the sts:AssumeRole API to assume the role:

aws sts assume-role --role-arn arn:aws:iam::<target-account-id>:role/<role-name> --role-session-name x_account_exploit

Extract the temporary credentials and use them to access resources in the target account.

Lateral Movement:

Once inside the target account, look for additional roles or resources to escalate privileges further.

3.2 Exploiting Azure Cross-Tenant Access

Enumerating Guest Users:

Use AAD PowerShell modules to list guest users and their assigned roles:

Get-AzureADUser | Where-Object {$_.UserType -eq "Guest"}

Escalating Privileges:

Exploit misconfigured roles assigned to guest users to gain access to sensitive resources:

az role assignment list --query "[?principalType=='User']"

Using Application Permissions:

Exploit poorly secured app registrations with delegated permissions to access other tenants.

3.3 Exploiting GCP Inter-Project Trust

Enumerating Permissions:

Use the GCP CLI to list IAM policies for external access:

gcloud projects get-iam-policy <project-id>

Service Account Impersonation:

Identify service accounts with permissions in external projects and impersonate them:

gcloud auth activate-service-account --key-file <keyfile.json>

Accessing Shared Resources:

Identify resources like shared buckets or databases with overly permissive ACLs.

3.4 Leveraging Stolen or Leaked Credentials

Credential Abuse:

- Test the credentials across multiple accounts using automation tools.
- **Example tools**: AWS CLI, AzCopy, or GCP gcloud CLI.

Pivoting:

Use the compromised account to identify additional misconfigurations or shared resources.

4. Tools for Cross-Account Exploitation

- **CloudSploit**: Multi-cloud misconfiguration scanner for detecting over-permissive roles or shared resources.
- **Pacu**: AWS exploitation framework for simulating cross-account attacks.
- **ScoutSuite**: Multi-cloud auditing tool for assessing cross-account trust and permissions.
- **ROADTools**: Focused on Azure AD misconfigurations and lateral movement opportunities.

5. Defensive Measures Against Cross-Account Exploitation

Restrict Trust Relationships:

- Use condition keys like source account, IP, or MFA to limit cross-account role assumptions.
- Regularly audit trust policies in AWS, Azure, and GCP.

Secure Shared Resources:

- Restrict access to shared resources by explicitly defining principals in policies.
- Enable logging for all access to shared resources.

Monitor for Unauthorized Access:

- Use CloudTrail (AWS), Azure Monitor, or GCP's Cloud Audit Logs to detect unauthorized cross-account activity.
- Set up alerts for role assumption events or changes in trust policies.

Rotate and Secure Credentials:

- Regularly rotate API keys, access tokens, and service account credentials.
- Use secrets management solutions to store and monitor credentials securely.

Implement Strong Identity Federation:

- Use strict SAML or OpenID Connect (OIDC) configurations.
- Regularly audit IdP configurations for security gaps.

Cross-account exploitation highlights the interconnected vulnerabilities in cloud environments. Misconfigurations in trust relationships, shared resources, or identity federation can provide attackers with paths to compromise multiple accounts. By understanding these exploitation techniques, red teamers can effectively simulate advanced adversary tactics, helping organizations identify and secure weaknesses before they are exploited by real attackers. Through proactive assessment and robust defense measures, organizations can maintain strong security postures across their cloud ecosystems.

9.4 Breaking into Hybrid Setups: Cloud and On-Premises

Hybrid cloud setups—where organizations integrate on-premises systems with cloud environments—offer flexibility and scalability, but also introduce a unique attack surface. The interconnection between cloud and on-premises infrastructure creates potential vulnerabilities that, if exploited, can provide attackers with pathways to compromise both environments. Breaking into hybrid setups requires understanding these interconnected systems, identifying weak links, and leveraging them for lateral movement and privilege escalation.

This chapter explores techniques for identifying and exploiting vulnerabilities in hybrid setups, focusing on weak integrations, misconfigurations, and trust mechanisms that bridge the gap between on-premises and cloud resources.

1. Anatomy of a Hybrid Setup

Hybrid infrastructures typically combine:

On-Premises Systems:

- Physical servers, data centers, and private networks.
- Identity providers like Active Directory (AD).

Cloud Services:

- Infrastructure-as-a-Service (IaaS) platforms like AWS, Azure, or GCP.
- Software-as-a-Service (SaaS) platforms integrated with on-premises systems.

Integration Layers:

- VPNs, direct connects, or service gateways for secure communication.
- Federation services for unified authentication (e.g., Azure AD Connect, ADFS).

2. Common Attack Vectors in Hybrid Setups

2.1 Exploiting Weak Identity Integration

Hybrid setups often integrate on-premises identity systems with cloud platforms for seamless user authentication. Key vulnerabilities include:

Azure AD Connect Sync Errors:

- Misconfigured Azure AD Connect setups may synchronize on-premises accounts with excessive privileges to the cloud.
- Attackers can exploit synchronization failures to escalate privileges in Azure AD.

Exposed Federation Services:

Services like ADFS may be misconfigured or exposed to the internet, allowing attackers to compromise tokens or credentials.

2.2 Misconfigured Network Bridging

Network connections between on-premises and cloud environments, such as VPNs or express routes, can serve as attack vectors if not properly secured.

Overly Permissive Network Rules:

Cloud-based virtual networks often allow unrestricted access to on-premises systems.

Insufficient Segmentation:

Lack of segmentation allows attackers who compromise one side (cloud or on-premises) to laterally move to the other.

2.3 Data Replication and Backup Flaws

Data synchronization between cloud and on-premises systems is a critical function of hybrid setups. Weaknesses in this process include:

Exposed Backup Endpoints:

Cloud storage buckets or databases used for backups may have public or unauthorized access.

Weak Encryption:

Data in transit between on-premises and cloud may be inadequately encrypted.

2.4 Leveraging On-Premises Access to Compromise the Cloud

Stolen Domain Credentials:

On-premises domain credentials can often be reused to access cloud resources through Single Sign-On (SSO).

Compromised Management Workstations:

Attackers who gain control of IT admin workstations can manipulate hybrid infrastructure through cloud management consoles.

3. Exploitation Techniques

3.1 Abusing Azure AD Connect

Enumerating Synchronization Errors:

- Identify misconfigurations in Azure AD Connect that can be exploited for privilege escalation.
- Look for accounts with elevated cloud privileges that originate from on-premises AD.

Extracting Synchronization Credentials:

Extract plaintext credentials stored by Azure AD Connect on compromised systems.

Get-ADSyncCredentials

Use these credentials to access Azure AD resources.

Forging SAML Tokens:

Manipulate ADFS configurations to generate forged SAML tokens for unauthorized cloud access.

3.2 Attacking Federation Services

Scanning for Exposed ADFS Endpoints:

- Use tools like Nmap or Shodan to locate ADFS servers exposed to the internet.
- Check for vulnerabilities in endpoints like /adfs/ls or /adfs/proxy.

Token Replay Attacks:

- Intercept SAML tokens using tools like Fiddler or Burp Suite.
- Replay or forge tokens to access cloud resources.

Credential Harvesting:

Use phishing campaigns targeting federation logins to steal credentials.

3.3 Exploiting Network Bridges

Identifying Misconfigured Routes:

Enumerate cloud VPC/VNet configurations to identify routes to on-premises networks.

aws ec2 describe-route-tables

az network route-table list

Look for routes with overly permissive CIDR ranges (e.g., 0.0.0.0/0).

Pivoting Through Hybrid Connections:

Use compromised cloud systems to scan on-premises networks for vulnerabilities.

nmap -Pn -p- <on-prem-IP>

Man-in-the-Middle (MitM) Attacks:

Exploit weakly encrypted or unencrypted connections between environments.

3.4 Leveraging Stolen On-Premises Credentials

Enumerating Cloud Access:

Use compromised domain credentials to authenticate against cloud services.

az login --username <user> --password <pass>

aws configure

Test for SSO configurations that extend on-premises credentials to the cloud.

Privilege Escalation in the Cloud:

Enumerate roles and permissions granted to the stolen credentials.

aws iam list-roles
az role assignment list

4. Tools for Breaking Hybrid Setups

- **BloodHound**: Analyzes Active Directory for attack paths, including Azure AD integration.
- **ROADTools**: Assesses Azure AD configurations and identifies weaknesses in hybrid setups.
- **Pacu**: Exploitation framework for AWS environments.
- **Mimikatz**: Extracts credentials from on-premises systems for hybrid attacks.

5. Defensive Measures for Hybrid Security

5.1 Strengthening Identity Integration

- Regularly audit Azure AD Connect configurations to ensure proper privilege management.
- Use conditional access policies to restrict synchronization processes to specific IP ranges or devices.

5.2 Securing Network Connectivity

- Implement strict segmentation between cloud and on-premises networks.
- Use zero-trust network principles to verify identity and context before granting access.

5.3 Hardening Federation Services

- Avoid exposing ADFS endpoints to the public internet.
- Regularly update and patch federation servers to address vulnerabilities.

5.4 Protecting Data Replication and Backups

- Encrypt data in transit and at rest between on-premises and cloud environments.
- Implement strict access controls for cloud storage buckets and backup endpoints.

Hybrid setups provide critical functionality for modern organizations, but their interconnected nature makes them attractive targets for attackers. By identifying and exploiting weak integration points, misconfigured trust relationships, and poorly secured network bridges, red teamers can simulate realistic threats to hybrid infrastructures. This insight is invaluable for helping organizations strengthen their hybrid environments, ensuring that both on-premises and cloud systems are resilient against advanced attacks.

10. Physical and Social Red Teaming

While digital attacks dominate the threat landscape, physical and social engineering tactics remain powerful methods of compromise. This chapter explores the intersection of psychology and security, focusing on how red teamers can use physical intrusion techniques and social engineering to bypass security measures. You'll learn how to exploit physical vulnerabilities like access control systems, locks, and surveillance, as well as how to execute convincing social engineering attacks such as pretexting, baiting, and impersonation. By mastering these non-technical attack methods, you'll understand how adversaries can manipulate human behavior and breach even the most secure environments.

10.1 Physical Intrusion Tactics: Bypassing Locks and Security Systems

Physical security is a cornerstone of an organization's overall defense strategy. However, even the most advanced digital security measures can be undermined by vulnerabilities in physical security controls. Physical intrusion tactics focus on bypassing barriers like locks, access control systems, and surveillance, allowing attackers to gain physical access to critical assets, including servers, workstations, and sensitive documents.

This chapter provides an in-depth look at techniques and tools used for physical intrusions, explores common vulnerabilities in physical security systems, and highlights strategies for evaluating and strengthening defenses against these threats.

1. Understanding Physical Security Layers

Physical security is often structured in concentric layers, each designed to deter or delay intruders:

- **Perimeter Security**: Fences, gates, and outdoor surveillance systems.
- **Access Control Points**: Keypad locks, biometric scanners, and RFID-based systems.
- **Internal Barriers**: Locked doors, safes, and secure enclosures for sensitive equipment.
- **Monitoring Systems**: CCTV cameras, motion sensors, and alarm systems.

Each layer presents potential points of failure that attackers can exploit.

2. Common Physical Intrusion Techniques

2.1 Lock Picking and Bypass Methods

- **Traditional Lock Picking**: Using tools like tension wrenches and picks to manipulate pin-tumbler locks.
- **Bump Keys**: Specially cut keys that exploit the mechanical design of pin-tumbler locks to open them quickly.
- **Shimming**: Inserting a thin shim to manipulate lock mechanisms, often used on padlocks or sliding doors.

Electronic Lock Hacking:

- Exploiting weak PINs on keypad locks.
- Using magnetic field emitters to bypass solenoid-based locks.

2.2 RFID and Proximity Card Exploits

Cloning RFID Cards:

- Using tools like Proxmark3 to read and replicate RFID card data.
- Exploiting weak encryption protocols in low-frequency (125 kHz) systems.

Replay Attacks:

- Capturing the signal from an RFID badge and replaying it to gain access.

2.3 Tailgating and Social Engineering

- **Tailgating**: Following authorized personnel through secure doors without authentication.

Social Engineering:

- Posing as delivery personnel, contractors, or employees to gain trust and access.
- Exploiting complacency or human error in access control enforcement.

2.4 Surveillance System Blind Spots

- Identifying and exploiting blind spots in CCTV coverage.
- Using laser pointers or IR emitters to temporarily blind or confuse cameras.
- Exploiting unsecured DVR or NVR systems to disable or delete footage.

2.5 Alarm System Manipulation

Tampering with Sensors:

- Blocking or bypassing motion detectors using thermal insulation materials.
- Jamming wireless sensors with radio frequency interference.

Disabling Control Panels:

- Accessing and disabling alarm panels, often located in unsecured areas.
- Exploiting default credentials or weak passwords to access system settings.

3. Tools for Physical Intrusion

3.1 Lock Picking Kits

- Tools for bypassing traditional locks, including picks, rakes, and tension wrenches.
- Advanced options like electric lock pick guns for rapid entry.

3.2 RFID Exploitation Tools

- Proxmark3: Versatile RFID tool for reading, cloning, and emulating RFID tags.
- ChameleonMini: Compact RFID emulator for field operations.

3.3 Surveillance Bypass Equipment

- IR LEDs: Mounted on clothing to create invisibility against infrared cameras.
- Laser Pointers: Disrupt optical lenses in CCTVs.
- Signal Jammers: Block wireless camera feeds or alarms.

3.4 Alarm Disabling Tools

- RF Jammers: Disrupt wireless communication between sensors and control panels.
- Multimeters and Wire Cutters: Identify and manipulate wired alarm systems.

4. Defensive Measures

4.1 Securing Locks and Access Points

- Use high-security locks with advanced pin mechanisms resistant to picking and bumping.
- Upgrade electronic locks to models with encryption and tamper-detection features.
- Implement anti-tailgating technologies like security turnstiles or mantraps.

4.2 Strengthening RFID Systems

- Use high-frequency (13.56 MHz) RFID systems with secure protocols like MIFARE DESFire or iCLASS SE.
- Implement multi-factor authentication (MFA) for access control points.

4.3 Improving Surveillance and Monitoring

- Overlap CCTV coverage to eliminate blind spots.
- Use motion-detection cameras with tamper alerts for real-time monitoring.
- Regularly audit surveillance equipment for vulnerabilities in software or physical placement.

4.4 Enhancing Alarm Systems

- Install tamper-resistant motion sensors with self-test capabilities.
- Use redundant communication channels (e.g., wired and cellular) to prevent jamming.
- Secure control panels in locked enclosures with access logs.

4.5 Employee Training and Awareness

- Conduct regular training on tailgating prevention and access control policies.
- Perform social engineering tests to assess and improve employee response to unauthorized individuals.

5. Red Team Considerations

For red teamers simulating physical intrusions:

Reconnaissance:

- Conduct surveillance to identify potential vulnerabilities in perimeter and internal security.
- Map access control systems and evaluate employee behavior.

Planning:

- Develop a strategy to exploit specific weaknesses in physical security.
- Prepare backup plans for contingencies, such as unexpected obstacles or enhanced security measures.

Execution:

- Execute intrusion attempts with minimal disruption or evidence of tampering.
- Document all techniques and tools used to replicate findings in reports.

Post-Intrusion:

- Securely return borrowed tools or bypassed systems to their original state.
- Provide actionable recommendations for improving physical security.

Physical intrusion tactics demonstrate how gaps in an organization's physical security posture can lead to breaches that bypass even the most robust digital defenses. By understanding the techniques attackers use to bypass locks, exploit RFID systems, and evade surveillance, red teamers can simulate real-world threats and provide valuable insights to fortify defenses. Implementing layered security, advanced technologies, and comprehensive employee training ensures that organizations can mitigate physical intrusion risks effectively.

10.2 RFID and Badge Cloning Techniques

Radio Frequency Identification (RFID) systems are widely used for secure access control in corporate offices, government facilities, and other high-security environments. However, these systems are often vulnerable to exploitation, especially when low-frequency or poorly secured RFID technologies are deployed. Badge cloning, the act of duplicating an RFID-based access card or tag, is a common tactic for bypassing access control systems. This chapter delves into the principles of RFID technology, the tools and techniques used for cloning badges, and strategies for identifying and mitigating these risks.

1. Fundamentals of RFID Technology

1.1 What is RFID?

RFID technology relies on electromagnetic fields to identify and communicate with tags embedded in access cards or badges. It typically consists of two components:

- **RFID Tag**: A chip and antenna embedded in cards or key fobs.
- **RFID Reader**: A device that emits radio waves to power the tag and read its unique identifier.

1.2 Types of RFID Tags

- **Low-Frequency (LF):** Operates at 125 kHz; commonly used in older access control systems.
- **Examples**: HID Prox, EM4100.
- **Vulnerabilities**: Weak or no encryption, making them easy to clone.

- **High-Frequency (HF):** Operates at 13.56 MHz; more secure with advanced encryption.
- **Examples**: MIFARE Classic, MIFARE DESFire.
- **Vulnerabilities**: Some versions (e.g., MIFARE Classic) have known encryption flaws.

- **Ultra-High-Frequency (UHF):** Operates at 300 MHz to 3 GHz; used in supply chain tracking and specialized applications.
- **Examples**: EPC Gen2.
- **Vulnerabilities**: Limited application in access control but susceptible to eavesdropping.

1.3 How RFID Systems Work

- An RFID reader emits a radio frequency signal.
- The RFID tag responds with its unique identifier.

The system checks the identifier against a database to grant or deny access.

2. Tools and Techniques for Badge Cloning

2.1 Tools for Cloning RFID Tags

Proxmark3:

- A versatile RFID research tool capable of reading, writing, and emulating tags.
- Supports both LF (125 kHz) and HF (13.56 MHz) tags.

Common commands:

lf search   # Scan for low-frequency tags
hf mf dump   # Dump high-frequency tag contents

ChameleonMini:

- A compact device that can emulate and clone RFID cards.
- Ideal for field operations requiring minimal equipment.

RFIDler:

- Open-source RFID tool for analyzing and cloning LF tags.
- Android Smartphones with NFC:
- Apps like Mifare Classic Tool allow reading and writing certain HF tags.

2.2 Badge Cloning Process

Tag Identification:

- Identify the tag type (LF or HF) using a tool like Proxmark3.
- Analyze the tag's response to determine its protocol and encryption.

Reading the Tag:

For LF tags:

lf read

Save the tag's unique identifier (UID) or memory contents.

For HF tags:

hf mf readblk

Extract data blocks for cloning.

Replicating the Tag:

Write the extracted data onto a blank card or key fob.

If write

hf mf writeblk

Test the cloned card on an RFID reader to ensure functionality.

Emulating the Tag:

Instead of cloning, use devices like Proxmark3 or ChameleonMini to emulate the tag in real-time.

2.3 Bypassing Encryption

Cracking MIFARE Classic:

Use tools like mfoc or Proxmark3 to exploit known vulnerabilities in MIFARE Classic's Crypto1 encryption.

mfoc -O dump.mfd

Replay Attacks:

Capture and replay RFID tag signals using Proxmark3 or a similar tool.

If t55xx sim

3. Advanced Badge Exploits

3.1 Passive Eavesdropping

Use a high-gain antenna to intercept RFID communications between a tag and reader. Analyze intercepted signals to extract UID or data blocks for cloning.

3.2 Relay Attacks

- Extend the range of RFID tags using relaying devices.
- **Example**: An attacker positions a relay device near a victim's badge and extends the signal to a reader.

3.3 Denial-of-Service (DoS)

- Jam RFID frequencies to prevent legitimate tag-reader communication.
- **Exploit**: Force security personnel to bypass the system or use manual overrides.

4. Defensive Measures

4.1 Deploying Secure RFID Systems

Upgrade to Secure Protocols:

- Use tags with advanced encryption, such as MIFARE DESFire or iCLASS SE.

Implement Mutual Authentication:

- Require both the reader and tag to authenticate each other before communication.

4.2 Protecting Badges

Shielding Cards:

Use RFID-blocking sleeves or wallets to prevent unauthorized reads.

Limiting Badge Exposure:

Avoid wearing badges in public spaces where they can be scanned.

4.3 Securing Readers

Place Readers in Secure Areas:

Avoid placing readers in locations accessible to the public.

Monitor Reader Activity:

Log and analyze failed access attempts for potential cloning attempts.

4.4 Network-Based Mitigations

Behavioral Analytics:

Monitor RFID access patterns for anomalies, such as duplicate tag use or unusual access times.

Multi-Factor Authentication (MFA):

Combine RFID badges with additional authentication factors, such as PINs or biometrics.

5. Red Team Considerations

When simulating RFID badge cloning attacks as part of a red team exercise:

Pre-Attack Reconnaissance:

Identify badge types used in the target environment by observing employees or inspecting discarded badges.

Controlled Execution:

Use cloning tools to replicate badges without disrupting legitimate operations.

Post-Attack Reporting:

Provide detailed documentation of vulnerabilities, tools used, and cloning methods. Offer actionable recommendations for mitigating identified weaknesses.

RFID badge cloning is a potent method for bypassing physical access controls, particularly when outdated or insecure technologies are deployed. By understanding the mechanics of RFID systems and employing advanced cloning tools, attackers can replicate legitimate badges and compromise secure environments. For defenders, upgrading to secure protocols, protecting badges from unauthorized scanning, and implementing layered security measures are critical steps to mitigate these risks.

10.3 Social Engineering Scenarios: Pretexting and Baiting

Social engineering is one of the most effective methods for bypassing technical security controls by exploiting human vulnerabilities. Two prominent tactics within this domain are pretexting and baiting, both designed to manipulate individuals into revealing sensitive information or granting unauthorized access. This chapter explores these tactics, providing real-world scenarios, methodologies, and mitigation strategies to protect against such attacks.

1. What is Pretexting?

Pretexting involves creating a convincing and often fabricated scenario to persuade a target to disclose sensitive information or take specific actions. Unlike other social engineering techniques, pretexting relies heavily on building trust and legitimacy.

1.1 Characteristics of Pretexting

- Relies on detailed research about the target to enhance credibility.
- Often involves impersonating a trusted individual or authority figure (e.g., an IT technician, HR representative, or executive).
- Targets may disclose confidential information, grant physical access, or perform tasks (e.g., resetting a password).

2. Pretexting Scenarios

2.1 Impersonating IT Support

Scenario: The attacker contacts an employee claiming to be from the IT department, citing a critical issue requiring immediate action.

Tactics:

- Requests login credentials to "fix" an account issue.
- Asks the employee to install remote desktop software for troubleshooting.
- Outcome: The attacker gains credentials or remote access to the target's workstation.

2.2 Fake Executive Requests

Scenario: The attacker pretends to be a senior executive using spoofed email or phone calls.

Tactics:

- Urgently requests a sensitive report or financial data.
- Persuades the victim to approve wire transfers under the guise of a business emergency.
- Outcome: Unauthorized access to sensitive data or financial loss.

2.3 Vendor or Partner Impersonation

Scenario: The attacker poses as a trusted vendor, citing ongoing business transactions.

Tactics:

- Requests updated payment information.
- Asks for access to company systems to "resolve" a technical issue.
- Outcome: Access to internal systems or redirection of payments to attacker-controlled accounts.

3. What is Baiting?

Baiting involves luring a target into taking a harmful action by offering something enticing. The bait can be a physical item, digital file, or online offer designed to exploit curiosity or greed.

3.1 Characteristics of Baiting

- Often exploits curiosity or desire for convenience.
- Can involve physical media (e.g., USB drives) or digital lures (e.g., fake downloads, free offers).
- Frequently includes malware deployment or credential theft.

4. Baiting Scenarios

4.1 Malicious USB Drive

Scenario: The attacker leaves USB drives labeled with enticing names (e.g., "Salary Information" or "Confidential") in visible locations such as parking lots or break rooms.

Tactics:

- When inserted, the USB executes malware that provides the attacker access to the target's network.
- **Outcome**: Compromise of the victim's system and potential lateral movement within the network.

4.2 Fake Software Updates

Scenario: The attacker emails targets with a link to download a "critical software update."

Tactics:

- Disguises malicious software as a legitimate update.
- **Outcome**: The victim unknowingly installs malware, enabling remote access or data exfiltration.

4.3 Online Offers and Downloads

Scenario: The attacker hosts fake ads or websites offering free software, eBooks, or movie downloads.

Tactics:

- Distributes malware hidden within downloads.
- Redirects users to phishing pages to collect login credentials.
- **Outcome**: Infection of the victim's system or credential theft.

5. Methodologies for Effective Social Engineering

5.1 Research and Reconnaissance

- Gather information about the target from open sources (OSINT) such as LinkedIn, company websites, or social media.
- Tailor the pretext or bait to align with the target's role, habits, or interests.

5.2 Building Credibility

- Use official-sounding language and provide verifiable, yet falsified, details to gain trust.
- Leverage tools to spoof caller IDs, email domains, or official branding.

5.3 Exploiting Psychological Triggers

- **Urgency**: Create a sense of time pressure to bypass critical thinking.
- **Authority**: Pose as a figure of authority to discourage questioning.
- **Reciprocity**: Offer something of value (real or perceived) to elicit cooperation.

5.4 Execution

- Initiate contact through emails, phone calls, or in-person interactions.
- Adapt the approach based on the target's responses to maintain the pretext or reinforce the bait.

6. Defensive Measures Against Pretexting and Baiting

6.1 Employee Awareness and Training

- Conduct regular security awareness programs to educate employees about common social engineering tactics.
- Emphasize the importance of verifying requests, especially those involving sensitive information or urgent actions.

6.2 Verification Protocols

- Implement multi-factor verification for sensitive requests (e.g., financial transfers, credential resets).
- Encourage employees to verify communications through independent channels (e.g., direct phone calls to known contacts).

6.3 Technical Safeguards

- Block the use of unauthorized USB devices through endpoint security policies.
- Deploy email filters to identify and quarantine suspicious messages.
- Use software whitelisting to prevent unauthorized programs from running.

6.4 Physical Controls

- Secure areas where employees might encounter physical bait, such as parking lots or shared workspaces.
- Ensure lost property policies discourage employees from using unclaimed devices.

7. Red Team Applications of Pretexting and Baiting

When simulating social engineering attacks as part of a red team assessment:

Pretexting:

- Identify potential targets with access to critical systems or data.
- Develop a believable scenario, such as a request from IT or an urgent email from an executive.
- Attempt to elicit sensitive information or actions, documenting all interactions.

Baiting:

- Deploy physical bait (e.g., USB drives) in strategic locations.
- Create fake emails or websites offering enticing downloads.
- Monitor responses to assess the organization's susceptibility.

Post-Engagement Reporting:

- Highlight gaps in awareness, verification processes, or technical controls.
- Provide actionable recommendations for addressing vulnerabilities.

Pretexting and baiting are powerful social engineering techniques that exploit trust, curiosity, and human error. By understanding how attackers craft scenarios and deploy bait, organizations can implement effective defenses, combining employee awareness, technical controls, and robust verification protocols. For red teams, leveraging these tactics ethically can provide invaluable insights into an organization's security posture, enabling meaningful improvements to counter real-world threats.

10.4 Exploiting Human Psychology for Gaining Trust

Human psychology plays a critical role in social engineering attacks. Attackers leverage psychological principles to manipulate individuals into trusting them, often bypassing technical security measures. By understanding the fundamental ways humans think and behave, social engineers can craft highly effective scams and fraud tactics. In this chapter, we will explore the psychological principles that underpin these attacks, the strategies attackers use to gain trust, and the countermeasures organizations can implement to defend against such tactics.

1. The Psychology of Trust

Trust is a powerful, but often fragile, component of human interactions. Social engineers exploit this fundamental aspect of psychology, creating situations where their targets are more likely to trust them, even when there is no valid reason to do so.

1.1 The Importance of Trust

- **Trust as a Social Glue**: Trust is essential in human relationships, especially in professional settings. People tend to trust those who appear authoritative, familiar, or similar to themselves.
- **Cognitive Biases**: Humans have a natural tendency to trust individuals who demonstrate certain traits, even if these traits are fabricated. These biases include reciprocity, social proof, and liking.

2. Psychological Principles in Social Engineering Attacks

2.1 Reciprocity

- **What is Reciprocity?:** The principle of reciprocity is the idea that people feel obliged to return a favor or a gift.
- **Example in Social Engineering**: The attacker might offer help, such as fixing a "computer issue," or provide small free services, only to later request something in return, like sensitive information or access to systems.
- **Psychological Lever**: Victims feel a subconscious obligation to reciprocate, even if they are unaware of the manipulation.

2.2 Authority

- **What is Authority?:** Humans are conditioned to obey figures of authority, especially those who appear knowledgeable or have official status.
- **Example in Social Engineering**: Attackers may impersonate executives, IT support staff, or other authority figures within the organization. They might use official-sounding language or spoof caller IDs to enhance their perceived authority.

- **Psychological Lever:** The victim trusts the "authority figure" and acts quickly without questioning the request, often resulting in the disclosure of sensitive data or the completion of a malicious task.

2.3 Social Proof

- **What is Social Proof?:** People tend to trust the actions or opinions of others, especially in uncertain situations.
- **Example in Social Engineering**: An attacker may send fake emails or messages from seemingly legitimate sources, such as colleagues, to create a sense of urgency or legitimacy. They may even exploit social media to appear more credible.
- **Psychological Lever**: When an attacker appears to be "in the know" or aligned with others in the organization, victims are more likely to follow their lead.

2.4 Liking

- **What is Liking?:** People are more likely to trust and comply with individuals they like or those who are similar to them.
- **Example in Social Engineering**: Attackers may create a false sense of camaraderie by pretending to share common interests or by flattering the target. They may build rapport over time to lower the target's defenses.
- **Psychological Lever**: The victim is more likely to trust the attacker and let their guard down if they feel they have a personal connection or shared interests with them.

2.5 Scarcity and Urgency

- **What is Scarcity and Urgency?:** The principle of scarcity suggests that people value things more highly when they perceive them to be in limited supply. Similarly, urgency motivates quick action, often without thinking through the consequences.
- **Example in Social Engineering**: The attacker may create a sense of urgency (e.g., "Your account will be locked unless you act now") or limited availability (e.g., "You must act before the offer expires") to pressure the victim into making hasty decisions.
- **Psychological Lever**: Victims feel compelled to act quickly, bypassing due diligence and rational thinking, which can lead to mistakes such as providing personal information or clicking on malicious links.

3. Crafting Effective Social Engineering Attacks Using Psychology

3.1 Tailoring the Attack to the Target

- Successful social engineering attacks often involve researching the target thoroughly to understand their psychological vulnerabilities. This can include studying their job role, interests, daily routines, and social interactions. Once these elements are understood, attackers can exploit them more effectively.
- **Example**: If an employee is known to be helpful or generous, an attacker might craft a pretext offering assistance or asking for a favor, knowing the victim will feel compelled to comply.

3.2 Building Rapport

- Attackers often engage in small talk or flattering behavior to establish a connection with the target. This behavior lowers the target's defenses and increases the likelihood of compliance.
- **Example**: An attacker might pretend to be a new employee or a contractor, offering compliments or asking for help to build a friendly relationship before attempting to gain sensitive information.

3.3 Exploiting Emotions

- Emotions like fear, greed, and empathy are powerful motivators. Social engineers often create scenarios that trigger emotional responses in their targets, making them more likely to act impulsively.
- **Fear**: The attacker may threaten consequences (e.g., an account being locked) to induce panic.
- **Greed**: The attacker might present an offer that seems too good to be true, such as a free vacation or a financial bonus.
- **Empathy**: The attacker may impersonate someone in need (e.g., a coworker having an emergency) to invoke compassion and prompt the victim to act without questioning.

3.4 Creating a Sense of Legitimacy

- Attackers often seek to enhance their perceived legitimacy by using official-sounding language, mimicking company policies, or employing authoritative communication channels like email or phone calls.
- **Example**: Using email signatures, company logos, or pretending to be from trusted departments (IT, HR, etc.) enhances the attacker's credibility.

4. Real-World Social Engineering Attack Example:

Scenario: An attacker impersonates an IT support technician and calls an employee, claiming there is an urgent security patch that needs to be applied immediately. The attacker uses official-sounding language, provides specific details about the employee's workstation, and pressures them to install remote access software to complete the update.

Psychological Tactics:

- **Authority**: The attacker poses as a trusted figure from the IT department.
- **Urgency**: The immediate need for action puts the target under pressure to comply quickly.
- **Reciprocity**: The attacker offers assistance by "helping" with the installation, making the victim feel obligated to trust them.

5. Defensive Measures Against Exploiting Psychology

5.1 Awareness and Training

- Regular training on social engineering tactics can help employees recognize psychological manipulation and resist the urge to comply with suspicious requests. Training should cover key psychological principles such as authority, reciprocity, and urgency.
- **Simulations**: Conducting simulated phishing and pretexting attacks as part of ongoing training can help employees recognize real threats in a safe environment.

5.2 Verifying Requests

- Establish a policy of verification for all sensitive requests, especially those involving financial transactions, account access, or privileged information. Employees should be encouraged to confirm the legitimacy of any request through independent channels, such as directly calling the purported source.
- **Two-Factor Authentication**: Ensure that critical systems require more than just a password, such as multi-factor authentication (MFA), to add another layer of protection.

5.3 Implementing Security Controls

- Use tools like email filters and firewalls to block phishing attempts and prevent malicious links or attachments from reaching employees.
- **Identity and Access Management (IAM):** Implement least-privilege access controls and role-based access to limit the impact of successful attacks.

Exploiting human psychology is at the heart of many successful social engineering attacks. By understanding the psychological principles of trust, authority, reciprocity, and urgency, attackers can manipulate their victims into making critical mistakes. To protect against these tactics, organizations must invest in employee awareness programs, implement strong verification processes, and utilize technical security measures to mitigate the risks posed by social engineering. The more an organization can train its people to recognize these psychological cues, the less vulnerable they will be to manipulation.

11. Collaboration with Blue Teams

Effective red teaming goes beyond just testing systems—it involves working with blue teams to strengthen defenses and build a more resilient security posture. This chapter focuses on the benefits and techniques of collaboration between red and blue teams, emphasizing the concept of purple teaming, where both offensive and defensive security professionals work together to identify weaknesses and improve detection and response capabilities. You'll learn how to structure engagements that provide actionable insights, communicate findings clearly, and foster a culture of continuous improvement. By understanding how to collaborate effectively, you'll help organizations build stronger, more adaptive security operations.

11.1 The Benefits of Purple Teaming Exercises

Purple teaming is an approach to cybersecurity that fosters collaboration between Red Teams (offensive security experts) and Blue Teams (defenders of the network) to improve an organization's overall security posture. Rather than working in isolation, both teams work together to simulate real-world attacks and defenses, creating a dynamic environment where both sides learn from each other. This chapter delves into the key benefits of purple teaming exercises, examining how this collaborative approach enhances security awareness, improves defense strategies, and strengthens the organization's overall resilience.

1. Bridging the Gap Between Offensive and Defensive Teams

The primary benefit of purple teaming is the creation of a feedback loop between the Red Team, which tests vulnerabilities, and the Blue Team, which defends against them. In traditional Red Teaming and Blue Teaming exercises, both teams work independently, which can sometimes lead to miscommunication or missed opportunities for improvement.

1.1 Real-Time Collaboration

- In purple teaming, Red and Blue Teams work together in real-time, with Red Teams launching simulated attacks and Blue Teams defending against them. This direct interaction fosters a deeper understanding of attack strategies and defensive techniques.

- The immediate feedback loop allows Blue Team members to adapt their defensive strategies quickly and improve their skills in real-time.

1.2 Knowledge Transfer

- Purple teaming promotes knowledge sharing between the teams. Red Team members share insights into attack techniques, while Blue Team members provide feedback on defensive mechanisms.
- This cross-pollination of expertise helps both teams refine their skills and gain a comprehensive understanding of both attack and defense.

2. Identifying and Addressing Gaps in Security Posture

One of the most significant advantages of purple teaming exercises is the ability to identify and address security gaps in a more dynamic and realistic way than traditional assessments.

2.1 Continuous Improvement of Defensive Strategies

- By simulating realistic attacks, Red Teams can expose vulnerabilities that might not be apparent during routine security assessments. Working together, Red and Blue Teams can identify weak spots in the organization's security infrastructure and immediately work on patching or mitigating those vulnerabilities.
- This iterative approach ensures that defensive strategies remain relevant and up-to-date with the evolving threat landscape.

2.2 Improving Detection and Response Times

- Purple teaming exercises are ideal for testing the efficiency of detection systems such as Security Information and Event Management (SIEM) and Intrusion Detection Systems (IDS). By launching simulated attacks, Red Teams provide a way to test how quickly and accurately the Blue Team can detect and respond to threats.
- This real-time testing improves the Blue Team's ability to detect threats, analyze them, and respond effectively, reducing detection times and enhancing response procedures.

3. Enhancing Communication and Coordination Between Teams

Effective communication between Red and Blue Teams is vital for improving security response times and coordination during real-world attacks. Purple teaming emphasizes the importance of collaboration, helping both teams better understand each other's roles and tactics.

3.1 Breaking Down Silos

- Often, Red and Blue Teams operate in separate silos, which can lead to misunderstandings and inefficiencies. Purple teaming fosters a shared understanding of objectives and strategies, breaking down these silos and promoting open dialogue.
- When both teams understand each other's methodologies and goals, they can collaborate more effectively during security incidents, making response efforts faster and more coordinated.

3.2 Improved Incident Response

- Through regular purple teaming exercises, Blue Teams can fine-tune their incident response protocols by working directly with Red Teams to identify how attacks unfold and where defense mechanisms fall short.
- Real-time collaboration enables both teams to develop and refine response strategies, ensuring that in the event of a real attack, the organization's defenses and response protocols are well-coordinated and efficient.

4. Training and Skill Enhancement

Purple teaming exercises provide an excellent opportunity for ongoing training and skill development for both Red and Blue Teams. By collaborating in a structured environment, both teams can sharpen their technical skills and learn new tactics, techniques, and procedures (TTPs).

4.1 Hands-On Training

- Purple teaming exercises give both teams the chance to practice real-world scenarios in a controlled environment. Red Teams can experiment with new attack vectors, while Blue Teams can test their defenses against evolving threats.
- This hands-on experience helps both teams become more adept at their roles and builds confidence in their ability to deal with real-world cyber threats.

4.2 Exposure to New Attack Techniques and Defense Mechanisms

- As Red Teams develop new tactics, the Blue Team learns to recognize these techniques and prepares defenses to counter them. Likewise, Red Teams are exposed to the latest defensive technologies and practices, allowing them to craft more sophisticated attacks.
- Both teams stay up-to-date with the latest cybersecurity trends, helping the organization stay ahead of emerging threats.

5. More Effective Use of Security Tools

Purple teaming allows for the testing and fine-tuning of security tools used by the Blue Team, including firewalls, intrusion detection systems, endpoint protection software, and more.

5.1 Fine-Tuning Defensive Tools

- By working alongside Red Teams, Blue Teams can better understand how their security tools perform under attack conditions. They can optimize these tools based on real-time feedback, ensuring that detection capabilities are enhanced, and defensive strategies are more effective.
- This includes configuring systems to better flag malicious activity, improving endpoint protection strategies, and ensuring the SIEM is properly tuned to detect specific threat patterns.

5.2 Attack Tools and Techniques

- Red Teams benefit from purple teaming exercises by gaining insight into how defensive tools interact with their attacks. This insight helps them develop more effective bypass techniques, which, in turn, improves their ability to simulate real-world attacks.
- By testing and refining their own attack techniques in collaboration with Blue Teams, Red Teams gain a better understanding of how attacks can be detected and mitigated, allowing them to craft more realistic simulations for training.

6. Building a Proactive Cybersecurity Culture

One of the most long-lasting benefits of purple teaming is the cultivation of a proactive cybersecurity culture within an organization. Purple teaming encourages collaboration and continuous learning, which can become a core part of the organization's security mindset.

6.1 Strengthening Collaboration Across Departments

- While purple teaming often involves Red and Blue Teams, it can extend to other departments within the organization, such as IT, HR, and legal teams. By engaging these departments, purple teaming fosters a broader, more collaborative approach to security.
- Engaging multiple departments ensures that everyone understands the role they play in maintaining security and that the entire organization is working together to mitigate threats.

6.2 Increasing Security Awareness

- Purple teaming exercises help raise awareness of security risks among employees. As Red and Blue Teams work together to identify potential attack vectors and defenses, employees across the organization become more educated about the types of threats they may encounter.
- Regular purple teaming activities help shift the organizational mindset from reactive to proactive, with employees continuously assessing their own roles in protecting the company from cyber threats.

Purple teaming exercises offer a unique and highly effective way to strengthen an organization's cybersecurity posture by encouraging collaboration, enhancing communication, and continuously improving both offensive and defensive strategies. Through these exercises, organizations gain the ability to identify security gaps, improve detection and response times, and ensure their security tools are operating at optimal effectiveness. Most importantly, purple teaming fosters a culture of continuous learning and adaptation, empowering both Red and Blue Teams to stay ahead of ever-evolving cyber threats. As the threat landscape becomes more complex, purple teaming will play a pivotal role in enabling organizations to build a robust, proactive defense against cyberattacks.

11.2 Conducting Adversary Simulations Together

Adversary simulations, commonly known as Red Team exercises, are a critical element in assessing an organization's security posture by mimicking real-world attacks. However, when Red and Blue Teams work together in adversary simulations, it transforms the process into a collaborative learning experience known as Purple Teaming. In this chapter, we will explore the benefits of conducting adversary simulations together, the steps involved, and how both teams can leverage this approach to enhance their effectiveness, improve defenses, and better prepare for real-world cyberattacks.

1. The Purpose and Benefits of Adversary Simulations

Adversary simulations are designed to test the security measures in place and simulate realistic attack scenarios that an organization could face. Traditionally, Red Teams simulate offensive attacks, while Blue Teams focus on defending against these attacks. The shift to purple teaming—where both teams collaborate—creates a more dynamic environment that allows for mutual learning, continuous feedback, and faster improvements in cybersecurity defenses.

1.1 Testing Real-World Attack Scenarios

- Adversary simulations allow teams to test the organization's ability to defend against the latest threats, such as Advanced Persistent Threats (APTs), insider threats, and zero-day exploits.
- In a purple teaming setup, the Red Team emulates these sophisticated attacks while the Blue Team defends, simulating a real-world attack scenario that provides actionable insights into how well the organization is prepared.

1.2 Improving Detection and Response

- Through adversary simulations, both teams can assess and improve the effectiveness of detection systems like Intrusion Detection Systems (IDS), Security Information and Event Management (SIEM) tools, and endpoint protection.
- This collaboration ensures that Blue Teams are not only identifying and mitigating threats more effectively but also adapting to the changing tactics used by adversaries in real time.

2. Collaborative Attack-Defense Cycle: How It Works

In adversary simulations conducted with a Purple Teaming approach, the exercise revolves around a collaborative cycle where the Red Team actively tests defenses, and the Blue Team counters these actions. Instead of working in isolation, the two teams share their findings, making this exercise a continuous loop of attack and defense.

2.1 Real-Time Attack Simulations

- The Red Team conducts attack simulations with the intent of exploiting vulnerabilities, while the Blue Team must detect, respond to, and thwart these attacks in real-time.
- The immediate collaboration between the teams ensures that Blue Team members can practice threat detection, incident response, and recovery in a controlled, real-time environment, which improves response times and effectiveness during actual attacks.

2.2 Feedback Loop for Improvement

- One of the most significant advantages of conducting adversary simulations together is the constant feedback loop that takes place during the exercise.
- Red Team's Feedback to Blue Team: The Red Team can provide immediate feedback on weaknesses in the Blue Team's detection mechanisms or defensive strategies.
- Blue Team's Feedback to Red Team: Blue Teams can inform Red Teams of successful defenses or detection strategies that thwarted the simulated attack, giving the Red Team an opportunity to refine their tactics and improve their methods.

2.3 Adjusting Tactics Mid-Simulation

The ability for both teams to adjust tactics mid-simulation based on real-time findings ensures that the simulation remains realistic and dynamic. If the Blue Team successfully detects a particular attack vector or technique, the Red Team may adapt their strategy to simulate a different attack, further testing the Blue Team's adaptability and knowledge.

3. Phases of Conducting Adversary Simulations Together

There are several phases involved in conducting adversary simulations with collaboration between the Red and Blue Teams. These phases ensure that both sides have clear objectives and can learn from each other's tactics and responses.

3.1 Pre-Simulation Planning

- **Defining Objectives**: Before starting the simulation, both teams must agree on the scope of the attack and defense objectives. The goals of the simulation might include testing specific vulnerabilities, validating defense strategies, or measuring the Blue Team's ability to detect and respond to a specific attack.

- **Rules of Engagement**: It is essential to define the rules of engagement to prevent unnecessary damage or disruption. Both teams should agree on acceptable targets, boundaries, and reporting structures.
- **Simulating Realistic Threats**: The Red Team should ensure that the attack scenarios mimic realistic threats based on the organization's threat model, considering the tools, techniques, and procedures (TTPs) used by actual adversaries.

3.2 Attack and Defense Execution

- During this phase, the Red Team launches simulated attacks, and the Blue Team defends. The Red Team may employ various tactics, including phishing, exploiting vulnerabilities, lateral movement, and privilege escalation techniques, while the Blue Team must detect, mitigate, and respond to these attacks.
- The collaboration should allow the Blue Team to respond dynamically. If a defensive strategy fails, the Red Team provides immediate feedback, while the Blue Team can adjust its defenses and attempt countermeasures to neutralize the attack.

3.3 After-Action Review and Knowledge Sharing

- Once the simulation is complete, both teams engage in a debriefing session where they discuss the effectiveness of their strategies and responses.
- The Red Team will share insights into how they managed to bypass defenses and which tactics were most successful. The Blue Team will discuss what defenses worked and where improvements are needed.
- This after-action review is critical for refining both offensive and defensive techniques, fostering a culture of continuous improvement and learning.

4. Skills and Tools Enhanced Through Collaboration

Purple teaming exercises provide an opportunity for both teams to enhance their skills and refine their tools and techniques in a real-world environment. The collaborative nature of adversary simulations strengthens not only individual skills but also teamwork and coordination.

4.1 Red Team Skill Enhancement

- Red Teams benefit from real-time feedback from the Blue Team on how their attacks are detected and mitigated. This allows Red Teams to refine their methods and adapt to evolving defensive mechanisms, ensuring their tactics remain relevant and effective.

- Collaboration also allows Red Teams to gain a deeper understanding of how defensive tools work, enabling them to devise more advanced attack strategies that can bypass detection.

4.2 Blue Team Skill Enhancement

- Blue Teams benefit by practicing real-time incident detection and response under pressure. In collaboration with Red Teams, they are exposed to advanced attack strategies and tools, which they can use to sharpen their defenses and increase their readiness for actual cyberattacks.
- In addition, Blue Teams gain firsthand knowledge of the weaknesses in their security tools and processes, which they can improve based on insights gathered during the simulation.

4.3 Tool Optimization

- During purple team exercises, both teams gain valuable insights into the strengths and weaknesses of their respective tools. Red Teams often use advanced attack frameworks (e.g., Metasploit, Cobalt Strike), while Blue Teams deploy detection tools (e.g., SIEM systems, firewalls, endpoint detection and response (EDR)).
- By seeing how these tools perform in real-time against simulated attacks, both teams can fine-tune their tools and processes to ensure optimal performance during actual security incidents.

5. Benefits for the Organization

While the collaboration between Red and Blue Teams is central to purple teaming, there are also substantial organizational benefits that stem from these adversary simulations.

5.1 Strengthening Organizational Resilience

- Purple team exercises help identify and mitigate security gaps in the organization's infrastructure, making it more resilient to real-world attacks. The continuous back-and-forth between offensive and defensive teams builds a stronger security posture.
- By fostering continuous learning, organizations can ensure they remain agile and responsive to emerging threats, reducing their exposure to risks.

5.2 Developing a Unified Security Culture

- One of the key organizational benefits of adversary simulations is the creation of a unified security culture where Red and Blue Teams are aligned in their common goal: protecting the organization from adversaries.
- Purple teaming emphasizes cooperation over competition, breaking down silos and encouraging communication and knowledge-sharing between traditionally separate security functions.

Adversary simulations conducted through purple teaming exercises offer significant advantages over traditional, isolated Red and Blue Team engagements. By working together, both teams gain a more comprehensive understanding of attack techniques and defense strategies, improving the organization's security posture as a whole. The collaborative nature of these exercises fosters an environment of continuous learning and adaptation, where both offensive and defensive techniques are refined in real time. As cyber threats become increasingly sophisticated, the ability to simulate and respond to realistic attacks in a dynamic, collaborative environment is a key component of maintaining a robust, resilient cybersecurity defense.

11.3 Building Resilience: Teaching Blue Teams to Defend

Building a resilient defense against cyber threats is one of the most critical objectives for any organization. While Red Teams often focus on exploiting vulnerabilities, Blue Teams are tasked with defending systems and networks from these attacks. In the context of Purple Teaming, the role of the Blue Team is not just to respond to simulated attacks but also to actively learn, adapt, and strengthen their defenses in real-time. This chapter explores how Purple Team exercises can be used as a training ground to teach Blue Teams the essential skills, strategies, and mindset required to defend against both known and unknown cyber threats, ultimately enhancing organizational resilience.

1. The Role of Blue Teams in Cyber Defense

Blue Teams are the backbone of an organization's cybersecurity efforts. Their primary responsibility is to detect, prevent, and respond to security incidents. However, to be effective in this role, Blue Teams must constantly evolve their defense strategies in response to an ever-changing threat landscape. The collaborative nature of Purple Teaming is crucial in building a defensive culture that fosters resilience, agility, and continuous improvement.

1.1 The Defensive Mindset

- Blue Teams must develop a mindset that prioritizes proactive defense rather than a reactive approach. In an increasingly complex cyber environment, the ability to anticipate potential threats and identify weaknesses in advance is essential.
- By working closely with Red Teams during Purple Team exercises, Blue Teams gain firsthand exposure to sophisticated attack techniques and learn how to counter them before they are ever deployed in the real world.

1.2 The Evolving Threat Landscape

- Modern cyber threats are diverse and ever-evolving. Attackers use a wide range of methods—ranging from phishing and social engineering to sophisticated zero-day exploits and ransomware attacks. Blue Teams need to stay ahead of these threats by constantly adapting their detection and response strategies.
- Purple Team exercises help simulate a variety of attack scenarios, allowing Blue Teams to practice defending against both common and advanced threats. This continuous exposure sharpens their skills and improves their readiness to face emerging risks.

2. Teaching the Fundamentals of Defense

To build a resilient Blue Team, it is essential to teach them the fundamental concepts of defense, detection, and response. In a Purple Teaming exercise, both teams collaborate to ensure that Blue Teams gain hands-on experience in defending against real-world attacks while learning the best practices to strengthen their defenses.

2.1 Network and System Monitoring

- A key element of Blue Team defense is the ability to effectively monitor network traffic, endpoints, and logs for signs of compromise. In a Purple Team setting, Blue Teams learn how to use various monitoring tools—such as Security Information and Event Management (SIEM) systems, Intrusion Detection Systems (IDS), and Endpoint Detection and Response (EDR) tools—to identify suspicious activity.
- Through Purple Team collaboration, Blue Teams learn how to fine-tune their detection systems to recognize indicators of compromise (IOCs) and anomalous behavior, increasing their ability to spot potential threats early.

2.2 Threat Hunting and Detection

- Threat hunting is the process of proactively searching for signs of malicious activity within the network, rather than waiting for alerts to be triggered. Purple Team exercises provide Blue Teams with the opportunity to practice threat hunting by actively searching for attack vectors, such as lateral movement or persistence mechanisms, that may evade detection tools.
- Red Teams simulate advanced attacks during Purple Team exercises, providing Blue Teams with real-world context to improve their threat-hunting skills and ensuring they can identify malicious activity even when it's disguised.

2.3 Incident Response and Mitigation

- Once an attack is detected, the Blue Team must respond quickly and effectively to minimize damage and contain the threat. Purple Teaming allows Blue Teams to practice real-time incident response, from identifying the attack's origin and scope to containing the threat and eradicating it from the network.
- In collaboration with Red Teams, Blue Teams learn to develop and refine incident response plans, improve their communication strategies during a crisis, and take swift, decisive action to neutralize threats.

3. Advanced Defensive Techniques: Building Resilience to Advanced Attacks

While basic defense mechanisms are essential, Blue Teams must also be equipped to defend against advanced, persistent, and evolving cyber threats. Through Purple Team exercises, Blue Teams gain exposure to sophisticated attack techniques, enabling them to build the necessary skills to detect, respond to, and mitigate these types of threats.

3.1 Advanced Threat Detection

- Red Teams often use advanced techniques such as fileless malware, living off the land (LotL) attacks, and covert command-and-control (C2) channels to bypass traditional detection methods. Purple Teaming exercises give Blue Teams a chance to detect these complex techniques by testing their security tools and refining their detection strategies.
- For instance, Blue Teams learn to spot unusual network traffic patterns, unexpected PowerShell scripts, or anomalous application behavior that could indicate a sophisticated attack.

3.2 Behavioral Analysis and Anomaly Detection

- Traditional signature-based detection methods are becoming increasingly ineffective against advanced threats. To stay ahead of attackers, Blue Teams need to shift toward behavioral analysis, which focuses on recognizing unusual activities and patterns rather than relying on known attack signatures.
- Purple Team exercises teach Blue Teams how to leverage machine learning, anomaly detection systems, and heuristic analysis to identify attacks that may not match predefined patterns but still exhibit malicious behavior.

3.3 Resilience Building: Hardening Defenses

- Purple Teaming helps Blue Teams develop strategies to harden their defenses against known attack vectors and advanced techniques. By simulating attacks and learning how to mitigate them, Blue Teams can strengthen firewalls, intrusion prevention systems (IPS), access control policies, and patch management processes to reduce vulnerabilities.
- In addition, Blue Teams learn how to deploy defense-in-depth strategies, ensuring that multiple layers of security are in place to protect critical assets and prevent attackers from moving laterally through the network.

4. Responding to Emerging Threats in Real-Time

One of the most significant advantages of Purple Team exercises is the opportunity for Blue Teams to respond to attacks in real-time. These exercises allow defenders to practice and refine their response protocols, ensuring they are prepared for the latest tactics, techniques, and procedures (TTPs) used by attackers.

4.1 Rapid Adaptation and Agility

- Cyber attackers are always adapting and evolving their tactics to bypass defenses. To counter this, Blue Teams must be able to quickly adapt to new attack methods and change their defensive posture as needed.
- During Purple Team exercises, Blue Teams practice responding to a variety of tactics and scenarios, developing agility and flexibility in their approach to cybersecurity. This continuous learning helps Blue Teams stay prepared for unforeseen threats.

4.2 Threat Intelligence Sharing

- Another critical aspect of building resilience is the ability to incorporate external threat intelligence into the defensive strategy. Blue Teams learn how to integrate real-time threat intelligence feeds into their security tools, enhancing their ability to detect and respond to emerging threats.

- By working with Red Teams in Purple Team exercises, Blue Teams can understand the value of threat intelligence in detecting and mitigating attacks quickly.

5. Building a Collaborative Cybersecurity Culture

The effectiveness of a Blue Team depends not only on their individual skills but also on the strength of their collaboration with other teams within the organization. Purple Teaming promotes a collaborative cybersecurity culture that bridges the gap between offensive and defensive security.

5.1 Cross-Team Communication

- Purple Team exercises encourage open communication between the Red and Blue Teams, ensuring that lessons learned during simulations are shared across the organization. Blue Teams gain valuable insights into how attackers think and operate, while Red Teams benefit from understanding the challenges faced by defenders.
- This collaborative approach fosters mutual respect and encourages teamwork, both of which are essential for creating a unified defense against cyber threats.

5.2 Training Across the Organization

- Building resilience isn't limited to Blue Teams alone. Purple Teaming can extend beyond technical teams to include other departments, such as HR, legal, and operations. Blue Teams can educate these departments on how to recognize and respond to cyber threats, creating an organization-wide culture of security awareness.
- In the long term, this results in a more secure and resilient organization, as all employees become better equipped to detect and respond to cyber threats.

Building a resilient Blue Team is not just about acquiring technical skills but also about developing the mindset and strategies necessary to defend against an ever-evolving threat landscape. Purple Team exercises play a pivotal role in this by providing a collaborative environment where Blue Teams can practice, learn, and improve their defensive strategies in real-time. By teaching Blue Teams to respond to attacks effectively, improve their detection capabilities, and harden their defenses, organizations can build resilience against even the most sophisticated cyber threats. Through continuous learning, collaboration, and adaptation, Blue Teams become better prepared to defend their networks, ultimately strengthening the organization's overall cybersecurity posture.

11.4 Bridging Gaps Between Offense and Defense

In the world of cybersecurity, the divide between offensive (Red Team) and defensive (Blue Team) operations has traditionally been wide. The two teams often function in parallel tracks, each focusing on different objectives: Red Teams simulate attacks to identify vulnerabilities, while Blue Teams work tirelessly to defend the organization from those same threats. However, the gap between offense and defense must be bridged to create a unified, dynamic approach to cybersecurity. Purple Teaming serves as the ideal model for breaking down this divide and fostering collaboration between these two distinct yet complementary functions.

This chapter will explore the importance of bridging the gap between offensive and defensive operations, focusing on how Purple Team exercises can create a continuous feedback loop, where the lessons learned from each side inform the other. By fostering collaboration, mutual understanding, and a shared mission, organizations can develop a more holistic and adaptive cybersecurity strategy.

1. The Historical Divide: Offense vs. Defense

Historically, Red and Blue Teams have worked in isolation, each with their own set of objectives, methodologies, and tools.

Red Teams focus on offensive techniques such as penetration testing, social engineering, and advanced exploitation methods. Their role is to simulate the tactics, techniques, and procedures (TTPs) of adversaries, probing the network for weaknesses and attempting to breach security defenses.

Blue Teams, on the other hand, are tasked with defense. Their objective is to monitor, detect, respond to, and mitigate security incidents. They deploy firewalls, intrusion detection systems, endpoint protection, and other defensive tools to protect the organization's assets.

The problem arises when the findings of Red Teams and the actions of Blue Teams are siloed. Red Teams might discover vulnerabilities without effectively communicating those weaknesses to Blue Teams, leaving the organization at risk. Similarly, Blue Teams may be unaware of the real-world attack techniques employed by adversaries, leading to gaps in detection and response. As cyber threats grow more sophisticated, this divide becomes increasingly problematic, especially in fast-moving environments where timely communication and collaboration are essential.

2. Purple Teaming: The Key to Bridging the Gap

Purple Teaming is a collaborative approach designed to bridge the divide between Red and Blue Teams. It emphasizes continuous feedback and joint efforts, encouraging the two teams to work together, share knowledge, and learn from each other in real-time. In a Purple Team environment, Red and Blue Teams interact directly during exercises, with the goal of improving the organization's security posture through mutual understanding and cooperation.

2.1 Shared Objectives

The primary objective of Purple Teaming is to improve an organization's overall security by aligning the goals of the offensive and defensive teams. While Red Teams focus on exploiting vulnerabilities and identifying weaknesses, Blue Teams concentrate on detecting, preventing, and mitigating attacks. The collaboration between the two teams is driven by a shared goal of improving defenses, making security more resilient, and ultimately reducing the risk of successful attacks.

2.2 Real-Time Feedback Loop

In a traditional Red Team exercise, attackers work in isolation, launching an attack and presenting their findings to the Blue Team once the exercise is complete. However, in a Purple Team exercise, feedback is continuous. Red Teams provide real-time guidance to Blue Teams during simulated attacks, helping them recognize weaknesses and adjust their defenses as the exercise progresses. This feedback loop accelerates learning and allows Blue Teams to refine their detection and response capabilities in response to evolving attack techniques.

2.3 Continuous Improvement

Purple Teaming fosters a culture of continuous improvement. Rather than waiting for periodic assessments or annual penetration tests, organizations can integrate offensive and defensive operations in an ongoing, iterative process. As Red Teams uncover new vulnerabilities, Blue Teams can immediately address them, learn new techniques for detection and response, and adapt their strategies based on the latest tactics employed by attackers. Over time, this constant evolution strengthens the organization's overall security resilience.

3. Building Mutual Understanding Between Red and Blue Teams

One of the biggest challenges in cybersecurity is ensuring that both Red and Blue Teams understand each other's perspectives and challenges. Each team has a distinct role and skill set, and without effective communication and collaboration, they may be working at cross purposes.

3.1 Red Teaming from a Defender's Perspective

For Red Teams to be effective in helping Blue Teams improve defenses, they must approach attacks from the mindset of defenders. Understanding how security teams monitor systems, detect threats, and respond to incidents is crucial. By understanding Blue Team challenges, Red Teams can simulate more realistic attack scenarios that mimic the tactics used by real-world attackers.

For example, when performing phishing attacks, Red Teams can craft emails and social engineering scenarios that reflect the actual types of attacks that Blue Teams might encounter in their environment. This gives Blue Teams the opportunity to fine-tune their detection strategies and response plans based on real-world intelligence.

3.2 Blue Teaming from an Attacker's Perspective

Likewise, Blue Teams benefit from gaining insight into how attackers think and operate. By collaborating with Red Teams, Blue Teams can better understand the tools and techniques employed by attackers, the stages of an attack, and how to detect indicators of compromise (IOCs). This perspective helps defenders anticipate attack strategies and improve the organization's defensive layers.

Blue Teams also learn how attackers exploit vulnerabilities, bypass security controls, and evade detection. This knowledge is invaluable for improving the overall effectiveness of defense mechanisms, including firewall rules, intrusion prevention systems (IPS), endpoint protection, and monitoring processes.

4. Shared Tools and Techniques for Collaboration

In a Purple Team environment, Red and Blue Teams not only share information but also tools and techniques to improve their collaborative efforts. Modern attack and defense tools can facilitate joint exercises, and many tools are designed to support both offensive and defensive activities.

4.1 Threat Intelligence Sharing

Purple Teaming encourages the exchange of threat intelligence between Red and Blue Teams. Red Teams provide valuable information on emerging threats, such as new malware strains or exploit techniques. Blue Teams, in turn, share data from their monitoring systems, including logs, alerts, and incident reports, which can help Red Teams identify patterns or refine attack strategies.

Effective threat intelligence sharing ensures that both teams are working with the most up-to-date information, improving the organization's ability to respond to emerging threats and ensuring that defensive measures are adapted to match the latest attack techniques.

4.2 Simulating Real-World Attacks

The collaboration between Red and Blue Teams allows for the creation of real-world attack simulations. These exercises are not limited to basic penetration testing but encompass a wide range of attack techniques, from phishing campaigns and network exploits to advanced persistent threats (APTs) and social engineering tactics. In a Purple Team environment, both Red and Blue Teams are involved in crafting realistic attack scenarios that closely resemble the kinds of threats organizations are facing today.

4.3 Automating Attack-Defense Simulations

In addition to manual Purple Team exercises, many organizations are increasingly leveraging automated platforms to simulate attacks and measure the effectiveness of defenses. These tools can simulate multiple attack scenarios simultaneously, giving both Red and Blue Teams insights into how their systems would respond under pressure. Automation also helps to scale the learning process, allowing organizations to run continuous simulations that provide both teams with regular feedback on their readiness.

5. Cultivating a Collaborative Cybersecurity Culture

The most significant benefit of bridging the gap between offense and defense is the development of a collaborative cybersecurity culture. In a collaborative culture, both Red and Blue Teams work toward the same overarching goal: to protect the organization from cyber threats. This shared mission promotes mutual respect, transparency, and trust between the teams.

5.1 Encouraging Open Communication

The foundation of effective Purple Teaming is open communication. By encouraging ongoing dialogue, Red and Blue Teams can discuss their methodologies, share insights, and provide constructive feedback. This transparency helps build trust between teams and improves overall effectiveness.

5.2 Collaborative Training

Another way to bridge the gap is by ensuring that both Red and Blue Teams are continuously learning from each other. Joint training sessions that involve both offensive and defensive tactics provide an excellent opportunity for cross-functional skill development. For example, Blue Teams can learn about the latest attack vectors and Red Teams can gain insight into new defensive strategies. Collaborative training enhances the overall skill set of both teams, ensuring they are always prepared for the next threat.

6. Conclusion: A Unified Approach to Cybersecurity

Bridging the gap between Red and Blue Teams is essential for creating a holistic and dynamic cybersecurity strategy. By adopting the Purple Teaming model, organizations can foster collaboration, mutual learning, and real-time feedback between offensive and defensive operations. This approach ensures that both Red and Blue Teams are working together toward a shared objective: improving the organization's security posture. Through continuous improvement, shared intelligence, and real-time exercises, organizations can develop a proactive, adaptive, and resilient defense strategy that is better prepared to handle the evolving cyber threat landscape.

12. Reporting and Legal Considerations

A red team's work is only as valuable as the insights it provides and how those insights are communicated. This chapter covers the crucial aspects of writing clear, actionable, and effective reports that not only highlight vulnerabilities but also offer solutions and remediation strategies. You'll learn how to structure your findings to make them impactful for both technical and executive audiences. Additionally, we'll explore the legal and ethical considerations of red teaming, including ensuring compliance with laws, managing sensitive data responsibly, and navigating the complex landscape of rules of engagement. Understanding these elements ensures that your work contributes to improving security without compromising legal or ethical standards.

12.1 Writing Effective Red Team Reports: Prioritizing Impact and Clarity

One of the most critical aspects of a successful Red Team engagement is the delivery of a clear, actionable, and well-structured report. After months of simulating sophisticated attacks, uncovering vulnerabilities, and testing security defenses, a Red Team's findings need to be communicated in a way that maximizes their impact and drives improvement in the organization's security posture. Writing effective reports requires not only technical proficiency but also the ability to present complex findings in a manner that can be understood and acted upon by various stakeholders, including technical teams, management, and non-technical decision-makers.

In this section, we will explore how to create impactful Red Team reports that strike the balance between technical detail and clarity, while prioritizing the most critical findings for immediate action. A well-written report serves not only as documentation of the engagement but also as a tool for improving security, guiding mitigation strategies, and fostering a culture of continuous improvement.

1. Structuring the Red Team Report: Key Sections

A Red Team report should follow a logical and structured format that ensures the findings are easy to follow and comprehend. While the precise structure may vary slightly depending on the organization or client, certain core sections should be included in every report. These sections provide clarity, context, and actionable insight, ensuring that the report delivers maximum value to its readers.

1.1 Executive Summary

The executive summary is the first section of the report, but it is often written last to ensure it accurately summarizes the key findings and recommendations. This section should provide an overview of the engagement, including:

- The scope of the engagement (i.e., what was tested and what was not).
- The overall risk or impact to the organization based on the findings.
- A high-level summary of critical vulnerabilities or successful attacks.
- Suggested actions or immediate priorities for the organization.

The executive summary should be concise, non-technical, and easy to read. Its goal is to inform senior leadership, non-technical stakeholders, or board members about the most significant risks and the overall effectiveness of their security defenses.

1.2 Scope and Methodology

This section provides transparency into how the Red Team conducted the engagement. It should clearly outline the scope of the exercise, including the systems, networks, applications, or processes that were tested. Additionally, the methodology section should explain the tactics, techniques, and procedures (TTPs) employed by the Red Team during the engagement, such as penetration testing, social engineering, phishing, or physical security testing.

This section helps readers understand the context of the findings and ensures that the Red Team's activities align with the agreed-upon rules of engagement and objectives. Providing details about the tools, frameworks, and exploit methods used also offers credibility to the findings.

1.3 Findings and Vulnerabilities

This is the core of the Red Team report and should include detailed descriptions of the vulnerabilities, attack paths, and successful exploits discovered during the engagement. For each finding, the report should answer the following:

- **What was the vulnerability?** A clear and concise explanation of the issue discovered.
- **How was it exploited?** A brief description of how the Red Team was able to exploit the vulnerability or weakness, including tools used or methods employed.

- **Risk and Impact**: The potential risk and impact to the organization if the vulnerability were to be exploited by a real-world attacker.
- **Evidence and Screenshots**: Where applicable, provide evidence, such as screenshots or logs, that demonstrate the existence of the vulnerability or successful attack.

This section should also prioritize the findings based on severity and likelihood, so that decision-makers can easily identify which vulnerabilities pose the most immediate risk to the organization.

1.4 Recommendations for Mitigation

After outlining the vulnerabilities and risks, the report should provide actionable recommendations for mitigation or remediation. These recommendations should be tailored to the organization's environment and should be realistic and feasible within the available resources. Key considerations for this section include:

- **Short-Term Mitigations**: These are immediate actions that can be taken to address high-risk vulnerabilities or prevent further exploitation. Examples include applying patches, modifying firewall rules, or disabling unnecessary services.
- **Long-Term Improvements**: This section focuses on broader security improvements, such as implementing multi-factor authentication, enhancing network segmentation, or improving employee training to mitigate social engineering risks.
- **Process or Policy Changes**: Recommendations on improving security processes or policies, such as reviewing access controls or conducting regular vulnerability assessments.

By including specific, actionable recommendations, the Red Team helps the organization take meaningful steps toward improving its security posture.

The conclusion of the Red Team report should summarize the overall findings, reiterate the most critical vulnerabilities and their potential impacts, and emphasize the importance of taking action. This section should reinforce the urgency of addressing the identified risks, while also acknowledging the strengths and positive security practices observed during the engagement.

2. Writing with Impact: Prioritizing Key Findings

A key principle of effective Red Team reporting is prioritization. Given that most organizations will not be able to fix every vulnerability identified immediately, Red Teams must provide guidance on which issues need to be addressed first. This is particularly important when reporting complex engagements with multiple findings.

2.1 Risk Rating Systems

To facilitate prioritization, many Red Teams use a standardized risk rating system, such as the Common Vulnerability Scoring System (CVSS) or custom scales developed by the Red Team or client. These ratings should take into account:

- **Severity**: The criticality of the vulnerability or exploit.
- **Likelihood**: The probability that the vulnerability could be exploited.
- **Impact**: The potential damage or consequences if the vulnerability is exploited.

By categorizing findings into risk levels (e.g., critical, high, medium, low), the Red Team helps the organization focus on the most important issues first. This rating system should be accompanied by clear explanations to ensure that the reasoning behind the prioritization is transparent.

2.2 Executive Focus

For executive stakeholders who may not have deep technical knowledge, it is essential to distill the technical findings into a narrative that highlights the most pressing business risks. In the executive summary and throughout the report, focus on the potential impact to the organization in terms of financial loss, reputational damage, legal implications, or compliance violations. Providing a clear business case for remediation helps senior leadership understand why addressing the vulnerabilities is critical for the organization's success.

2.3 Balancing Technical Detail with Readability

The body of the report should strike a balance between technical detail and readability. While security professionals will need the technical specifics to understand and address the findings, non-technical stakeholders may need higher-level summaries. Effective Red Team reports will therefore include:

Technical Appendices: For security experts, include appendices that provide additional technical detail, such as proof-of-concept (PoC) code, detailed logs, or a list of tools used.

High-Level Summaries: For non-technical readers, provide summaries of each finding, avoiding excessive jargon and focusing on the potential impact of each issue.

The goal is to ensure that all stakeholders can digest and act on the report's findings, regardless of their technical expertise.

3. Communicating Complex Findings Clearly

Clear communication is vital for ensuring that the Red Team's findings lead to effective action. Use concise language and avoid unnecessary complexity in the report. In particular:

- **Avoid Overloading with Technical Jargon**: Use plain language whenever possible and define technical terms when they are unavoidable.
- **Provide Context**: Help readers understand why a particular vulnerability or exploit is critical by describing its real-world implications, including potential consequences like data breaches or system downtime.
- **Visual Aids**: Where appropriate, include diagrams, flowcharts, or visual representations of attack paths, which can simplify complex ideas and help illustrate the attack chain.

4. Conclusion: The Role of the Red Team Report

Red Team reports play a pivotal role in driving security improvements within an organization. A well-crafted report not only highlights vulnerabilities but also provides clear, actionable recommendations for mitigation, ultimately helping the organization improve its defenses. By prioritizing impact, clarity, and conciseness, Red Team reports can foster a culture of continuous improvement, turning each engagement into an opportunity to strengthen the organization's security posture against evolving threats.

12.2 Communicating Risks to Stakeholders and Decision-Makers

Effectively communicating risk is one of the most crucial aspects of a Red Team engagement. After a comprehensive series of simulated attacks, a Red Team report will typically outline vulnerabilities and tactics that pose potential threats to an organization's security. However, these technical findings need to be translated in a way that resonates with a wide range of stakeholders, from C-suite executives to non-technical decision-makers. The primary goal is to ensure that the risks identified are understood, prioritized, and acted upon by the appropriate individuals within the organization.

In this section, we will discuss strategies for communicating risk to various stakeholders, how to frame the potential impact in a way that aligns with business objectives, and the importance of fostering an environment where security is seen as a shared responsibility.

1. Understanding the Audience: Tailoring the Message

The first step in effective risk communication is understanding the audience. Different stakeholders will have varying levels of technical knowledge, and their concerns and decision-making priorities will differ. As a Red Teamer, it's essential to tailor the message for each group to ensure it's received and understood in the right context.

1.1 Executives and C-Suite

C-suite executives and senior leadership are primarily concerned with the business risks, not the technical specifics of the vulnerabilities. These stakeholders often focus on high-level outcomes, such as:

- **Financial impact**: How would an exploit impact revenue, brand value, and regulatory fines?
- **Reputation damage**: What would be the consequences for the organization's reputation if a successful attack were to occur?
- **Operational disruption**: Would the identified vulnerabilities result in a breach that disrupts business continuity or productivity?

When presenting findings to executives, focus on the business impact rather than the technical details. The goal is to connect the Red Team's findings with potential financial, reputational, and operational consequences. It's crucial to frame the risk in terms of probability and impact: "There is a 70% chance that this vulnerability could be exploited, leading to a potential loss of $5 million in revenue."

1.2 Technical Teams (IT, Security Engineers, SOC)

Security professionals and technical teams will likely have the expertise to understand the technical details of vulnerabilities and exploits. For these stakeholders, the focus should shift to:

- **Mitigation strategies**: Detailed instructions on how to fix or remediate the vulnerabilities found.
- **Impact on system integrity**: How the discovered vulnerabilities could be leveraged by an adversary to compromise the system, escalate privileges, or exfiltrate sensitive data.
- **Tactics, Techniques, and Procedures (TTPs):** A deeper dive into how the Red Team executed the attack and how it might be mitigated or detected.

Technical teams will appreciate a detailed breakdown of the attack vectors and a thorough analysis of how vulnerabilities can be exploited, allowing them to take immediate steps toward remediating the issues.

1.3 Business and Non-Technical Stakeholders

Business decision-makers, including legal, compliance, and HR teams, will likely have little to no technical knowledge of cybersecurity. These stakeholders are more concerned with the business continuity, legal implications, and regulatory compliance related to security risks. When addressing these stakeholders:

- **Compliance risks**: Highlight whether the vulnerabilities could result in non-compliance with industry regulations such as GDPR, HIPAA, or PCI-DSS.
- **Operational risks**: Explain how security weaknesses might affect the day-to-day operations, such as data loss, system downtime, or unauthorized access to critical business assets.
- **Legal ramifications**: Describe the potential for data breaches, intellectual property theft, or lawsuits resulting from the exploitation of vulnerabilities.

For this audience, you'll need to focus on risk quantification in business terms—how vulnerabilities could result in legal exposure, loss of customers, or non-compliance penalties.

2. Framing Risks in Terms of Business Impact

When communicating risks to stakeholders, especially non-technical decision-makers, it's crucial to frame vulnerabilities and exploits in terms of business impact rather than the technical details of the vulnerabilities themselves. This can significantly improve the likelihood of gaining support for necessary mitigation efforts.

2.1 Risk Rating and Prioritization

Red Team reports often include a risk rating system that categorizes vulnerabilities based on severity (e.g., critical, high, medium, low) and the likelihood of exploitation. It's important to explain the methodology behind the ratings and provide clear justifications for why certain risks are higher priority than others.

For example, if a critical vulnerability allows attackers to escalate privileges within the network, it should be communicated as a high-risk, high-priority issue. Conversely, lower-risk vulnerabilities should be communicated with the understanding that they might not have immediate consequences but still warrant attention over time.

A risk matrix, using a scale from 1 to 10 or "low", "medium", and "high" categories, can be an effective way to prioritize vulnerabilities and simplify the communication of risk levels.

2.2 Connecting Risks to Business Outcomes

The primary concern for decision-makers is how these vulnerabilities could impact the business. Red Teams should help stakeholders understand the potential outcomes in terms of the organization's strategic goals, including:

- **Revenue loss**: "Exploiting this vulnerability could enable attackers to steal sensitive financial data, potentially resulting in a loss of $X in revenue or fines due to regulatory violations."
- **Brand and reputation damage**: "A breach stemming from this vulnerability could make the company a target for media attention, damaging trust with customers and partners."
- **Operational disruption**: "Exploitation of this vulnerability could lead to a ransomware attack, bringing business operations to a halt and disrupting critical services."

By framing the risk in terms of what it means for the organization's bottom line, Red Teams can drive home the importance of addressing security issues promptly.

2.3 Using Scenarios and Real-World Analogies

To make the risks more relatable to non-technical stakeholders, it can be helpful to use real-world analogies or scenarios. For example:

- "Think of this vulnerability like an unlocked door to your server room. If attackers gain access, they could steal valuable company data or plant malware that could cause long-term damage."

- "This vulnerability is similar to leaving a key under the doormat. While it might seem harmless, it could allow attackers to gain unauthorized access to your most sensitive information."

These scenarios help bridge the knowledge gap and create a sense of urgency around risk mitigation, even for individuals who may not fully understand the technical nuances.

3. The Importance of Ongoing Communication and Collaboration

Effective risk communication doesn't end with the report delivery. Continuous dialogue between Red Teams, stakeholders, and decision-makers is critical to ensure that identified risks are addressed and that the organization is moving toward a stronger security posture.

3.1 Regular Updates and Reporting

After the initial report, Red Teams should offer to conduct follow-up meetings or presentations with stakeholders to provide updates on remediation efforts. This ensures that all parties remain engaged and that the company is actively addressing risks. It can also help to communicate interim steps the organization is taking to mitigate the identified vulnerabilities while working on long-term solutions.

3.2 Aligning Security with Organizational Goals

Security should be viewed as a critical enabler of business success, rather than an isolated IT concern. By consistently showing how security measures tie back to the organization's objectives—whether through protecting customer data, ensuring regulatory compliance, or maintaining operational continuity—Red Teams can position themselves as vital partners in the organization's long-term success.

4. Conclusion: Building a Security-Conscious Culture

The key to effective risk communication is not just informing decision-makers of risks but fostering an ongoing, collaborative relationship between technical teams and business leaders. By clearly articulating the potential consequences of vulnerabilities in terms that resonate with non-technical stakeholders and framing the conversation around business impact, Red Teams can play an important role in driving positive change across an organization. This approach ensures that security becomes an integral part of organizational decision-making, ultimately contributing to a more resilient and secure environment.

12.3 Legal and Ethical Boundaries in Red Teaming

Red teaming plays a crucial role in strengthening an organization's security posture, but it also involves significant ethical and legal considerations. Red teamers simulate real-world cyberattacks to identify vulnerabilities, weaknesses, and blind spots within an organization's defenses. However, these activities often involve actions that could potentially harm the organization's systems, compromise sensitive data, or cause operational disruption if not properly controlled. Therefore, it is essential that Red Team engagements adhere to legal guidelines, ethical standards, and rules of engagement (ROE) to ensure that their actions do not result in unintended consequences or legal ramifications.

This section explores the key legal and ethical boundaries that Red Team professionals must navigate, including how to conduct security testing responsibly, the importance of obtaining proper authorization, and ensuring compliance with local and international laws.

1. Legal Considerations in Red Teaming

Legal boundaries are one of the most significant concerns for Red Teams. Unauthorized penetration testing or simulated attacks can be illegal and can lead to criminal charges, financial penalties, or damage to the organization. It is therefore critical to ensure that Red Team activities are conducted in a controlled, transparent, and legally compliant manner.

1.1 Authorization and Written Agreements

The cornerstone of any Red Team engagement is explicit authorization. Before performing any kind of testing or attack simulation, the Red Team must receive written permission from the organization's leadership or the designated representatives. This is typically formalized through a Rules of Engagement (ROE) document that outlines:

- **Scope of testing**: What systems, networks, applications, or employees are within the engagement's scope and what are explicitly out of scope.
- **Testing limits**: What kinds of tactics, techniques, and procedures (TTPs) can and cannot be used. This ensures that all parties are aligned on the boundaries of the engagement.

- **Duration and timing**: When the engagement will take place, the duration of the testing, and any limitations on when testing can occur to minimize impact on business operations.
- **Point of contact**: Who within the organization is responsible for communicating with the Red Team during the engagement, and who is responsible for responding to any issues or incidents.

Without clear, written authorization, Red Teaming activities can easily cross the line into unauthorized hacking, which can be prosecuted under various computer crime statutes, such as the Computer Fraud and Abuse Act (CFAA) in the United States or equivalent laws in other jurisdictions. Even if the Red Team's intentions are ethical, engaging in unauthorized activities is still illegal.

1.2 Data Privacy and Confidentiality Laws

When conducting Red Team activities, testers often have access to sensitive or confidential data, whether it's customer information, internal documents, or intellectual property. It is essential to understand and comply with data privacy and confidentiality laws that govern how this data can be handled. These may include:

- **General Data Protection Regulation (GDPR):** This European regulation sets strict guidelines for data handling and privacy for EU citizens, including rules about collecting, storing, and sharing personal data. If Red Teamers access personally identifiable information (PII), they must ensure that they comply with GDPR's requirements, including the need to obtain consent for processing such data.
- **Health Insurance Portability and Accountability Act (HIPAA):** In healthcare environments, Red Team members must ensure compliance with HIPAA regulations when accessing protected health information (PHI).
- **Payment Card Industry Data Security Standard (PCI DSS):** If the engagement involves testing systems that store, process, or transmit payment card data, Red Teamers must follow the relevant PCI DSS requirements for safeguarding cardholder information.

In all cases, Red Team members must ensure that any data accessed or compromised during testing is protected and securely handled, and they must refrain from using this data for any unauthorized purposes.

1.3 Jurisdictional Considerations

Red Team engagements often take place across multiple geographical locations, which can introduce complex legal and jurisdictional issues. The legal status of certain activities, like testing specific systems or networks, can vary significantly depending on the country in which the organization operates. It is crucial to:

- **Understand local laws**: Testing that is legal in one country may be illegal in another. Red Team members should be familiar with both domestic and international laws regarding cyberattacks, data privacy, and hacking.
- **Coordinate with legal teams**: Red Teams should always work closely with the organization's legal department to ensure compliance with all applicable laws, including obtaining advice on legal risks and requirements for the engagement.

Given the global nature of the internet and the complexity of international law, Red Teams need to be aware of cross-border legal implications. Activities that might seem harmless in one jurisdiction could violate laws in another.

2. Ethical Boundaries in Red Teaming

Ethics in Red Teaming refers to maintaining a high standard of integrity, professionalism, and responsibility in the course of an engagement. Ethical considerations ensure that Red Team activities are conducted with respect for the organization's employees, data, and systems, and with the broader goal of strengthening cybersecurity.

2.1 Protecting Organizational Reputation

One of the primary ethical concerns during Red Team engagements is the protection of the organization's reputation. While the goal is to uncover vulnerabilities, testers should never intentionally cause harm to the organization's systems, reputation, or relationships with customers, partners, or the public. This includes:

- **Avoiding disruption**: Red Team activities should not interfere with business operations or cause downtime, except when explicitly authorized or agreed upon in the ROE. Testers should also avoid activities that could impact customer-facing systems, which could damage the brand's trust.
- **No public disclosure**: Any vulnerabilities discovered during a Red Team engagement should be reported directly to the organization and should not be publicly disclosed or discussed with third parties unless authorized. Ethical Red Teamers avoid using discovered vulnerabilities as a way to gain public recognition or attention.

2.2 Minimizing Risk of Harm

Ethically, Red Teamers must take steps to minimize harm and ensure that their simulated attacks do not inadvertently damage critical systems, leak sensitive data, or compromise the integrity of business operations. This includes:

- **Contingency planning**: Red Teamers should have a contingency plan in place in case their activities cause unintended consequences. For example, if an attack leads to system downtime or a data leak, the team must be prepared to mitigate the issue immediately.
- **No real exploitation**: The goal of a Red Team engagement is to simulate attacks in a controlled environment to identify weaknesses, not to exploit those weaknesses for personal gain or to cause damage. Red Teams should never perform activities like data theft, creating malware, or damaging systems, even if they could theoretically do so.

2.3 Respecting Individuals and Privacy

A significant ethical responsibility is to respect the privacy and rights of individuals within the organization. This includes:

- **Social engineering and employee interaction**: Red Teams often use social engineering techniques, such as phishing, pretexting, or baiting. While these techniques are effective at testing human vulnerabilities, they must be used ethically. Red Teamers should never deceive or manipulate employees in a way that could cause emotional distress, harm, or loss of trust in the organization's security team.
- **Respecting employees' personal information**: Any personal data acquired during testing should be handled with the utmost care and only used within the bounds of the engagement. Red Teamers should avoid targeting or accessing personal data that is not relevant to the engagement.

2.4 Reporting and Transparency

Transparency is key to maintaining ethical integrity. Red Teams should:

- **Provide accurate findings**: The final report should be an honest and accurate reflection of the findings, without exaggeration or omission of critical details. Misrepresentation of results or the scope of the testing could lead to unnecessary panic or misguided decision-making.

- **Foster trust**: Building trust between the Red Team and the organization is essential for ensuring that vulnerabilities are addressed and not ignored. This trust is maintained through open communication, transparency in methodologies, and a shared commitment to improving security.

3. Conclusion: Maintaining Ethical and Legal Integrity

Navigating the legal and ethical boundaries in Red Teaming is essential to ensure that simulated attacks are both effective and responsible. By adhering to legal requirements such as obtaining proper authorization, respecting data privacy, and ensuring compliance with relevant laws, Red Teams help organizations improve their defenses without crossing any legal lines. At the same time, ethical Red Teamers respect the organization's systems, employees, and reputation by minimizing harm and promoting trust. When these boundaries are carefully followed, Red Team engagements can serve as a powerful tool in strengthening an organization's cybersecurity resilience while maintaining integrity and professionalism.

12.4 Handling Sensitive Data: Confidentiality and Storage Protocols

In Red Team operations, the handling of sensitive data is a critical responsibility that demands careful attention. As Red Teamers simulate real-world attacks, they often gain access to sensitive information, ranging from personal data to proprietary business details. Ensuring that this data is handled with the utmost confidentiality and stored securely is not only a best practice but also a legal and ethical obligation. Mishandling sensitive data could lead to reputational damage, regulatory fines, and even legal action.

This section delves into the importance of data confidentiality in Red Team engagements, outlining the protocols and best practices for securely handling, storing, and transmitting sensitive data during and after testing. By understanding and implementing effective data management strategies, Red Teams can minimize risk and ensure the integrity of the testing process.

1. Data Classification and Identification

Before starting any Red Team engagement, it is vital to understand the type of sensitive data that may be encountered during testing. Sensitive data can be classified into several categories, each with different levels of protection required:

1.1 Types of Sensitive Data

- **Personally Identifiable Information (PII):** This includes any information that can be used to identify an individual, such as names, addresses, phone numbers, and social security numbers.
- **Protected Health Information (PHI):** Health-related data that is governed by laws like HIPAA in the United States, which must be handled with strict confidentiality.
- **Payment Card Information (PCI):** Data related to payment cards, including card numbers and transaction details, which must comply with PCI DSS requirements.
- **Proprietary Business Data**: Information such as trade secrets, intellectual property, and sensitive business strategies or financial records that are crucial to the organization's competitive position.
- **Credentials and Authentication Data**: Login credentials, passwords, API keys, and other authentication mechanisms that could be used to gain unauthorized access to systems.

1.2 Identifying Sensitive Data During the Engagement

During a Red Team engagement, sensitive data could be discovered unintentionally through vulnerability exploitation or social engineering techniques. As such, it is essential for Red Teamers to have protocols in place to identify and handle sensitive information immediately. This includes:

- Documenting the type and source of the data.
- Notifying the organization if sensitive data is discovered, especially if it was not part of the original engagement scope.
- Taking immediate steps to secure the data to prevent it from being exposed, lost, or mishandled.

It is also important to avoid intentionally collecting or exposing sensitive data unless explicitly authorized by the organization's leadership as part of the engagement's scope. Any collection or interaction with PII, PHI, or other sensitive information should only be for the purpose of testing and improving the organization's security posture.

2. Confidentiality and Non-Disclosure Agreements (NDAs)

To ensure that sensitive data is not disclosed to unauthorized parties, confidentiality agreements are essential. These agreements set the foundation for how sensitive data is handled, shared, and protected during the Red Team engagement.

2.1 Confidentiality Agreements (CAs)

Before beginning a Red Team engagement, Confidentiality Agreements (CAs) or Non-Disclosure Agreements (NDAs) should be signed between the Red Team, the organization being tested, and any third parties involved. These agreements ensure that all parties are legally bound to protect any sensitive data discovered during the engagement.

Key elements typically found in NDAs or CAs include:

- **Scope of confidentiality**: Clearly stating the types of information covered under the agreement (e.g., personal data, trade secrets, network credentials).
- **Data protection**: Ensuring that all sensitive data is handled in accordance with applicable data protection laws and organizational policies.
- **Usage limitations**: Outlining what can and cannot be done with sensitive data, including restrictions on storing, sharing, or distributing the data.
- **Duration of confidentiality**: Specifying how long the obligations of confidentiality last, which may extend beyond the engagement itself, especially if sensitive data is uncovered.

NDAs and CAs not only provide legal protection but also demonstrate a commitment to protecting the data and ensuring ethical Red Team operations.

3. Data Storage and Encryption

Once sensitive data is identified, it is critical to store it securely to prevent unauthorized access. Data storage protocols should follow industry best practices, and encryption should be used to ensure the confidentiality of sensitive information.

3.1 Secure Storage of Sensitive Data

Sensitive data should be stored in secure environments that adhere to the organization's security policies. This could involve:

- **Encrypted storage**: Encrypting sensitive data both at rest (while stored on disk) and in transit (while being transmitted over networks).
- **Access controls**: Implementing strict access controls to limit who can access sensitive data, with permissions granted only to authorized Red Team members.

- **Data minimization**: Avoid storing sensitive data unless absolutely necessary for the engagement. If Red Teamers do not need to retain data, they should delete it immediately following the test.

3.2 Encryption Protocols

To ensure the confidentiality and integrity of sensitive data, strong encryption protocols should be used for storing and transmitting data. Common encryption methods include:

- **AES-256**: A widely accepted standard for encrypting sensitive data, offering strong protection for stored data.
- **RSA and ECC (Elliptic Curve Cryptography):** Used for securely encrypting data in transit, particularly when exchanging sensitive data between systems.
- **TLS/SSL**: Used to encrypt data transmitted over networks, ensuring secure communication channels between the Red Team and the organization.

Red Teamers must verify that all sensitive data is encrypted both when stored locally and when transmitted over the network, especially if the engagement involves remote access or cloud environments.

4. Secure Transmission of Sensitive Data

During a Red Team engagement, there may be instances when sensitive data must be shared between the Red Team, the organization's security team, or other stakeholders. This transmission must be carried out securely to prevent interception or unauthorized access.

4.1 Using Secure Communication Channels

Sensitive data should always be transmitted through secure, encrypted channels to prevent interception by unauthorized parties. This includes:

- **Encrypted email**: Using services such as PGP (Pretty Good Privacy) or S/MIME (Secure/Multipurpose Internet Mail Extensions) to encrypt email communications containing sensitive data.
- **Secure file transfer protocols**: Using secure protocols like SFTP (Secure File Transfer Protocol) or SSH (Secure Shell) to transfer files containing sensitive data.
- **Virtual Private Networks (VPNs):** If Red Team members need to communicate remotely or access an organization's internal network, using a secure VPN

connection helps ensure that all transmitted data is encrypted and protected from eavesdropping.

4.2 Sharing with Authorized Personnel Only

When transmitting sensitive data, it is critical that it is only shared with authorized personnel within the organization. This could include:

- Security team members who need the data for remediation purposes.
- Compliance officers or legal teams if the data is relevant to regulatory concerns.
- C-suite executives who need to understand the business impact of discovered vulnerabilities.

Red Teamers must ensure that any data shared is done so securely and only with those who need it to make informed decisions regarding risk mitigation or compliance.

5. Data Retention and Disposal

Data retention refers to how long sensitive data is kept, while data disposal refers to how it is securely deleted once it is no longer needed. Both practices are vital in ensuring that sensitive data is not left vulnerable after an engagement concludes.

5.1 Data Retention Policies

Red Teamers should adhere to strict data retention policies that specify:

- How long sensitive data will be stored: Only for as long as necessary to complete the engagement and provide actionable insights.
- Retention schedules: Documenting when data will be destroyed or anonymized after the engagement ends, ensuring compliance with organizational policies and regulatory requirements.

5.2 Secure Data Disposal

When sensitive data is no longer needed, it must be securely disposed of to prevent any potential data breaches or unauthorized access. Secure disposal methods include:

- **File shredding**: Using software tools that overwrite sensitive data multiple times to ensure it cannot be recovered.

- **Physical destruction**: In cases where physical media, like hard drives, are involved, destroying the media completely is a guaranteed method to ensure data is unrecoverable.

Organizations should have clear protocols for the disposal of data following a Red Team engagement to ensure that no sensitive data is left vulnerable after the conclusion of testing.

6. Conclusion: Prioritizing Security and Ethical Responsibility

Handling sensitive data is a fundamental part of Red Team operations and must be approached with the highest standards of security, confidentiality, and ethical responsibility. By classifying data correctly, using encryption, maintaining proper storage protocols, and adhering to legal and organizational requirements, Red Teamers can protect sensitive information and ensure the success and integrity of their testing efforts. Ensuring secure and ethical data handling not only mitigates the risk of data breaches or legal violations but also builds trust between the Red Team and the organization, contributing to the overall security posture.

13. Evolving as a Red Teamer

The world of cybersecurity is dynamic, and staying ahead of evolving threats requires continuous growth and adaptation. This chapter focuses on how red teamers can evolve in their craft by staying up-to-date with the latest tools, techniques, and attack methodologies. You'll learn how to engage in lifelong learning through certifications, hands-on practice, and active participation in the cybersecurity community. We'll also discuss the importance of developing a red teamer's mindset—how to think critically, embrace creativity, and stay ethical while constantly pushing the boundaries of your knowledge. Whether you're looking to sharpen your skills, lead larger teams, or shape the future of red teaming, this chapter provides a roadmap for your continued professional growth.

13.1 Staying Ahead: Researching New Attack Techniques

In the ever-evolving landscape of cybersecurity, Red Teamers must consistently stay ahead of emerging threats and attack techniques. The field of offensive security is dynamic, with adversaries constantly innovating and refining their tactics, techniques, and procedures (TTPs). To remain effective and provide value to organizations, Red Team professionals must engage in continuous learning and research to adapt to new vulnerabilities, exploits, and attack methodologies.

This chapter emphasizes the importance of researching new attack techniques, understanding how cybercriminals and nation-state actors evolve their tactics, and applying these insights to Red Team engagements. Staying ahead of the curve is critical not only for the success of Red Team operations but also for ensuring that organizations can effectively defend against the latest and most sophisticated threats.

1. Monitoring Emerging Threats and Vulnerabilities

The first step in staying ahead of emerging attack techniques is to continuously monitor the cybersecurity landscape for new vulnerabilities, exploits, and attack methods. With the rapid pace of technological advancements, new security flaws are discovered daily, and Red Teamers need to keep track of these developments to simulate realistic, up-to-date threats.

1.1 Leveraging Vulnerability Databases and Alerts

One of the most effective ways to stay informed about emerging vulnerabilities is through vulnerability databases, such as:

- **CVE (Common Vulnerabilities and Exposures):** The CVE database provides a detailed list of publicly known security vulnerabilities. Red Teamers can use CVE data to identify critical flaws in widely used software and hardware.
- **NVD (National Vulnerability Database):** This U.S. government-supported database includes CVE data and provides security professionals with critical information on newly discovered vulnerabilities, including severity scores and potential mitigations.
- **Security Mailing Lists**: Subscribing to mailing lists like Full Disclosure or Bugtraq can provide real-time alerts on newly discovered vulnerabilities or zero-day exploits.
- **Exploit Databases**: Platforms like Exploit-DB and Packet Storm host information on known exploits, including proof-of-concept code, which can help Red Teamers understand current attack techniques.

1.2 Threat Intelligence Feeds

Red Teamers can utilize threat intelligence feeds from sources like MISP (Malware Information Sharing Platform) or Anomali to stay updated on emerging TTPs used by cybercriminals, hacktivists, or advanced persistent threats (APTs). These feeds provide insights into active attack campaigns, tactics, and attack indicators that can inform Red Team testing strategies. Threat intelligence feeds help Red Teamers simulate attacks using methods seen in the wild, making their engagements more realistic and aligned with real-world threats.

2. Engaging with the Offensive Security Community

The cybersecurity community is full of passionate professionals sharing new findings, research, and exploit techniques. To stay ahead, Red Teamers must actively engage with this community and learn from the work of others.

2.1 Participating in Conferences and Capture-the-Flag (CTF) Events

Attending industry conferences and participating in Capture-the-Flag (CTF) competitions is an excellent way to stay at the forefront of offensive security techniques. These events often showcase cutting-edge attack techniques and provide opportunities to test new skills in a controlled environment. Popular conferences such as Black Hat, DEF CON, and RSA Conference offer hands-on workshops, talks, and demonstrations by top security researchers, providing insights into the latest attack methods and trends in cybersecurity.

2.2 Contributing to Open-Source Projects

Contributing to or studying open-source projects related to penetration testing and Red Teaming can provide invaluable exposure to new techniques and tools. Communities such as GitHub and GitLab host a wealth of offensive security repositories where Red Teamers can contribute, share, and learn about the latest tools, scripts, and techniques used by the security community. Projects like Metasploit, Cobalt Strike, Empire, and BloodHound regularly update their frameworks with new exploits and attack techniques, making them essential resources for keeping up with offensive tactics.

2.3 Collaborating with Researchers and Penetration Testers

Networking with other penetration testers, security researchers, and Red Team professionals allows for knowledge sharing and learning about the latest techniques. Engaging in online forums, Slack channels, or Discord servers dedicated to cybersecurity topics is an excellent way to exchange ideas, ask questions, and keep informed about the latest research and trends.

3. Exploring New Attack Vectors and Technologies

As technology advances, new attack vectors and security technologies emerge, which Red Teamers must explore to remain effective. It's essential to keep an eye on how evolving technologies, such as artificial intelligence (AI), machine learning, cloud environments, and IoT, impact the landscape of cybersecurity.

3.1 Artificial Intelligence and Machine Learning

The rise of AI and machine learning has opened up new opportunities for both attackers and defenders. Adversaries may use AI to automate tasks like phishing or credential stuffing, and Red Teamers must stay informed about these techniques to simulate these types of automated attacks. At the same time, AI can be used for threat detection and analysis, requiring Red Teams to understand how adversaries might counter these technologies and evade detection.

New attack methods leveraging AI/ML could involve:

- **Automated social engineering**: Using machine learning algorithms to craft more convincing phishing messages based on a target's behavior or language patterns.
- **Adversarial machine learning**: Exploiting weaknesses in machine learning models, such as causing misclassifications or evading detection by manipulating inputs in a targeted way.

Red Teamers should be aware of these developments to effectively emulate sophisticated attacks.

3.2 Exploiting Cloud and Hybrid Environments

With the growing adoption of cloud technologies, Red Teamers need to adapt their techniques to target cloud infrastructures like AWS, Microsoft Azure, and Google Cloud Platform (GCP). Cloud environments introduce new attack surfaces and misconfigurations, such as improperly set IAM roles, exposed S3 buckets, or weak security policies, which can be exploited.

In hybrid cloud environments (a mix of on-premises and cloud infrastructures), attackers can move seamlessly between different systems and take advantage of misconfigurations or inadequate security controls. Red Teamers must understand how to exploit these configurations and simulate attacks across both cloud and on-prem environments.

3.3 Internet of Things (IoT)

The proliferation of IoT devices, from smart thermostats to connected industrial equipment, has expanded the attack surface. Red Teamers need to research how IoT devices can be compromised and used as entry points into networks. This might involve exploiting weak default credentials, insecure communication protocols, or vulnerabilities in IoT-specific firmware. Understanding how attackers can compromise IoT devices and pivot through networks is critical for comprehensive Red Team assessments.

4. Developing and Testing Custom Attack Techniques

While off-the-shelf tools and techniques are essential, Red Teamers should also develop and test their own custom attack techniques tailored to the unique environments they are simulating. This can involve:

- Crafting novel social engineering scenarios that reflect emerging threats.
- Building custom exploits for zero-day vulnerabilities or flaws in specific software or hardware.

- Simulating complex attack chains that combine multiple attack techniques (e.g., initial access via phishing, followed by lateral movement and privilege escalation).

Developing custom techniques requires an in-depth understanding of both the target environment and the broader cybersecurity landscape. Red Teamers should dedicate time to exploring new tactics and testing them in real-world scenarios to refine their skills.

5. Continuous Training and Self-Education

Staying ahead of new attack techniques requires ongoing self-education. This includes reading the latest research papers, blogs, and books related to offensive security, as well as participating in ongoing training and certification programs. Some well-known certifications and training programs include:

- **OSCP (Offensive Security Certified Professional):** Focuses on practical penetration testing and Red Teaming.
- **GIAC (Global Information Assurance Certification):** Offers certifications such as the GIAC Penetration Tester (GPEN), which cover advanced Red Team and penetration testing techniques.
- **SANS courses**: Offering specialized training in areas such as cloud security, ethical hacking, and adversarial simulations.

By dedicating time to ongoing learning, Red Teamers can ensure they are well-prepared for the rapidly changing threat landscape.

Staying ahead of new attack techniques is an essential component of effective Red Teaming. By continuously researching emerging vulnerabilities, engaging with the cybersecurity community, exploring new attack vectors, and developing custom attack techniques, Red Teamers can simulate realistic, cutting-edge threats that challenge organizations' defenses. Ultimately, this continuous learning ensures that Red Teams remain relevant and capable of identifying and exploiting vulnerabilities in today's ever-evolving cyber threat landscape.

13.2 Continuous Skill Development: Certifications and Communities

In the fast-paced world of cybersecurity, Red Teamers must commit to lifelong learning and skill development to remain effective. As new attack methods and defensive technologies emerge, Red Team professionals need to continuously refine their knowledge, master new tools, and stay ahead of evolving threats. This chapter explores the importance of continuous skill development through certifications and active participation in professional communities, two key components that help Red Teamers stay sharp and relevant in the field.

1. The Importance of Continuous Skill Development

The cybersecurity landscape is dynamic, with new technologies, vulnerabilities, and attack techniques emerging regularly. For Red Teamers, staying proficient requires an ongoing commitment to professional development. The rapidly evolving nature of cyber threats means that even experienced Red Teamers must keep learning to handle new challenges effectively.

Red Teaming demands a broad set of skills, including technical expertise, creativity, problem-solving, and the ability to think like an adversary. Therefore, continuous learning isn't just about technical skill improvement; it's also about adapting to new thinking models, understanding emerging tools, and staying updated on new attack trends. By focusing on skill development through certifications and communities, Red Teamers can ensure they remain valuable assets to organizations looking to strengthen their defenses.

2. Certifications: Formalizing Knowledge and Gaining Recognition

Certifications play a crucial role in validating a Red Teamer's expertise and providing structured pathways to mastering new skills. For Red Team professionals, certifications demonstrate proficiency in areas ranging from penetration testing to offensive security and threat simulation. They help ensure that practitioners have up-to-date knowledge of the tools, tactics, and techniques required to conduct effective and realistic Red Team engagements.

2.1 Offensive Security Certified Professional (OSCP)

One of the most well-known certifications in the cybersecurity community is the Offensive Security Certified Professional (OSCP). The OSCP certification is offered by Offensive Security, a leading provider of cybersecurity training. This certification focuses on hands-on, practical skills in penetration testing and is highly regarded by the Red Teaming community.

The OSCP exam requires candidates to hack into a series of machines in a controlled environment within a limited time frame. This certification emphasizes not just theoretical knowledge but the practical application of exploitation techniques, making it particularly valuable for Red Teamers looking to strengthen their core offensive skills.

The OSCP is particularly well-suited for those looking to specialize in penetration testing, but it also provides valuable skills that can be applied in Red Team operations, such as vulnerability scanning, exploit development, and post-exploitation.

2.2 GIAC Penetration Tester (GPEN)

The GIAC Penetration Tester (GPEN) certification, offered by the Global Information Assurance Certification (GIAC), focuses on the broader scope of penetration testing, including reconnaissance, exploitation, and post-exploitation strategies. It is ideal for Red Teamers who need to demonstrate their proficiency in testing network security, web application security, and wireless networks.

The GPEN exam tests an individual's ability to assess vulnerabilities and understand penetration testing tools and techniques. Unlike the OSCP, which focuses on practical hacking skills, the GPEN also covers important foundational knowledge, such as network architecture, ethical hacking methodology, and risk management. It's an excellent certification for Red Team professionals looking to establish credibility in the field.

2.3 Certified Red Team Professional (CRTP)

For those specifically interested in Red Teaming, the Certified Red Team Professional (CRTP) certification offered by Pentester Academy is a highly specialized credential. It covers key concepts related to Red Team operations, including advanced attack simulation, lateral movement, privilege escalation, and command-and-control infrastructure.

The CRTP focuses on tools and techniques used during real-world adversary simulations and tests a candidate's ability to perform Red Team-style assessments in an offensive security context. This certification is ideal for Red Team professionals who want to specialize in simulating high-level, persistent threats and adversary tactics.

2.4 Certified Ethical Hacker (CEH)

While not as specialized as other certifications like OSCP, the Certified Ethical Hacker (CEH), offered by EC-Council, is still valuable for Red Teamers. The CEH program covers a wide range of topics, including network security, cryptography, hacking techniques, and attack tools. It is an entry-level certification for those new to the cybersecurity field or Red Teaming and is designed to help professionals understand the basics of ethical hacking.

For Red Teamers, CEH provides a solid foundation in common attack techniques and tools, such as Metasploit, social engineering, and wireless network attacks. It can be a useful stepping stone for those aiming to pursue more advanced Red Team certifications.

3. Communities: Networking, Collaboration, and Knowledge Sharing

In addition to certifications, participation in cybersecurity communities is essential for Red Team professionals. Cybersecurity communities provide platforms for knowledge exchange, collaboration, and networking. Through these communities, Red Teamers can share their experiences, stay informed about new trends, and learn from others in the field.

3.1 Online Forums and Discussion Boards

Online forums like Reddit's /r/Netsec, Stack Exchange's Information Security community, and Black Hat's community platform are great places for Red Teamers to engage with peers, ask questions, and discuss the latest trends and techniques. These forums host discussions on everything from specific exploits to the ethical considerations involved in Red Teaming. Engaging with these forums allows professionals to stay informed about the latest attacks and defense strategies and also provides a space to share knowledge and ask for advice.

3.2 Capture the Flag (CTF) Competitions

Capture the Flag (CTF) events are competitions where participants solve security-related challenges to capture virtual "flags." CTFs are a fantastic way for Red Teamers to practice and improve their skills in a fun, competitive, and hands-on environment. They cover a wide range of topics, such as reverse engineering, web application security, cryptography, and forensics.

Not only do CTFs help sharpen technical skills, but they also encourage creativity and collaboration. Many top-tier CTF events, such as DEF CON Capture the Flag (CTF) or PicoCTF, are hosted by security professionals and researchers, providing Red Teamers with opportunities to learn about emerging attack methods and sharpen their problem-solving abilities.

3.3 Security Conferences

Attending industry conferences like Black Hat, DEF CON, RSA Conference, and ShmooCon allows Red Teamers to network with industry experts, learn about the latest research, and get hands-on training. These events often feature workshops, keynote speeches, and vendor exhibitions, which cover topics such as advanced penetration testing techniques, Red Team operations, and new security tools.

Security conferences provide valuable opportunities for skill development and professional networking. Red Teamers can attend talks on offensive security, participate in workshops, and collaborate with fellow cybersecurity professionals to stay current on the latest trends and techniques.

3.4 Local and Regional Meetups

In addition to large-scale conferences, Red Team professionals can benefit from participating in local or regional cybersecurity meetups and user groups. These smaller, more intimate events allow professionals to build relationships with others in the cybersecurity field, exchange ideas, and discuss local security challenges. Many cities have regular meetups for security professionals, such as OWASP chapters, local InfoSec groups, or meetups organized through platforms like Meetup.com.

4. Embracing Lifelong Learning

The cybersecurity field is ever-evolving, and Red Teamers must view their education as a lifelong journey. Regularly engaging with the cybersecurity community, pursuing advanced certifications, and experimenting with new tools and attack techniques ensures that Red Team professionals are not just passive consumers of knowledge but active contributors to the broader security ecosystem.

By embracing continuous learning through certifications, engaging with communities, and participating in hands-on activities like CTFs, Red Teamers can stay at the cutting edge of their craft. This commitment to personal and professional growth ensures that Red Teamers remain adept at simulating realistic attacks, identifying vulnerabilities, and ultimately helping organizations defend against emerging threats.

Continuous skill development is essential for Red Team professionals who aim to stay relevant in the ever-evolving cybersecurity landscape. By earning specialized certifications, engaging with professional communities, and participating in hands-on events, Red Teamers can continuously improve their technical expertise, creativity, and problem-solving skills. This ongoing commitment to learning and collaboration ensures that Red Team professionals remain prepared for the increasingly sophisticated adversarial tactics they will encounter in the field.

13.3 Navigating Ethical Dilemmas in Red Teaming

Red Teaming, by its very nature, involves simulating real-world cyberattacks and exploiting vulnerabilities in order to identify weaknesses in an organization's defenses. While Red Team operations play a crucial role in improving cybersecurity, they often involve actions that could, under different circumstances, be considered illegal or unethical. This chapter delves into the ethical considerations and dilemmas that Red Teamers may encounter during engagements and how to navigate these challenges while maintaining professionalism and adhering to legal boundaries.

1. The Nature of Ethical Dilemmas in Red Teaming

Unlike traditional penetration testing, where the scope and objectives are generally well-defined and agreed upon, Red Team engagements are often broader and more aggressive. A Red Team operation might involve tactics such as social engineering, physical intrusion, and extensive exploitation of network and system vulnerabilities—methods that can be controversial if not approached carefully.

At the core of many ethical dilemmas in Red Teaming are questions about consent, the potential for collateral damage, and the balance between achieving a realistic attack simulation and causing harm. The critical issue here is ensuring that Red Teamers understand the legal and moral boundaries of their work while maintaining the effectiveness of their engagements.

The role of a Red Teamer requires them to think and act like an adversary, but unlike real-world attackers, they are bound by rules of engagement (ROEs) that define the scope of their actions. Operating within these boundaries ensures that their actions remain ethical and lawful, protecting both the organization's security and the Red Team professional's integrity.

2. Balancing Risk with Reward

One of the primary ethical considerations in Red Teaming is the balance between pushing the limits of an organization's defenses and minimizing the risks involved. While the goal of a Red Team engagement is to uncover vulnerabilities and simulate real-world attacks, the actions taken must be carefully weighed to prevent undue harm.

2.1 Impact on Business Operations

Red Teamers must be mindful of how their activities affect business operations. While an engagement might involve exploiting system vulnerabilities, this should not be done at the expense of damaging critical business infrastructure or services. For instance, an attack designed to disable a service or compromise an organization's ability to operate may expose the team to liability, especially if the attack causes long-term disruptions or financial losses.

To mitigate this risk, Red Teamers must have clearly defined Rules of Engagement (ROEs) that establish the boundaries of the operation. These boundaries can include exclusions such as off-limits systems, critical infrastructure, or sensitive customer data. Operating within these ROEs ensures that Red Teamers can still conduct effective testing without jeopardizing the organization's ability to function.

2.2 Psychological and Emotional Effects on Employees

Social engineering and phishing simulations can be particularly controversial in Red Team engagements. These tactics often target employees directly, manipulating them into taking actions they would not normally take, such as divulging sensitive information or clicking on malicious links. While these methods are effective in demonstrating an organization's vulnerability to human error, they can also cause emotional distress, embarrassment, or loss of trust among employees.

Red Team professionals must exercise caution when conducting social engineering campaigns. Transparency and clear communication about the objectives of these tests are essential. The organization should always be informed in advance about the potential for emotional or psychological impact, and efforts should be made to minimize harm. Post-engagement debriefings and lessons learned can help alleviate any negative feelings and ensure employees are better prepared for future threats.

3. Navigating Legal and Compliance Challenges

Another significant ethical challenge in Red Teaming is ensuring that the engagement complies with legal requirements and regulations. Unauthorized access, data breaches, or the deployment of malicious tools without proper consent could lead to legal consequences for both the Red Team and the organization. This is particularly relevant in industries with stringent data privacy regulations, such as healthcare (HIPAA) or finance (GDPR, PCI-DSS).

3.1 Legal Boundaries

Red Teamers must operate within the boundaries of the law, which includes obtaining explicit permission to conduct penetration testing and simulating attacks. A Red Team engagement should always be authorized by the organization and should follow legal guidelines, such as obtaining a signed contract that clearly outlines the scope, objectives, and limitations of the test. Engaging in activities beyond the agreed-upon scope, or testing without the explicit consent of the organization, could lead to accusations of hacking or cybercrime.

Red Team professionals must understand the legal implications of their actions, especially when it comes to accessing sensitive or protected data. Engaging in activities that violate privacy laws or data protection regulations is a breach of both legal and ethical standards and can expose individuals to legal liability.

3.2 Consent and Transparency

One of the most important ethical principles in Red Teaming is the concept of informed consent. Red Teamers must ensure that the organization is fully aware of the scope of the engagement and consents to the tactics, techniques, and procedures (TTPs) used during the assessment. This includes detailing the methods of attack, the systems involved, and any potential risks. Clear communication is essential to prevent misunderstandings and ensure the organization has realistic expectations.

Red Teamers should also be transparent about the potential consequences of their actions. This transparency is particularly important in cases where an attack may result in temporary system outages, disruptions, or other negative effects. By being open about the potential impacts, Red Teamers can gain trust from stakeholders and ensure that all parties are aligned in terms of goals and expectations.

4. Professional Ethics: Upholding Integrity in Red Teaming

In addition to legal and operational considerations, Red Teamers must also adhere to professional ethics and personal integrity. The field of cybersecurity is built on trust, and maintaining that trust requires Red Team professionals to act responsibly, ethically, and with a sense of duty to protect the systems and individuals they are testing.

4.1 Respecting Privacy

Privacy is one of the most important ethical considerations when conducting Red Team operations. Red Teamers often have access to sensitive information, such as customer data, corporate secrets, and personal employee details. Respecting the confidentiality of this information is paramount, and it is crucial that Red Teamers do not misuse or expose sensitive data during the engagement.

A Red Team's responsibility is to identify vulnerabilities and provide actionable recommendations without compromising privacy. To ensure this, Red Teamers must follow stringent guidelines for data handling, maintain confidentiality agreements, and avoid accessing unnecessary information.

4.2 Ethical Responsibility to the Organization

While Red Teamers simulate adversarial attacks, their ultimate responsibility is to improve the security posture of the organization. As such, they must exercise caution and avoid exploiting vulnerabilities in ways that go beyond the scope of the engagement. This includes being mindful of how vulnerabilities are disclosed, ensuring that sensitive findings are shared only with the appropriate stakeholders, and providing clear, actionable recommendations to mitigate the risks uncovered.

Red Teamers should also ensure that their work does not undermine the organization's efforts to protect its assets or tarnish its reputation. They must work collaboratively with other security teams, like the Blue Team, to ensure that lessons learned from the engagement are implemented in a manner that strengthens overall security.

5. Conclusion: Striking the Right Balance

Red Teaming is a powerful tool for identifying vulnerabilities and strengthening defenses, but it also presents numerous ethical challenges. Navigating these challenges requires a careful balance between performing realistic, high-impact simulations and maintaining responsibility and professionalism. Red Teamers must adhere to legal and ethical guidelines, communicate transparently with stakeholders, and ensure that their actions lead to positive outcomes without causing harm or jeopardizing trust.

By maintaining a strong ethical framework, Red Teamers can ensure their engagements contribute to a more secure and resilient environment while upholding the principles of integrity, respect, and professionalism.

13.4 Building a Reputation in the Cybersecurity Industry

In the fast-paced and highly competitive world of cybersecurity, reputation is everything. For Red Team professionals, building a solid reputation can lead to career advancement, more opportunities, and the chance to work on high-profile engagements. A strong reputation is built not just on technical skills but also on professionalism, ethical conduct, and contributions to the community. This chapter explores how Red Teamers can strategically build and maintain a positive reputation in the cybersecurity industry.

1. Mastering Core Technical Skills

The foundation of a strong reputation in Red Teaming is, of course, expertise. A Red Teamer's ability to conduct thorough, effective, and innovative security assessments is key to gaining recognition in the field. The cybersecurity industry is results-driven, and technical competence speaks louder than anything else.

1.1 Continuous Learning and Specialization

Red Teamers must commit to ongoing education and training to stay ahead of evolving threats and defense mechanisms. Whether through certifications, training courses, or hands-on experience, developing deep expertise in niche areas—such as social engineering, cloud security, or exploitation techniques—can distinguish a Red Teamer from others in the field. Specializing in a high-demand area allows you to build a reputation as a subject-matter expert, making you a go-to professional for complex engagements.

By participating in capture-the-flag (CTF) competitions, bug bounty programs, and regular red teaming exercises, professionals can continually test and refine their skills. Mastering the latest tools, frameworks (like Metasploit, Cobalt Strike, or Empire), and tactics used by real-world adversaries will ensure that your technical abilities remain sharp and relevant. The ability to execute sophisticated engagements that push the boundaries of offensive security while maintaining operational integrity will earn you respect in the cybersecurity community.

1.2 Reputation Through Results

Proving that your engagements consistently uncover critical vulnerabilities, identify security gaps, and ultimately strengthen an organization's security posture is a powerful way to build a reputation. Be it through well-documented reports, measurable improvements to an organization's defenses, or real-world success in breaching defenses (without causing harm), showcasing tangible results of your work will make a strong case for your skills.

A reputation for producing actionable insights that lead to effective risk mitigation will enhance your credibility and position you as a trusted partner in security, rather than just an external contractor.

2. Ethics and Integrity: A Pillar of Reputation

While technical expertise is essential, ethical conduct and integrity are arguably the most critical aspects of building and maintaining a reputable career in Red Teaming. The reputation you build is as much about how you conduct yourself as it is about your abilities to perform.

2.1 Building Trust with Clients

Red Teaming involves simulating cyberattacks that could have real-world consequences, and trust is crucial. Ensuring that clients feel confident in your professionalism, discretion, and ability to deliver ethical, legal, and constructive assessments is key to long-term success.

Always adhere to the agreed-upon rules of engagement (ROEs) and operate within the defined scope. Avoid causing any harm—whether physical, financial, or reputational—and be transparent about your methods and intentions. Clear communication with clients about what can and cannot be done, along with setting expectations at the outset of each engagement, will help cultivate trust and enhance your professional reputation.

2.2 Handling Sensitive Information

Red Teamers are often exposed to sensitive or confidential data, including intellectual property, customer information, and internal communications. Ethical handling of this information is paramount. Never misuse or leak sensitive data you encounter during engagements. The trust you build by keeping proprietary data secure is an essential part of your professional reputation.

Similarly, sharing findings with clients should be done in a way that helps them improve their security posture. This includes avoiding unnecessary sensationalism or fear-mongering and instead providing clear, actionable recommendations. Being known for your integrity and responsibility in handling confidential information will lead to long-lasting relationships and repeat business.

3. Community Engagement and Knowledge Sharing

Building a strong reputation is not just about what you do within an organization but also about how you contribute to the broader cybersecurity community. Active involvement in the community helps establish your credibility, allows you to collaborate with peers, and gives back to the industry.

3.1 Participating in Open-Source Projects

Contributing to open-source security tools or Red Team frameworks is an excellent way to gain recognition. Many Red Teamers make their mark by creating or contributing to tools that are widely used in the cybersecurity community. Whether it's improving an existing framework or developing a new tool, your contributions can highlight your expertise and commitment to the craft.

Open-source projects are also a great way to connect with other cybersecurity professionals and get feedback on your work. These contributions not only enhance your skill set but also position you as a thought leader in the field.

3.2 Writing Articles, Blogs, and Whitepapers

Publishing technical articles, blog posts, or whitepapers is another powerful method for showcasing your knowledge. Writing on topics like advanced penetration testing, offensive security, threat simulation, or Red Team methodologies allows you to share your experiences, insights, and lessons learned with the wider community.

By publishing your work, you demonstrate your expertise, communicate new ideas, and stay on the radar of other industry professionals. Blogs, technical articles, and thought leadership pieces will help build your personal brand and elevate your reputation as a trusted expert in the field.

3.3 Speaking at Conferences and Webinars

Public speaking engagements, such as presenting at industry conferences (e.g., DEF CON, Black Hat, RSA, or OWASP) or hosting webinars, can significantly enhance your professional reputation. Speaking engagements allow you to share your knowledge, discuss emerging trends, and engage with others in the community. Being recognized as a speaker at prominent cybersecurity events establishes you as an authority in your field.

Additionally, these engagements allow you to network with other professionals, collaborate on future projects, and learn from others. Building a reputation as a knowledgeable speaker also enhances your visibility in the cybersecurity space.

3.4 Mentorship and Collaboration

Mentorship is an important aspect of building a lasting reputation. By offering mentorship to junior Red Teamers, security enthusiasts, or newcomers to cybersecurity, you not only help others grow but also establish yourself as a leader who is invested in the future of the profession.

By giving back to the community through mentorship, collaborative projects, and knowledge sharing, you will build a reputation as someone who not only excels in the field but also strives to help others succeed.

4. Networking and Building Relationships

Your professional reputation also hinges on the relationships you build with others in the cybersecurity industry. Building a strong network of trusted colleagues, partners, clients, and mentors can have a significant impact on your career.

4.1 Industry Networking

Attending conferences, participating in online forums, and joining cybersecurity groups on platforms like LinkedIn, Twitter, or Slack enables you to connect with others in the industry. Networking with fellow Red Team professionals, Blue Teamers, and security leaders provides opportunities for collaboration, sharing knowledge, and discovering job opportunities.

Developing a reputation as a reliable, knowledgeable, and approachable professional within these circles will help establish your credibility. Networking can also open doors to high-profile engagements and partnerships that contribute to career growth.

4.2 Building Personal Brand

Your personal brand plays a critical role in your reputation. A strong online presence through platforms like LinkedIn, Twitter, GitHub, or personal blogs allows you to showcase your work, share your expertise, and interact with others in the cybersecurity community. A personal brand built on transparency, expertise, and ethical conduct will help you stand out in a crowded industry.

5. Conclusion: Reputation as a Career Asset

A strong reputation is one of the most valuable assets a Red Teamer can possess. Building and maintaining a positive reputation requires a combination of technical excellence, ethical integrity, community engagement, and strong professional relationships. By continually honing your skills, sharing knowledge, and contributing to the field, you can position yourself as a trusted expert in Red Teaming and cybersecurity.

As you build your career, remember that reputation is built over time through consistent, ethical actions. Whether through mastering new techniques, publishing insightful content, mentoring others, or speaking at industry events, every effort you make to contribute positively to the community strengthens your standing and creates new opportunities for growth. Ultimately, your reputation will speak for itself and open doors to a long and successful career in cybersecurity.

In a world where cyber threats evolve faster than ever, staying ahead of attackers demands more than basic penetration testing. **The Red Teamer's Handbook: Advanced Penetration Testing Techniques** is your definitive guide to mastering the art of offensive security.

This book takes you beyond the fundamentals, providing advanced strategies, tools, and insights to emulate real-world adversaries. Across 13 comprehensive chapters, you'll dive deep into:

- Crafting sophisticated attack scenarios using the latest tactics and techniques.
- Exploiting vulnerabilities across on-premises, cloud, and hybrid environments.
- Navigating the psychology of social engineering and physical intrusion.
- Collaborating effectively with blue teams to build more resilient defenses.

Whether you're a red team veteran or an ethical hacker looking to elevate your skills, this book offers the knowledge and practical advice you need to excel in today's high-stakes cybersecurity landscape.

The Red Teamer's Handbook isn't just a manual—it's a call to action for security professionals to think creatively, adapt quickly, and act decisively. Arm yourself with the mindset and tools to challenge assumptions, uncover blind spots, and defend against even the most advanced threats.

Are you ready to think like the adversary? Open this book and begin your journey into the cutting edge of cybersecurity.